HERITAGE STUDIES

4

Third Edition

bju press®

Greenville, South Carolina

Note

The fact that materials produced by other publishers may be referred to in this volume does not constitute an endorsement of the content or theological position of materials produced by such publishers. Any references and ancillary materials are listed as an aid to the student or the teacher and in an attempt to maintain the accepted academic standards of the publishing industry.

Heritage Studies 4
Third Edition

Authors
Carol Arrington Ardt
Eileen Berry
Ethan Birney
Brian C. Collins, PhD
Annittia Jackson

Consultant
Charlene McCall

Bible Integration
Bryan Smith, PhD

Project Editors
Kaitlyn Chisholm
Maria S. Dixson

Page Layout
Bonnijean Marley

Designer
Michael Asire

Cover Design
Elly Kalagayan

Cover Art
Ben Schipper

Cover Photography
Craig Oesterling

Project Coordinators
Michele White
Kendra Wright Winchester

Illustrators
Paula Cheadle
Zach Franzen
Preston Gravely
Cynthia Long
Kathy Pflug
John Roberts

Permissions
Sylvia Gass
Sarah Gundlach
Brenda Hansen
Carrie Walker

Photo credits appear on pages 489–92.

Produced in cooperation with the Bob Jones University School of Education and Bob Jones Academy.

© 2015 BJU Press
Greenville, South Carolina 29614
First Edition © 1985 BJU Press
Second Edition © 1997, 1999 BJU Press

ISBN 978-1-60682-728-4

15 14 13 12 11 10 9 8 7 6 5 4 3 2

Contents

What Is Heritage Studies?

The BJU Press Heritage Studies materials are a presentation of social studies that integrates civics, culture, economics, geography, and history. *HERITAGE STUDIES 4* includes an age-appropriate study of civics and government and evaluates historical events in United States history from the first Americans through World War II, all from a Christian worldview. This study highlights the role of significant Christians in American history and their viewpoints on historical events. Eye-catching artwork, maps, graphs, photos, review questions, and timelines enhance learning.

1 Justice and the Fear of God

Focus

Leaders should rule justly and in the fear of God.

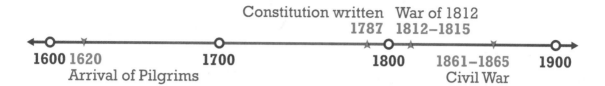
What Makes a Good Ruler?

If you were asked to rank the presidents of the United States from best to worst, how would you decide what makes a good president? A good place to start is 2 Samuel 23:3–4. God gave this prophecy to David at the end of his life. David was God's choice to be king over Israel.

God gave David these words to teach other rulers what a good ruler is like: "He that ruleth over men must be just, ruling in the fear of God. And he shall be as the light of the morning, when the sun riseth, even a morning without clouds; as the tender grass springing out of the earth by clear shining after rain."

These words from God teach what a ruler must be. They also paint a picture of how good it is for people to be ruled over by a good ruler. Have you ever awakened in the morning after a rain to see the sun shining through a window? The clouds have moved away, and the sun shines on the green grass. Mornings like these can make your heart happy. God says that is what it is like being ruled over by a good ruler.

But what is a good ruler like? God says we can identify a good ruler by two things. First, the ruler must be just. Second, he must fear God.

A **just** ruler always does what is right toward people. For example, if a wicked person offers the ruler money to escape punishment, a just ruler would not accept the money. Instead, he would give the wicked person the punishment he deserves. A greedy person might want land that does not belong to him. He might promise to support a ruler if the ruler will get him that land. A just ruler would refuse. A wealthy **employer**, or boss, might treat his workers however he pleases.

"Honour thy father and thy mother: that thy days may be long upon the land which the Lord thy God giveth thee."
Exodus 20:12 (KJV)

But a just ruler would make sure employers treat their workers as people made in God's image. A just ruler would obey Jesus' second great commandment and love others as he loves himself.

David says that a just ruler rules in the fear of God. The fear of God is not like the fear that a slave has toward an angry master. The fear of God is more like what a child feels toward his father. A child should love his father. A child does not want his actions to disappoint his father. A child also knows that a good father teaches him to love and obey God. The father corrects his child when the child does not do right. The child desires to always please his father.

A ruler who fears the Lord loves God and wants to please God in all he does. A just ruler obeys the greatest commandment. He loves God with all his heart. A just ruler will read his Bible. He will want to know what the Bible says about how to be a good ruler. When a ruler loves God and loves others, he will be a great blessing to those he rules.

Students who are studying history should ask whether their rulers today are just and fear God. These are good questions to ask about presidents. But presidents are not the only rulers in the United States. Members of Congress and judges are also rulers. Governors of states and mayors of cities are rulers. And in some ways, the nation's people are rulers because they vote to decide who will rule.

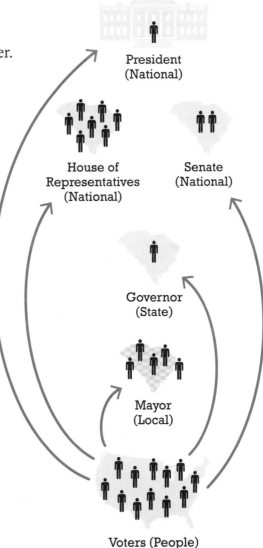

Voting for Government Leaders

President
(National)

House of
Representatives
(National)

Senate
(National)

Governor
(State)

Mayor
(Local)

Voters (People)

What are two things that identify a good ruler?

People Come to America
The First Americans

Early in the world's history, God scattered people all over the earth. Some people found their way to North and South America. Most historians think the people traveled across the Bering Strait.

Some people found their way to Central America. There they built large cities. Thousands of people lived in these cities, which were filled with beautiful statues and buildings. Today people still travel to see the pyramids these early Americans built. The early people in Central America also knew how to grow food. Maize, or corn, was not good food for people to eat at first. But early Central Americans learned ways to grow it and make it into a good food.

The early Americans built great civilizations. Christians should not be surprised by this. People are able to do great things because God created people in His image. Because they bear His image, people are able to rule over His creation. But although these civilizations inspire wonder and astonishment, the people in them were not always good. Sin hurt the civilizations. People worshiped false gods. Sometimes they sacrificed other humans to these gods. Christians can learn two things from these civilizations. People have the ability to do great good because God created them in His image. But people often do great evil. This is because they are sinners.

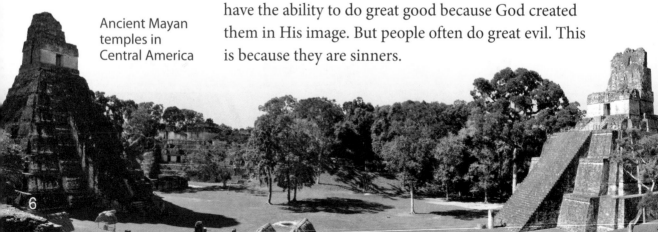

Ancient Mayan temples in Central America

Europeans

Europeans discovered the Americas in 1492. Christopher Columbus was trying to sail around the world to Asia. Instead he landed on an island in the Caribbean. He thought he had arrived in the Indies in Southeast Asia. So he called the people on that island Indians.

Many European countries were interested in the new lands that Columbus discovered. These lands were called the New World. Some countries sent explorers there to look for gold, furs, or other natural resources. Some countries also sent people to live in these newly discovered lands. These people were called colonists.

Some colonists came to the New World because they could not find work in their home country. Some came because they could not worship God the way the Bible taught in their home country. This is why the Pilgrims and the Puritans came to America.

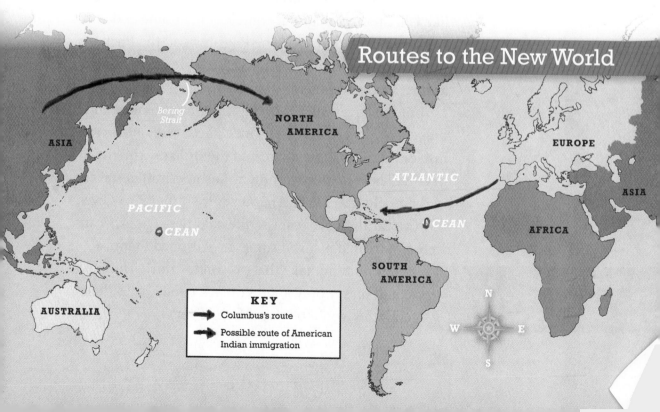

Routes to the New World

KEY
- Columbus's route
- Possible route of American Indian immigration

People are not naturally good. This is one reason they need governments. Government is God's way to keep people from acting wickedly. The colonies in the new world were under governments in Europe. But Europe was a long way away. Government was needed in the colonies too.

The Pilgrims and the Puritans in America wanted a government that pleased God. They wanted their leaders to be Christian. They wanted people to live like Christians, not just at church but at home and at work and in all they did. The Pilgrims and the Puritans made good laws that tried to keep people from sinning against God and others.

But the governments in the American colonies did not always do what pleased God. They were not always just. Sometimes they mistreated the Indians who lived nearby. These early governments also permitted slavery in their colonies. Many Africans were brought as slaves to work for the Europeans in the colonies. The Africans were not treated justly. If someone wronged them, they could not take that person to court. They could marry only another black person, and their children would be slaves for life also.

Why were early Americans able to build great civilizations?

The Great Awakening

The Pilgrims and the Puritans came from England. The king there told people how to worship. But the Pilgrims and Puritans wanted to follow the Bible in their worship of God. They traveled to the New World to live there and worship God the right way.

But not all their children became followers of Jesus. There were also other people who moved to the colonies who were not followers of Jesus. After a while, many people who did not follow Jesus lived in the colonies.

George Whitefield preaching from his folding pulpit

Soon false ideas from Europe began spreading to the American colonies. Some important people in Europe said that the Bible was not God's Word. They also said that Jesus was only a man. They denied that He is God. They said that reason and experience were better ways of learning how to live than learning from the Bible. This concerned the leaders of some colonies. The Pilgrims and Puritans wanted their communities to please God. God is not pleased if people do not love Him and obey Him.

God did something special in the colonies. An English evangelist named **George Whitefield** traveled to the American colonies. He preached everywhere he went. Large crowds of people went to hear him. The Holy Spirit worked in the hearts of people, and they saw they were sinners. As a result, many trusted Christ to be their Savior. This special time when many people turned to Christ for salvation is called the **Great Awakening**. God sent the Great Awakening early in American history. This is one of God's blessings to America.

The Revolutionary War

Great Britain claimed much land in North America. Most of the colonists who lived along the Atlantic Ocean were British. Other countries also claimed land in the Americas. The Spanish claimed Florida, Mexico, and much of South America. The French claimed Canada and lands west of the British colonies.

As British colonists in America moved west, they faced conflict with the French. Both sides claimed the land as theirs. This disagreement caused the French and Indian War. The Indians fought with the French against the British. The British won the war, but it cost them much money. The government in Britain thought it only just that the British colonists help pay for the war. The government said the war was fought for their benefit.

The Declaration of Independence was signed on July 4, 1776.

The British colonists did not agree. They said paying taxes to Britain for the war was not just. The colonists had done much of the fighting themselves. Also, since they did not get to vote on laws the British government made for them, the colonists said they should not have to pay.

By now the British colonists were known as Americans. In 1774 representatives from the American colonies met. Their meeting was called the First Continental Congress. They sent the British king a letter asking him to correct the wrongs being done to them, but the king did not listen.

The British and the Americans went to war against each other. Great Britain had the strongest army in the world. The Americans lost many battles. But in the end, they defeated the British. The Americans founded their own nation: the United States of America.

The United States needed to create its own government. The first attempt did not work well. But in 1787 Americans wrote the Constitution of the United States. The Constitution set up a government that has lasted over 200 years.

Why has the US Constitution lasted so long? One reason is that God gave the United States wise founders. One of them was George Washington.

Washington was a general who helped fight the war against the British. Many successful generals seize power after a revolution. George Washington did not do this. The Americans elected him to be president for two terms. Washington decided not to run for a third term. He set a precedent for American leaders to give up their power after a certain amount of time. Washington was also careful not to use his power to help himself. He used his power to help the entire nation. He was a president who ruled justly. Because he was a just ruler, he was a great blessing to his nation.

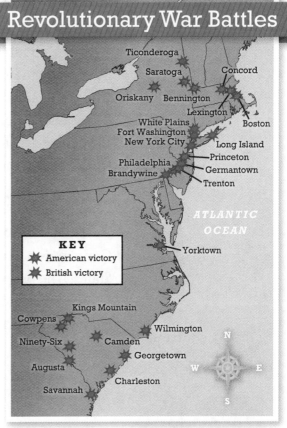

Revolutionary War Battles

Ticonderoga
Saratoga
Concord
Oriskany   Bennington
Lexington
White Plains
Fort Washington
New York City
Boston
Long Island
Princeton
Philadelphia
Germantown
Brandywine
Trenton

ATLANTIC OCEAN

KEY
✹ American victory
✹ British victory

Yorktown

Kings Mountain
Cowpens
Wilmington
Ninety-Six   Camden
Georgetown
Augusta
Charleston
Savannah

N
W   E
S

America's first president

How did George Washington rule the nation justly?

Early Years as a Nation
Creating a New Government

Some countries are ruled by a king. The king must be virtuous. This means he must be a person who wants to do what is right. He must be just, wise, honorable, generous, merciful, loyal, and brave. If the people are not virtuous, the king can stop them from doing wrong. If the people are proud, greedy, or violent, the king can make laws that stop the people from living wickedly.

The United States does not have a king. The Constitution gave power to the people of the United States. The people help choose the president of the United States. The people choose representatives to Congress. The people also choose leaders for their state governments.

The United States Constitution gave power to the people.

Because the American people elect their leaders, it is important that the people be virtuous. If the people are wicked, they will not choose just and wise men to lead them.

Would the American people be good and virtuous? People did not know in the early days of the nation. During and after the Revolutionary War, there was a time of unbelief in the people. Many American leaders began to reject the Bible as God's Word. They thought they could believe only parts of the Bible. They accepted parts that taught about being good. They refused to accept parts they thought were foolish. Some leaders thought that in the future nobody would believe the Bible was God's Word.

God once again showed goodness to the United States. He sent a **Second Great Awakening**. Evangelists, or traveling preachers, took the gospel to different parts of the country. Pastors preached the gospel in their churches. In the West, people gathered in camp meetings to hear the gospel preached. And many Americans became Christians who fully trusted God's Word.

These Christians often looked for ways to do great good in their communities. Christians formed groups called voluntary societies. These groups helped raise money for printing Bibles. Voluntary societies also helped orphan children who needed care, encouraged better treatment of prisoners, and worked to end drunkenness in their communities.

God used Asahel Nettleton's preaching to bring many Americans to true faith in Christ. Nettleton always insisted that God brought revival. Nettleton would not preach for churches that thought he created revivals.

The War of 1812

The Americans worked hard at setting up a good government. God blessed the United States with many Christian people.

At this time the United States was still a young nation. It did not have the respect of other countries yet. Great Britain and France were a couple of these countries.

Great Britain and France were at war with each other. The United States wanted to trade goods with both of them. But neither Great Britain nor France wanted the United States to trade with the enemy. Both the British and the French stopped American ships from trading with the other country. The British also forced some American sailors to fight for the British Navy.

The Americans thought Great Britain was still treating them like a colony. The Americans also said that the British were stirring up trouble with the American Indians. In 1812, America declared war on Great Britain. Neither side was ready for war. The British were busy fighting the French, and the Americans had only a small military.

Battle of North Point in Maryland on September 12, 1814

In America, Congress would not raise taxes to help Americans pay for the war. Without good roads, troops had difficulty moving around the country to fight. The battles that were fought often went badly for the Americans. In the end, the British and the Americans agreed to sign a peace treaty that would end the war.

General Andrew Jackson commanding his troops against General Pakenham and the British troops at the Battle of New Orleans, January 8, 1815

News of the treaty traveled slowly. One important battle occurred after the treaty had been signed. The soldiers at the Battle of New Orleans had not heard about the peace treaty. The British attacked the city of New Orleans in Louisiana. The American general, **Andrew Jackson**, had built strong defenses. He defeated the British and became an American war hero.

But Jackson did not always do right. During the war he had defeated the Creek Indians who fought for the British. But the treaty he made with the Creek Indians afterward was unjust. The treaty took lands away from the Cherokee and the Creek Indians, even though some of these Indians had helped Jackson during the war.

President Madison told Jackson that the treaty was illegal. He said Jackson needed to correct the treaty. The land Jackson took from loyal Cherokees and Creeks must be returned. But Jackson angrily refused. Since Jackson was a popular war hero, the president backed down. He did not force Jackson to return the land to the Indians.

General Andrew Jackson

How did American Christians help their communities?

America Grows
Growth of Democracy

Andrew Jackson was able to get away with doing something unjust because he was popular. This shows that democracy, or rule by the people, is not a perfect form of government. The majority is not always right. A bad leader or ruler can cause the people to make unwise decisions.

The American founders knew democracy had weaknesses. So they made the United States a republic. The people had an important role. They chose their leaders for the House of Representatives. But the people did not choose all of their leaders directly. The state legislatures chose senators. The president chose the judges. And the Electoral College had a large part in choosing the president.

This system was put to the test in 1824. Four men ran for president. None of them won more than half the votes in the Electoral College. The Constitution has a plan when this happens. The House of Representatives elects the president. Jackson had won the most electoral votes. But the Speaker, or leader, of the House of Representatives was concerned about Jackson's disobedience of the law. The Speaker of the House thought John Quincy Adams would make a better president. The Speaker encouraged the representatives to elect Adams. John Quincy Adams became president instead of Andrew Jackson.

How the American Republic Works

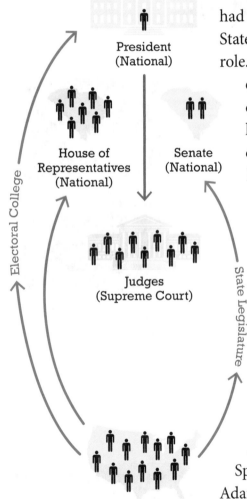

President
(National)

House of
Representatives
(National)

Senate
(National)

Judges
(Supreme Court)

Electoral College

State Legislature

Voters (People)

Jackson won the next election for president. The president is responsible to uphold the law. But President Jackson was willing to break the law. Worst of all, he broke treaties the United States had made with the Indian peoples.

The Cherokees were the best known of these groups. They had their own constitution, written language, and towns. They never fought with the Americans after the Revolutionary War. Many of them had become Christians.

Trail of Tears

But Jackson said he would not keep the treaties. He would not protect the Cherokees from people who came on their lands illegally. Jackson said the Cherokees should move to lands west of the Mississippi. Finally, the US Army forced the Cherokees to move west. About four thousand Cherokees died in the move that became known as the Trail of Tears. Jackson was not ruling justly or in the fear of God.

Christian leaders spoke out against breaking the treaties. They said the United States should treat the Cherokees justly. Some missionaries were thrown into prison for defending the Cherokees.

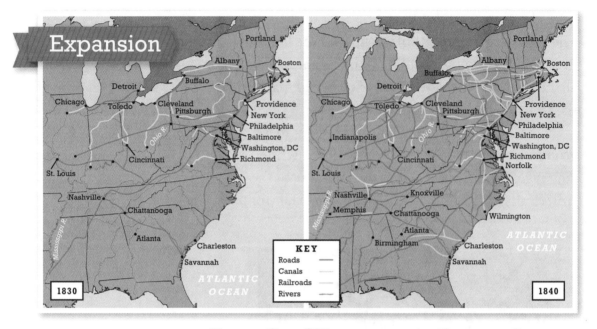

Expansion

1830

1840

KEY
Roads
Canals
Railroads
Rivers

Growth of Transportation and Inventions

All this time the United States grew as a nation. It started with thirteen states along the coast of the Atlantic Ocean. By the 1840s the United States stretched from the Atlantic Ocean to the Pacific Ocean. Most Americans still lived east of the Mississippi River. But they were moving west.

The United States grew in many ways. Transportation increased. Roads, canals, and railroads connected American towns and carried resources and goods across the nation. The number of inventions grew. In the 1840s Samuel Morse developed the telegraph. It allowed instant communication from one place to another. Steam engines powered factories that could produce many goods for the American people. And reapers and steel plows helped American farmers grow more food.

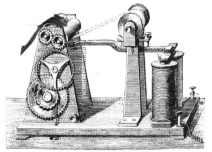
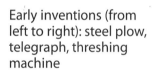

Growth of Territory

The United States also grew in its number of towns. It grew in miles of railroad track. It grew in the number of factories. And it grew in the number of people who lived within its borders. Some Americans thought the nation should keep growing. To the south and west of the United States lay the country of Mexico. Some Americans thought the United States should own the parts of Mexico that lay west of the United States.

At this time James K. Polk was the US president. Polk purposely stirred up a conflict. He sent soldiers to the Mexican border to cause trouble. He also sent soldiers disguised as explorers to California. Polk wanted the soldiers to take California from Mexico. The United States and Mexico went to war against each other. The war was known as the Mexican-American War. The United States won, and President Polk received much of the territory he wanted. Many Americans said Polk was wrong in getting land this way. Some Christians were afraid that God would judge America for Polk's actions.

It is sad that not all of America's leaders have ruled justly. But it is a great blessing that many Christians lived in the United States and called on their nation to turn from its sins and do right.

Early inventions (from left to right): steel plow, telegraph, threshing machine

In what ways did Andrew Jackson fail to rule justly?

Slavery and the Civil War
Slavery

The United States gained new land after winning the Mexican-American War. But this new land caused problems. Slavery was a big part of these problems. The Southern states allowed slavery. The Northern states did not allow slavery. Southerners wanted to bring slaves into the new land. Northerners did not want to see slavery spread.

Southerners did not want more free states to form in the new land. That would mean more senators and representatives from free states in Congress. Then Congress might try to outlaw slavery.

Northerners did not want more slave states to form. The Northerners thought the slave states had too much power.

Sadly, Christians disagreed about slavery. Some Christians said slavery must be right. They said the

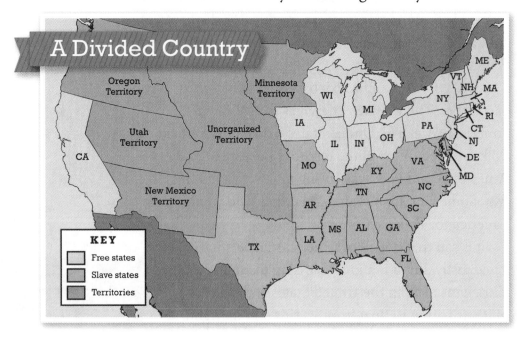

A Divided Country

KEY
Free states
Slave states
Territories

Slave family

Bible permitted slavery. It did not say people could not own slaves. They said the Bible simply required that masters treat their slaves well.

Other Christians said slavery was wrong. They said that the **ancestors** of most slaves were kidnapped from Africa. The Bible said kidnappers and slavers, or people who enslaved other people and sold them, deserved death.

During Bible times, some people in Israel served as slaves because they could not pay their debts. They paid their debts by serving for six years. After six years, slaves were set free. Then their old master helped them set up their own farm or business. This is not how American Southerners treated their slaves. These slaves were made slaves because of the color of their skin. Slaves in the South and their children were made slaves for life.

Many Americans were wrong about slavery. They were wrong to buy kidnapped people. They were wrong to make people and their children slaves forever. They were wrong to mistreat people because of their skin color.

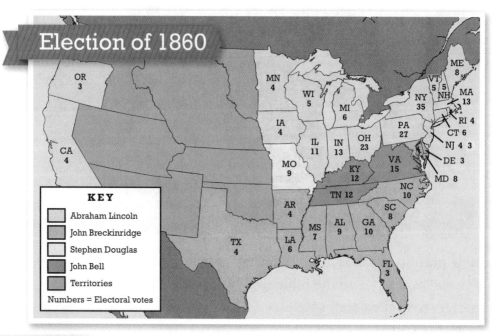

Election of 1860

KEY
- Abraham Lincoln
- John Breckinridge
- Stephen Douglas
- John Bell
- Territories

Numbers = Electoral votes

1860s photo of Abraham Lincoln

The Civil War

In 1860 Abraham Lincoln won the election for president. All of his votes were from free states. He did not win a single electoral vote in the slave states. He opposed the spread of slavery.

This election concerned the slave states. They saw that Northern voters could win elections without Southern votes. Southerners feared that Northern voters might not allow any more slave states. Then the South would never win elections. If slavery could not spread, the slave states would one day be outnumbered by the free states.

South Carolina declared its independence. It said it was no longer part of the United States. South Carolina believed that the free states were breaking the Constitution's laws about runaway slaves. The free states were making it difficult for slave owners to get their slaves back.

Five other slave states also declared their independence. Lincoln asked the other states for troops to deal with this rebellion. This angered more Southern states. Four other states declared independence. The **Civil War** had begun.

The Civil War was a long and bloody war. The South did not have as many resources as the North. But since most of the battles were fought in the South, Southern soldiers did not have to travel far. They had the easier task of defending their own land. The South also had better generals. They were often able to outsmart the Northern forces. The North, however, had more men. It also had more factories that could produce equipment for the army.

Large weapons called mortars were used during the Siege of Yorktown in 1862.

At first President Lincoln had a hard time finding a general who would fight and who could win. But later he found the right general: Ulysses S. Grant. The South suffered a heavy loss of men and materials over the four years of war. In the end the North won the Civil War. The United States remained a single nation.

One great good came of the war. The Civil War ended slavery in the United States. During the war, Lincoln announced that slaves who were in the Confederate areas, or areas that had rebelled against the United States, were free. At the end of the war, Congress passed a Constitutional Amendment. It ended slavery throughout the United States.

Conclusion

This book tells the history of the United States from the end of the Civil War through the end of World War II. During this time the United States faced many new challenges. It needed to rebuild itself after the Civil War. It continued to expand westward. It needed to learn to manage growing cities. It had to learn how to root out corruption in government and businesses. During this time Christians faced challenges from unbelief and wickedness in the culture. Still, evangelists crossed the country preaching the gospel. Pastors faithfully led their churches to follow Christ. Missionaries were sent to carry the gospel around the world. Christian colleges trained Christian young people to stand against unbelief. Christians faithfully served God in government and businesses. They also served God at home and in their communities.

Think carefully as you study American history. Did Americans fear God? Did they act justly toward others? Are there lessons you can learn from them? You may also be an American citizen. You will vote in elections. You will have to think about what actions are best for the nation. You will need to fear God. You will need to help America act justly.

How was slavery in the South unbiblical?

Activity

Make a Timeline

A timeline lists key events that happened in history. A timeline shows these events in the order they happened and shows the amount of time that passed between the events.

A timeline can record events that happen in your life, family, class, or in the life of a famous person. Use resources and choose pictures to make your own timeline.

2 Rebuilding the Nation

Focus

Americans needed to rebuild their nation with liberty and justice for all.

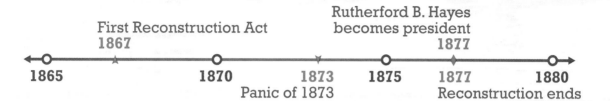

First Reconstruction Act
1867

Rutherford B. Hayes
becomes president
1877

1865   1870   1873   1875   1877   1880
                    Panic of 1873   Reconstruction ends

Looking to the Future

After the Civil War ended, Americans had to live in a country that was far different from the one only five years earlier. The period from 1865 to 1877 is called **Reconstruction**, which means to rebuild. The Reconstruction was both a time period and a process of rebuilding the South and reuniting the nation. During this time, Americans had to rebuild their nation physically, socially, and politically.

Even after the fighting from the Civil War stopped, many Americans still did not feel like one people. The three main groups of Americans were freedmen, Southerners, and Northerners.

The **freedmen** were people who used to be slaves but were now free. Many freedmen were joyful and hopeful about freedom. Some were concerned about finding a home or a job. Most freedmen praised God for delivering them from bondage.

27

At the end of the Civil War, most Southerners were hurt and confused. Invading armies had destroyed their states. Many men had died in battle or of disease. Without slavery, many Southerners were concerned about who would work in the fields. The war had brought peace. But Southerners did not feel that the war had helped them. It only left them with new problems.

Northerners celebrated the war's end. They had accomplished their goals. The Union, or the states that had remained in the United States, stayed together and slavery ended. Although many Northern soldiers had died, their deaths were not in vain. Northerners looked forward to a better future.

Everyone hoped Reconstruction would form America into a better nation. However, they did not agree on exactly what a better America was.

Reconstruction Begins

Freedmen began to enjoy life as free people. Some left their plantations, looked for family, or looked for work. When the freedmen had been slaves, they could not leave their plantations without a written pass. Now the freedmen could go where they liked.

Freedmen realized that to enjoy their freedom, they needed to work. They hoped to be repaid for the many years they had worked as slaves. Most freedmen wanted land so that they could raise their own food. They did not want to work for someone else.

Southerners hoped to rebuild the South as it had been before the war. Although Northern armies had destroyed Southern cities, bridges, and railroads, Southern culture remained. Southerners planned to reopen their schools and colleges. They also wanted to rebuild their plantations and cities. And even though slavery had ended, many Southerners still wanted to direct the freedmen's work.

The effects of the Civil War in the South on Carey Street in Richmond, Virginia

The war had little effect on the North in Broadway, New York.

Most Northerners felt pleased. Their states suffered little physical damage from the war. Factories kept running. Many immigrants had arrived during the war. The number of people in the North continued growing. Many in the North hoped to help the freedmen make new lives. Many Northerners wanted to change the way Southerners treated freedmen.

Northerners also wanted to change Southern industry. **Industry** is the making of things or providing of services for the purpose of making money. Some industries get materials to sell to people or factories. Some industries manufacture goods. Other industries provide services like education.

Northerners, Southerners, and freedmen each had their own hopes and plans for Reconstruction. Not all these goals could be met. Southerners wanted life to return to what it was like before the war. This would stop the changes the freedmen wanted. Northerners wanted to make the South more like the North. But changing the South might destroy the old Southern culture. Most freedmen wanted freedom to control their own work, families, and social groups. Few Northerners and Southerners thought the freedmen could care for themselves. During Reconstruction, each of these groups tried to change the country. Each group succeeded in some ways. None of the groups succeeded in everything.

Who were the three groups of Americans after the Civil War?

Healing the Nation
Reconstruction and Lincoln

As Reconstruction began, Americans faced many questions. The biggest question was about the states that used to be the Confederacy, or the Confederate States of America. Before the Civil War, these states had voted to secede from the nation. Now that the war was over, were these states still part of the United States? If they were not, how could they rejoin? Americans wondered who was in charge of making the decision. Could the president accept these states? Did Congress get to decide?

The confusion about who was in charge made Reconstruction hard. At this time, the president seemed to be in favor of what most congressmen wanted. But both the president and Congress wanted to be in charge of the process of Reconstruction.

As the Civil War ended, President Lincoln wanted to be sure the country healed quickly. He said that all Americans should "bind up the nation's wounds; to care for him who shall have borne the battle, and for his widow, and his orphan." Lincoln also wanted to be sure the freedmen were treated fairly. He hoped that all Americans, black and white, would enjoy a peaceful and successful country.

The New President

At Ford's Theatre in Washington, DC, John Wilkes Booth assassinated President Abraham Lincoln.

Sadly, President Lincoln was **assassinated**. On the evening of April 14, 1865, Lincoln took his wife to see a play. The Civil War was coming to an end. Since the main Confederate army had surrendered,

the Union's victory seemed sure. The president could finally enjoy a night of relaxation. It seemed as though victory was almost complete. But John Wilkes Booth, an actor who liked the South, burst into Lincoln's theater box and shot him.

Lincoln's vice president, Andrew Johnson, became president. Johnson was very angry about Lincoln's assassination. He promised to punish the people who did it. Many Americans believed that the leaders of the Confederacy were to blame for Lincoln's death. Johnson said that the leaders of the South would pay for their crimes.

Andrew Johnson

Johnson believed that he should be in charge of Reconstruction. Most of the men in Congress hoped Johnson would do a good job. These men were from the North and were members of the Republican Party. They believed that leaders of the Confederacy should be punished for fighting against the Union. When Johnson talked with these congressmen, they thought he agreed with their ideas.

Laws for Slaves	New Southern Laws for Freedmen
• Slaves must work under a master.	• Freedmen must have a job with an employer.
• Slave contract gives the master ownership of the slave and his family.	• Work contract requires a freedman along with his family to work for an employer.
• Children of slaves are also slaves and belong to the master.	• Children of freedmen can be apprenticed without their parents' permission.
• Slaves have no choice of living quarters; they are told where to live.	• Freedmen cannot live in some towns.

Instead, Johnson treated the Southerners mildly. He pardoned almost all the Confederate leaders. He did not make rules to protect the freedmen. He let Southern states hold elections to choose representatives to send to Congress. These representatives were often men who had supported the Confederacy. Johnson claimed to be doing what Lincoln wanted.

While most white Southerners were happy with Johnson's choices for Reconstruction, many freedmen suffered. Southern states passed harsh laws. These laws seemed to be set up to make the freedmen almost slaves again. Few people in the North knew about the new Southern laws.

Although slavery had ended, most freedmen did not seem much better off than before they were emancipated, or freed from slavery. Instead, Reconstruction under President Johnson seemed to help mainly the Southerners.

What were some of President Johnson's decisions for Reconstruction?

FREEDOM

INEQUALITY

Congress Takes Over Reconstruction
A Report on the Freedmen

In 1865 the president sent Carl Schurz to tour the South. Schurz had to report back to the president on how Reconstruction was doing in the South. After Carl Schurz returned to Washington, DC, his report helped change Reconstruction.

Schurz's report said that Johnson's decisions for Reconstruction did not work. Southerners seemed convinced that they could go back to living as they had before the war. The Southerners were also mistreating freedmen, Northern soldiers, and Northern civilians who had moved south to help the freedmen. A civilian is someone who is not serving in the army.

Schurz was an abolitionist. In his report he was most concerned about how freedmen were treated. Throughout the South there were leaders who used to be Confederates. They passed many laws. These laws made the freedmen work as if they were still slaves.

Many Southerners wanted to make the freedmen start working on plantations again. These Southerners tried to make this happen by passing laws. Often freedmen could not live in cities. They also had to have a job. If a freedman had no job, he could be forced to work. Those who hired freedmen were allowed to whip them.

The Southern laws also made freedmen unequal with other people in society. Freedmen were required to show extra respect to white people. Freedmen could not serve on juries. They were not allowed to testify in court against white people.

Congress Takes Action

When Northerners heard Schurz's report, they grew angry. They thought of the deaths of thousands of soldiers and Abraham Lincoln. The Northerners wanted those deaths to count for something. Most Northerners knew people who had fought in the Civil War. The North expected Southerners to admit to losing the war. Northerners believed that since the South lost, it should change.

Government officials met with freedmen in North Carolina to see how the Freedmen's Bureau was working.

Congress met in late 1865. Northern congressmen wanted Reconstruction to change. First, they said certain men could not join Congress. These men who could not join were the newly elected representatives and senators from states that used to be Confederate. The Northern congressmen's decision made President Johnson unhappy.

Then Congress passed two laws that caused Reconstruction to change. The first law strengthened a government organization called the **Freedmen's Bureau**. This powerful organization was supposed to help anyone who had lost his home during the Civil War. The second law Congress passed was the Civil Rights Bill. This law said that the freedmen were free from unjust Southern laws.

Passing a Law After a Veto

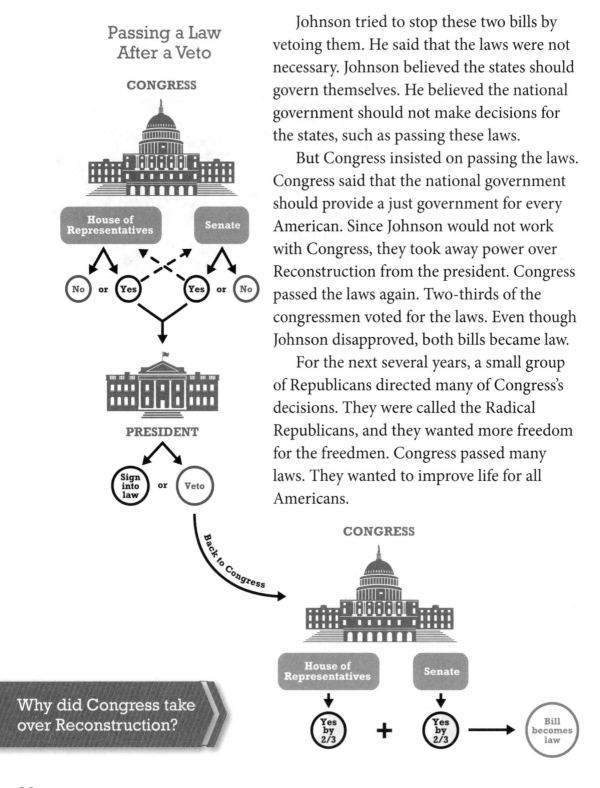

CONGRESS

House of Representatives | Senate

No or Yes | Yes or No

PRESIDENT

Sign into law or Veto

Back to Congress

CONGRESS

House of Representatives | Senate

Yes by 2/3 + Yes by 2/3 → Bill becomes law

Johnson tried to stop these two bills by vetoing them. He said that the laws were not necessary. Johnson believed the states should govern themselves. He believed the national government should not make decisions for the states, such as passing these laws.

But Congress insisted on passing the laws. Congress said that the national government should provide a just government for every American. Since Johnson would not work with Congress, they took away power over Reconstruction from the president. Congress passed the laws again. Two-thirds of the congressmen voted for the laws. Even though Johnson disapproved, both bills became law.

For the next several years, a small group of Republicans directed many of Congress's decisions. They were called the Radical Republicans, and they wanted more freedom for the freedmen. Congress passed many laws. They wanted to improve life for all Americans.

Why did Congress take over Reconstruction?

Congress Tries to Help
The Freedmen's Bureau

Throughout Reconstruction, many in Congress tried to improve life in the South. Sometimes Congress forgot how different the South was from the North. This made Congress's changes hard for Southerners. Still, Congress tried to help.

One of the main ways Congress tried to help was by starting the Freedmen's Bureau, also called the Bureau. It began at the end of the Civil War. The Bureau's job was to help anyone in the South who suffered from the war. The Bureau helped settle people who had lost their homes during the war.

As time went on, the Bureau did much more. It sent aid to the needy. It provided schools for freedmen. It improved treatment of black workers by their employers. It ran hospitals. The Bureau also had power to give away abandoned land.

Although the Bureau was set up to help all Southerners, its work focused on the freedmen. Because the Bureau was closely tied to black people, few white Southerners wanted its help. The Bureau spent much energy to improve the freedmen's conditions.

Tolson's Chapel was built in 1866 in Sharpsburg, Maryland. This historic African American church was used as a Freedmen's Bureau school for black students after the Civil War.

The Bureau probably did the most good by helping to organize schools for freedmen's children. Many Northerners wanted to help the freedmen. These Northerners sent money and teachers to the South. The Bureau made sure the people and funds went to help projects that the Bureau thought were good.

African American legislators—Robert Smalls, Joseph Rainey, and Blanche Bruce

Military Oversees Reconstruction

Congress also tried to help Reconstruction through the military. Congress put Northern soldiers in the South. This displeased the Southerners. But the army's presence helped encourage better behavior toward the freedmen and Republicans.

Early in 1867 Congress passed a new law. The First Reconstruction Act set up five military districts throughout the South. A general was put in charge of each district. State governments that were already in power were allowed to continue. However, the general could overrule them if he thought it was necessary.

The generals were in charge of overseeing political reconstruction. First, each state had to write a new constitution. This would allow a state to get back its political independence. The constitution had to give freedmen the right to vote. Also, some former Confederates would not be allowed to vote. Second, a majority of legal, or lawful, voters must approve the new constitution. Then a state could send representatives to Congress and be part of making laws for America.

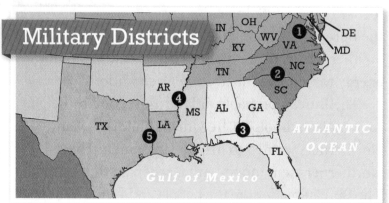

Military Districts

Constitutional Amendments

During Reconstruction, Congress also passed three amendments, or changes, to the United States Constitution. These helped to make sure Americans were treated fairly and equally. Congress said that the Southern states had to approve the amendments. If they did not, they could not rejoin the Union.

The Thirteenth Amendment abolished slavery. Congress passed this amendment before the Civil War ended. In late 1865 enough states voted in favor of the amendment, and it became law.

The Fourteenth Amendment made the freedmen citizens. It stated that anyone born in the United States was a citizen. The amendment also promised that all citizens of the United States would receive equal treatment under the law. Congress proposed this amendment in 1866. It took two years for the amendment to become law. Many states in the South voted against it at first. But in the end they all accepted it to rejoin the United States.

Even after the Fourteenth Amendment passed, some states refused to let freedmen vote. The Fifteenth Amendment was the last Reconstruction amendment. It said that a person's race or skin color was not a legal reason to prevent anyone from voting. A citizen of any race could vote.

Through the Freedmen's Bureau, the military overseeing Reconstruction, and the Reconstruction amendments, Congress tried to make life more fair for the freedmen. Some results happened right away. Some results took many years to make a difference.

Reconstruction Amendments

Slavery is abolished.

Freedmen are citizens.

All adult male citizens can vote.

What was one way that Congress tried to improve life in the South?

Changes in Daily Life
Education

Reconstruction brought much change to the South. Some changes lasted. Some did not. However, during the Reconstruction years, life for most Southerners was very different from life before the war.

One of the biggest changes was in the growth of education. Freedmen sent their children to schools. New colleges helped educate black Americans. Churches restarted colleges that had closed during the Civil War.

African American students at the Hampton Institute in Virginia

Children's Education

Before the Civil War, few slaves were allowed to learn to read or write. During Reconstruction, the children of freedmen began to receive an education. Throughout the South, thousands of schools opened.

States also began to pay for public education. Most schools served either white or black children. Even though some white Southerners treated Northern teachers badly, teaching continued. Freedmen wanted their children to receive an education. Parents gave what money they could to pay for schools and teachers.

Colleges

Colleges at this time rarely permitted black students to attend. Because of this unjust treatment, colleges opened for black people in the South.

Christians realized that the freedmen's pastors needed to be well educated, so churches often paid to meet this need. These colleges educated leaders in religion, politics, and other fields. Several of these colleges still exist today.

After the Civil War, white Southerners supported colleges too. Many students and teachers had died fighting in the war. Some colleges had loaned their money to the Confederate government. After the war, these colleges had nothing. Many religious groups gave money to colleges. Several new schools were founded. Almost all of them began as religious schools.

A mathematical geography class at the Hampton Institute in Virginia in 1899

Daniel Payne

What: bishop, teacher, author

When: 1811–1893

Where: South Carolina

Daniel Payne was born a free black American. He started a school when he was eighteen. But he had to close the school after laws would not allow the teaching of reading and writing to black people. During the Civil War Payne became the first black American to be the president of an American college. After the war he worked hard to provide education and churches to the freedmen.

Carpetbaggers and Scalawags

Northerners moving south also changed Southern life. Many wanted to help rebuild the South. Some Northerners came as businessmen. Others came to teach.

Northerners often found the South unfriendly. People from the North thought Southerners should realize they had lost the war and accept that they were wrong. Northerners believed the South should be remade to make it more like the North. Most Southerners disagreed. They knew they had lost the war. But they did not admit that they were completely wrong. They often believed that God had let them lose to punish their sin. But few thought slavery was their sin. They did not like Northerners telling them they were wrong.

Northerners in the South had to find jobs. Southerners rarely wanted to work with them.

An 1860s American wool carpetbag with leather handles

Many Northerners tried to get government jobs. Southerners called these northern men **carpetbaggers**. A carpetbag was a cheap suitcase. Southerners said that carpetbaggers were poor people from the North who went South because they could not find jobs up North.

Before the Civil War not all Southerners wanted to leave the Union. After the war some of them worked with Northerners. Other Southerners called these Southerners **scalawags**. Scalawags and freedmen often voted for carpetbaggers to be in government. Scalawags, freedmen, and carpetbaggers usually joined the Republican Party. During Reconstruction, the Republicans controlled many Southern states.

Churches

Churches also changed during Reconstruction. Before the Civil War, most Southern churches had a mix of white and black people who attended. Enslaved people attended church with their masters. But black people had to sit in the back or in balconies. At that time, most pastors were white.

After the war, churches split into churches for either white or black people. These churches often split when people in them treated each other unequally.

Freedmen wanted the situation in churches to change. Freedmen wanted their own black pastors. Freedmen wanted to be able to sit anywhere in church. White Southerners did not want change. They wanted churches to function as they always had. Because of this, most freedmen began their own churches. They started many Baptist and Methodist churches.

Slave benches in the balcony of a church

The freedmen's churches needed help. They usually had no land or buildings. And few black men had studied to become pastors. Some Southern white churches gave land to black churches. The Southern Methodists helped set up black Methodist churches. Some Northern churches sent money for land to the new black churches. These Northern churches also often sent missionaries and pastors. Later, Northern churches gave black men licenses to preach in their own churches.

Southern Society

By the end of Reconstruction, society in the South was splitting into two groups. A **society** is a group of people who live and work together and have similar cultures and beliefs.

By now few freedmen attended white churches. Both white and black Southerners claimed to be Christians, but the two communities rarely met together in church. White Southerners usually stayed in the Democratic Party. Freedmen joined the Republican Party. Even in schools, white and black Southerners were separated.

What were some of the changes Reconstruction brought to the South?

Problems During Reconstruction
Corruption

Besides the division in Southern society, there were other problems during Reconstruction. Some of the biggest problems were corruption, violence, and finding jobs for the freedmen.

During Reconstruction, both the North and the South suffered from **corruption**, or dishonesty, in government. Corruption occurs when people use their influence, or authority, to help themselves instead of doing their job. One example of corruption happened in the Midwest. Some tax collectors sent only half of the money they collected to the government and kept half for themselves.

Many Southerners claimed that corruption was the Republicans' fault. In 1868 America elected a new president, Ulysses S. Grant. He had been a successful general during the Civil War. He was also a Republican. Many of President Grant's friends were corrupt. The president himself was not.

Political cartoon by Thomas Nast showing President Grant weighed down with the burdens of government and corruption

In the South several state lawmakers were corrupt. Sometimes these lawmakers took bribes. A **bribe** is a gift of money or favor to cause someone to make a decision. For example, many Southern states built railroads after the war. The owner of a railroad company might bribe state lawmakers to let his company build the tracks. But some companies did not finish the job. Then the state had to pay to finish the work. Corruption hurt the Southern states.

Political cartoon by Thomas Nast of Democratic watchdog standing against the corrupt Southern wolf

There was also much corruption in the North. In New York City a small group of men tried to control the entire city. They wanted people to pay them money. In return the men said they would vote in favor of certain laws and building projects that the people wanted. This was not an honest way to vote. America suffered from the corruption.

Most Americans opposed corruption. One man named **Thomas Nast** drew pictures making fun of corrupt people. When newspapers printed his pictures, people learned about the corruption. Over time Americans passed new laws to stop corrupt behavior.

Violence

Violence became another major problem during Reconstruction. In the South, white people did not like the freedmen to act as if they were equal with white people. Most white Southerners did not want black people to vote. They wanted black people to obey white people. To make this happen some white people began groups to threaten and hurt freedmen. The most infamous group was the Ku Klux Klan. *Infamous* means being known for doing wrong or bad things.

Bad white men hurt freedmen to stop them from voting. Enemies of freedmen's voting rights sometimes blocked black people from voting. They beat or shot black men who tried to vote. Sometimes these people went to freedmen's houses at night. They burned crosses in the yards and even burned the freedmen's houses. Freedmen often had to hide to be safe.

For a while Northern army officers protected the freedmen. As long as a Northern army was in a Southern state, the Freedmen's Bureau told the army about problems there. But as Reconstruction ended, problems got worse. When a Northern army left a Southern state, white men there threatened and killed freedmen. By the end of Reconstruction, many freedmen stopped voting. Even though the Fifteenth Amendment promised them the right to vote, voting had become too dangerous.

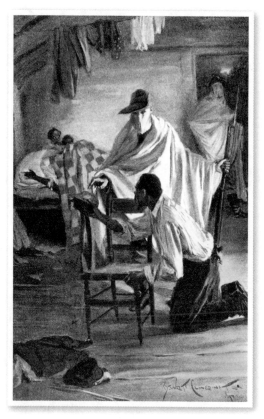

Some former Confederate soldiers formed a secret group called the Ku Klux Klan. They tried to scare freedmen to keep them from voting.

Jobs for Freedmen

Finding work for the freedmen was another major problem. Before the Civil War the South had few factories. Afterward most Southerners expected to continue to make a living by growing crops. Many freedmen hoped to become independent farmers. They believed that the government would give each family land and a mule. Freedmen hoped that the national government would take land from Confederate leaders who owned large plantations. These freedmen hoped the land would be divided up among those who used to be slaves there. Many freedmen believed that since they and their ancestors had helped build the plantations, they should receive the land.

White Southerners viewed land and work differently. They believed that the land belonged to them. Even though the slaves had been freed, white Southerners did not think the freedmen should get the land. Many Southerners thought most freedmen were lazy. White Southerners wanted to force freedmen to work on the white people's plantations.

The national government did not give either side what they wanted. Only some freedmen were given land. The government said that it could not take people's land. Land was only taken from landowners if they did not pay their taxes.

However, the government did not let Southern white people force the freedmen to work. When Southern states passed laws that required the freedmen to work, the national government said the laws were illegal.

Eventually the South developed a way to grow crops. This system was called **sharecropping**. Landowners allowed poor white and black farmers to rent plots of land. In return the farmer gave the landowner a share of the crops. A farming family might borrow money to buy seeds and farm tools. When the crop was harvested, they had to pay back their landlord and pay him rent. Few poor Southerners made much money sharecropping. Many ended up owing lots of money to their landlords. The system of sharecropping lasted in the South for many decades. A **decade** is a period of ten years.

① Farmer **rents** land in exchange for **share** of crops.

② Farmer **borrows** money to buy seeds and tools.

③ Farmer **plants** and **harvests** the crop.

The Sharecropping Cycle

④ Farmer **shares** harvest and **repays** debt.

⑤ Farmer usually **owed** more than he could pay.

⑥ Farmer **promised** to share more and repay more next time.

What were three big problems during Reconstruction?

The End of Northern Reconstruction
Different Hopes and Goals

When Reconstruction began, the three major groups of Americans each had different hopes and goals. Freedmen wanted to be independent. They wanted to be treated fairly and to have the chance to own their own land. Southerners wanted to govern their own states again. They hoped to restore, or bring back, the South as closely as they could to how it was before the war. Northerners wanted to make sure that the Civil War was not in vain. They hoped to rebuild the South and make it like the North. They also wanted to make sure the freedmen were treated fairly.

But as problems grew in the South, Northerners became less interested in changing the South.

Changes in the North

In 1877 Rutherford B. Hayes became president. By this year things had changed. Events in the North made Northerners rethink their views of Southern politics. The corruption during Ulysses S. Grant's eight years as president made Northerners focus on their own problems. It also made them more likely to agree with Southerners when they complained that Republicans in the South were corrupt. Since Southern Republicans were mainly freedmen, scalawags, and carpetbaggers, some Northerners began to think that Southern Democrats should be allowed to take over Southern government again.

President Ulysses S. Grant

The Northern economy also took Northerners' minds off the Reconstruction. Starting in 1873 many businesses closed. Some banks had to shut down. Several railroads went bankrupt. Going **bankrupt** means not being able to pay money that is owed. During this time many people lost their jobs. These events were known as the Panic of 1873. Northerners were too busy worrying about work and business to try to keep helping the South.

Northerners also wondered why the freedmen still needed help. Some Northerners thought that since the slaves had been free since 1865, they should be able to take care of themselves.

For many Northerners enough time had passed since the Civil War that the fighting was a memory. Their cities had never been burned. Their railroads had not been destroyed. The war seemed far away. Northerners struggled to understand why the freedmen kept wanting more help.

Progress

The freedmen's position had improved a little since the war ended. Some owned land. Many more rented small pieces of land. Their children went to school. However, anyone with black skin was treated as less important than someone with white skin. The freedmen feared that if Northerners stopped caring about the South, the freedmen's lives would become worse. As Northern influence left the South, most freedmen tried to fit into the new situation. It was not as good as what they hoped for at emancipation, or freedom from slavery. However, their new situation was not as bad as slavery.

End of Reconstruction

By the end of the 1870s, Reconstruction ended. Southern Democrats now controlled all the state governments in the South. The end of Reconstruction fulfilled some of the white Southerners' hopes. When Northern troops left the South, freedmen lost their

Activity

Displaying the Reconstruction

Museums have creative exhibits that teach us about many different things. In history museums, exhibits show objects from the past that people can observe and study. Most of the objects and documents you see in history museums are primary sources.

For this activity, you will be designing a display about the time of Reconstruction in America. The display should include a title, artifacts, visuals, and maps.

"Shall I trust these men,   and not this man?"

protection. Many who used to be leaders of the South came back to power. But the Southerners' new world was different from the old. The South was not the same as before. Railroads and industry had entered the South. Cities like Atlanta, Georgia, began to bring factories and businesses to the South.

In the end Reconstruction did not exactly fulfill anyone's goals. President Lincoln in his Second Inaugural Address said that he wanted Americans to "achieve and cherish a just, and a lasting peace, among [themselves]." The peace in America was not complete or completely just, but by the end of Reconstruction in 1877, more Americans enjoyed more liberties than in 1860.

Thomas Nast's political cartoon contrasting Confederate leaders asking for pardons with a Union soldier who could not vote

What is one reason that Northerners stopped caring about Reconstruction?

3 The Wild West

Focus

The settlement of the American West brought opportunity to some people and loss to others.

First transcontinental
railroad completed
1869

Oklahoma Land Rush
1889

1860 1862   **1870**   **1880**   **1890**

Homestead Act   Battle of Wounded Knee

The West Beckons

Now more and more Americans turned their eyes to the West. During the Civil War and Reconstruction, the nation had worked on settling problems and rebuilding its torn land. But changes were taking place in other parts of the country too. With the war over, many people now had time to look westward.

White Americans looked at the West as a wild land to be tamed and settled. This way of looking at the West was partly good. God made people to fill and rule the earth. But the problem was that the land in the West was not empty. Native Americans had been there for centuries. As you read this chapter, you will see that white Americans did not act out of love for these first Americans. Trouble and sadness came because Americans did not obey God's command to love.

Tracks Across the Continent

One of the most exciting changes in the West was the growth of railroads. Before the Civil War, the United States had more than 30,000 miles of railroad track. But all this track lay east of the Mississippi River. In 1862 Congress approved the building of the first **transcontinental** railroad—a railroad that would cross the entire continent.

The railroad project began in two different places. The Central Pacific Railroad Company began laying a track eastward from Sacramento, California. The Union Pacific Railroad Company laid its track westward from Omaha, Nebraska. The two railroads would meet somewhere between the two cities.

Building a railroad was not a quick and easy task. Railroad workers had to be strong. They also had to be good at solving problems. Sometimes the workers had to stop and deal with landforms in their way. Sometimes they had to build a curved track around a mountain. At other times they used dynamite to blast through rock and carve out a tunnel. In winter they had to cut their way through deep snowdrifts.

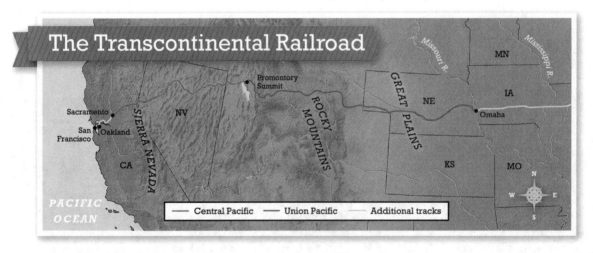

The Transcontinental Railroad

Many Irish and Chinese immigrants worked on the railroad. The Irish came mostly from America's eastern cities. The Chinese came either from California mining towns or all the way from China. Former Civil War soldiers also found jobs on the tracks.

The Chinese on the Central Pacific line were some of the best workers. They did their job quickly, quietly, and diligently. They ate seafood and vegetables and drank tea throughout the day. Because of their diet, they stayed healthier than the Irish workers. But even with these good qualities, the Chinese received less pay than the Irish. They also endured many insults and jokes because they were Chinese. Yet they kept working hard. It was not long before they earned the respect of those in charge. They were given the hardest jobs and were trusted to do them well.

These Chinese railroad workers are shown wearing traditional cone-shaped hats to shade their heads from the sun.

Indian Conflicts

The Indian tribes of the plains were troubled by the growth of the railroad. Fast, noisy trains would now come steaming through their lands. Towns would spring up on their hunting grounds. The buffalo would not be able to live there any longer.

Union Pacific workers often had conflicts with the Plains Indians. Fighting broke out from time to time. People on both sides were killed. Many railroad workers lived in fear of raids by the Cheyenne or the Sioux tribes. But one tribe, the Pawnee, was friendly to the railroad workers. The Pawnee people helped guard the tracks from attacks by other tribes, and the work went on.

Railroad workers and officials celebrate the meeting of the two tracks at Promontory Summit.

Today the original Golden Spike is displayed at the Cantor Arts Museum at Stanford University.

The Golden Spike

As the Central Pacific and the Union Pacific tracks drew near to each other, excitement grew. Where would the tracks meet? Workers on both tracks pushed themselves harder and worked even faster. Sometimes the two lines had contests to see which one could lay the most track. Near the end of the Central Pacific line, railroad workers laid ten miles of track in one day!

On May 10, 1869, the two tracks met at **Promontory Summit, Utah**. The last spike that joined the rails together was a special spike made of gold. Heads of the railroad companies took turns tapping the golden spike into place. Then the golden spike was replaced with an iron one and put in a museum.

The first transcontinental railroad was finished. With this new and faster route now open, more and more people traveled west. The West beckoned all kinds of people. Some went west to look for work. Some went west to look for gold. And many families went west to settle.

> Where did the two railroad tracks meet?

Cowboys and Longhorns
The Frontier

The open land in the West was called the frontier. A **frontier** is land that has not been settled. At the end of the Civil War, Americans had settled most of the country east of the Mississippi River. Gold hunters had rushed to California, and pioneers had settled in Oregon. The Mormons had settled in Utah. Some Americans lived in Texas. But much of the land in western America still had not been tamed.

As Americans began to settle the West, whole tribes of Indians were forced off their lands. Many of them now lived in the Oklahoma Territory. Buffalo still roamed the plains, and these Indians followed the herds. They used the buffalo for their food, clothing, and shelter. They needed the buffalo to live.

Buffalo were not the only wild animals on the frontier. Millions of wild cattle called **longhorns** also roamed freely in Texas. Spanish settlers had brought the first of these animals to America long ago. The cattle had long, sharp horns. They were strong and dangerous. The bulls would attack anyone who came near them.

Both eastern cities and western towns wanted these cattle. Longhorn hides were used to make leather. Their fat was used in products like candles and soap. Their beef was used for food. American ranchers in Texas began rounding up longhorns to sell. The cattle could be herded north to towns along the railroad. There they could be sold and taken by train to other places. But herding cattle was not easy. The ranchers needed some brave young men to drive the cattle north to the railroad towns.

Life as a Cowboy

In the 1860s and 1870s, many men went west to work as cowboys. Boys as young as twelve years old found jobs herding cattle. Immigrants from Europe, white Americans, black freedmen, Mexicans, and Indians worked as cowboys.

Cowboys had to have important skills. They had to be good with horses. Some cowboys had to be able to tame wild horses for riding. They had to be able to throw a lariat, or rope, around the horns of a stray longhorn. They had to be tough enough to survive long, hot days and chilly nights on the frontier. They had to be men who loved adventure.

Moving a herd of longhorns north was called a **cattle drive**. An average herd had 2,000 to 3,000 cattle. A **trail boss** was in charge of a cattle drive. It was his job to get the entire herd safely north to the railroad.

Cowboys learned their skills and their style of dress from Mexican cattle herders, or *vaqueros*. The English word *buckaroo* comes from the Spanish word *vaquero*.

A Cattle Drive

The trail boss often rode out in front of the herd. He also rode along the sides or looked for lost animals. He sometimes sent a scout ahead to search for the next place to camp.

Point rider

The cook drove the chuck wagon with all the food supplies.

Point riders led the herd. They rode at the front on each side.

Swing riders rode along the sides of the herd.

Flank rider

Swing rider

Drag riders rode behind the herd. They kept the stragglers moving with the rest of the herd.

Flank riders rode near the back of the herd. Both swing and flank riders kept cattle from wandering off to the left or right.

Wranglers rode with the extra horses. Each cowboy needed eight to ten horses for the cattle drive.

Cattle Brands

Each longhorn in a herd had a special symbol on its hide. These symbols, called **brands**, stood for the ranches the cattle had come from. Cowboys burned the symbol onto each cow's hide with a hot branding iron. Brands helped cowboys know whom each longhorn belonged to. Brands also made it hard for thieves to steal cattle.

A branded longhorn bull

As the herd moved along, cowboys had to stay alert. Many things could upset the cattle, especially at night when they could not see well. A loud clap of thunder or a gunshot could scare them. They could be surprised by a leaping jackrabbit or deer. Even small sounds like the clatter of a tin pan or the snap of a twig sometimes spooked the herd. When the herd became frightened, a **stampede** might take place. Stampeding cattle scattered and ran wildly away from the trail, sometimes for miles. It might take the cowboys days to round up the herd again after a stampede.

A cowboy's work was tiring. When they stopped to camp, cowboys could relax and enjoy some free time. They often held contests, told jokes and stories, and sang songs. Some of these cowboy songs are still sung today.

Relaxing around the campfire was a cowboy's reward at the end of a long day's work.

Why did cowboys drive cattle north?

Cattle Trails and Cow Towns

At first, cattle were taken mainly to towns in Missouri to meet the railroad. But settlers in Oklahoma and Missouri did not like the longhorns coming through their lands. The settlers were trying to raise cattle of their own. The longhorns often carried ticks. These ticks caused a fever in the settlers' cattle.

A cattle buyer named Joseph McCoy had an idea. He set up a cattle shipping yard in the small town of Abilene, Kansas. Since the railroad had made its way west, Abilene was now located by the railroad. Many cowboys were glad to be able to bring their cattle to a town farther west. The route to Abilene was straight north from Texas, and there was no danger of harm to the settlers' cattle.

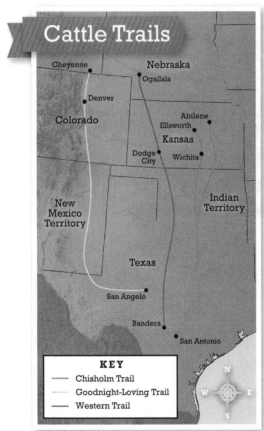

Cowboys used the same trails for cattle drives again and again. The trail used to go to Abilene was called the **Chisholm Trail**. This trail was named after a trader, **Jesse Chisholm**. He had used the trail to carry goods to his trading posts. For many years the Chisholm Trail was the most popular cattle trail. Another trail, the Goodnight-Loving Trail, went even farther west. Charles Goodnight and Oliver Loving created this trail as a way to get cattle to Colorado and Wyoming.

As the cattle trade grew, several more Kansas railroad towns were used as shipping points. Abilene, Wichita, Ellsworth, and Dodge City were some of the best-known **cow towns**.

Most cow towns had no local government to make laws. Without laws, cow towns quickly became some of the roughest towns in the West. Cowboys were paid at the end of a cattle drive. A cow town provided many ways for a cowboy to spend his money. Businesses such as gun shops, boot sellers, and general stores did well in cattle towns. But there were also many ways to spend money on things that were not good or wise. Dance halls and saloons where cowboys could gamble and drink whiskey moved into cow towns. These towns became places of much temptation to evil for young cowboys.

Many cow towns hired lawmen to help keep order. **Tom Smith** was one of the first lawmen, or marshals, of Abilene. He believed in using his hands as his weapon more often than his guns. Athletic and fearless, he stood up to the toughest men in town. He was killed while on duty. But he is still remembered as a lawman who commanded respect.

Bill Tilghman was the marshal of Dodge City for two years. Like Smith, he rarely used his guns unless he had to. He was known for his honesty and courage. He later worked as a lawman in Oklahoma, where he helped arrest two dangerous outlaws.

Tom J. Smith, Abilene marshal

Bill Tilghman, Dodge City marshal

Wild Bill Hickok

Not every lawman had the kind of character that everyone admired. **"Wild Bill" Hickok** was probably the most famous lawman of the West. He was the marshal of Abilene after Tom Smith. Hickok was a gambler who spent much of his time in saloons. But he was also an expert shooter and quick to deal with trouble. Feared by many and hated by some, he died of a gunshot wound.

By the late 1800s, many cow towns had become calmer places. For the most part, large cattle drives had ended. More and more settlers planted crops and put up fences. Open land for driving cattle was hard to find. Railroads were more common and easier to reach. More ranchers and cowboys took care of cattle on privately owned land.

But Americans have not forgotten the days of the cowboys. Some of the cow towns, such as Wichita and Dodge City, are large cities in the state of Kansas today. And the cowboy himself is a symbol of the spirit of adventure in America's Old West.

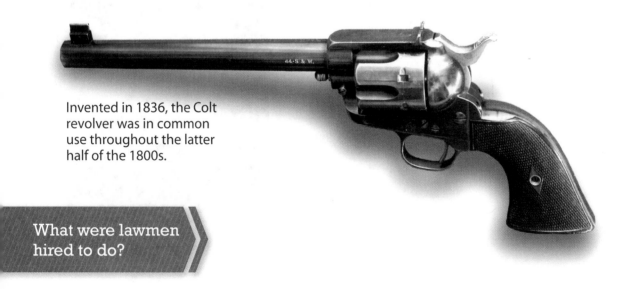

Invented in 1836, the Colt revolver was in common use throughout the latter half of the 1800s.

What were lawmen hired to do?

Miners and Missionaries
Gold Seekers

Some of the people who traveled west were looking for treasure. Gold had already been discovered in California in 1848. About ten years later, gold was found in the Rocky Mountains near Pikes Peak. Gold seekers rushed to the area that is now Colorado. Some of them painted the words "Pikes Peak or Bust" on their wagons. The saying meant a person would get to Pikes Peak or spend all his money trying to get there.

About the same time, a discovery of both gold and silver brought miners rushing to Nevada. This rich source, or **lode**, of precious metals was named the Comstock Lode.

In the 1870s, the richest lode of gold was found in the Black Hills, a mountain range in what is now South Dakota. At the time, the Black Hills belonged to the Sioux Indians. The US government had promised that white Americans would stay out of this land. The gold there did not belong to them. But miners did not keep the agreement to stay off the Indians' land. Many rushed to the Black Hills in hopes of getting rich quickly.

A mining camp near Pikes Peak

Gold Mining

Miners set up camps in the West. These camps quickly grew into towns and cities. Railroads made travel to many of these places easy. Merchants began to open stores in mining towns. Post offices and lumber mills were set up. A town that grew quickly was called a **boomtown**. Like the cow towns, mining boomtowns were often rough places. But as more and more families came to these towns, the towns settled down. Boomtowns like Denver and Boulder grew because of the Pikes Peak Gold Rush. Denver and Boulder are now large cities in Colorado.

Not all boomtowns became lasting cities. Some towns that grew from mining camps were later abandoned. People left when they could no longer make a living from mining. These deserted towns with their empty buildings and silent streets were called **ghost towns**.

A western ghost town

Soul Seekers

Some Christians went west seeking a different kind of treasure. They remembered that Jesus had taught His followers to lay up treasure not on the earth but in heaven. Preachers, missionaries, and teachers took His words seriously. They went west to bring the gospel to people. They were looking for lost souls who were ready to trust Christ. By seeking these people they were laying up treasure in heaven.

Ezra Fisher was one of the missionaries to the West. Fisher had been the pastor of Baptist churches in Vermont, Indiana, Illinois, and Iowa. In the 1840s, he and his family traveled west across the plains to Oregon.

Ezra Fisher preached in Oregon and California for the next thirty years. His health was poor, and money and food were scarce. But God always met his needs. Fisher worked hard to support himself and his family. With people pouring into the western lands to look for gold, he was able to share the gospel widely. He even worked in the gold mines himself for a few months to raise money for his family. Many were so caught up in their desire for gold that they wanted nothing to do with Christ. But Fisher did not give up. He traveled throughout southern Oregon preaching. He helped organize several Baptist churches. More important, he saw many lives changed by the saving power of Christ.

Ezra Fisher

"I could walk this country all over for my Master, if I could only be successful in winning souls to Christ."

What two kinds of treasure did people find in the West?

Homesteaders
Sodbusters on the Plains

The West beckoned more than cowboys and treasure seekers. Many people headed west to set up homes there. In 1862, President Lincoln signed the **Homestead Act**. This important act opened land in the west to settlers. Each settler could have 160 acres of land. The settler had to build a house, live on the land, and improve the land over the next five years. Improving the land meant building a house or growing crops. After the five-year period, the land, called a homestead, belonged to him. People who gained land this way were known as **homesteaders**.

Many flocked to the West to claim land on the plains. Among them were freedmen and even some single women and widows. Some of these people owned land for the first time in their lives.

Railroad companies also sold land cheaply along the tracks. Word spread in Europe about the land for sale in America. Immigrants from Europe came to America to buy land in the West.

A large group of African Americans called "Exodusters" settled in the community of Nicodemus, Kansas.

Most of the early homesteaders on the plains made their living by farming. Recent inventions like the steel plow and the reaper were a great help to farmers. Prairie farmers grew corn and wheat and raised cattle and hogs. People called the prairie farmers **sodbusters**.

Turkey Red wheat growing on the Kansas plains

Immigrants from Russia brought an important product to America's Great Plains. The immigrants' Turkey Red wheat grew well on the prairie, even in the bitterly cold winters. The wheat could be ground into flour for making bread. Wheat became one of the main cash crops of the plains. Farmers grew wheat to sell and sent it by railroad to cities in the East. The Great Plains came to be called "America's Breadbasket."

Homesteaders on the dry, windy plains had to learn new ways of living and working. Because few trees grew on the plains, many did not use wood to build their houses. They built their homes out of sod. A sod house, or "soddy," was made of strips of thick prairie grassland. These sod pieces were fitted tightly together. Some families added doors and put glass panes in the windows. Soddies were comfortable homes. Now and then the roof leaked during heavy rains or a bit of sod fell out of the walls. But soddies kept settlers warm in winter and cool in summer.

This pioneer family added a sturdy wooden door to their sod house.

Very little rain fell on the plains. Many farmers began using the windmill to pump water. Windmills were powered by the strong prairie winds. The windmills drew water up from deep underground.

Laura Ingalls Wilder

What: homesteader, author

When: 1867–1957

Where: the American West

Laura lived in several different places during her childhood. She and her family spent time homesteading in Kansas, Minnesota, and the Dakota Territory. When Laura grew up, she married another homesteader, Almanzo Wilder. Later she wrote a series of books based on her childhood experiences. *Little House on the Prairie* is her best-known book. Her work has helped people all over the world understand what life was like for homesteaders on America's frontier.

One farmer named Joseph Glidden invented a new material for fences. His barbed wire worked well for keeping cattle out of the corn and wheat fields. It also helped keep Texas longhorns from crossing the settlers' land during cattle drives.

Sodbusters faced many other challenges. Storms, fires, and swarms of grasshoppers sometimes destroyed their crops and homes. In some parts of the frontier there were problems between the homesteaders and the Indians. The sodbusters could have given up. But most did not. Few settlers had come west expecting an easy life. Those who trusted God took comfort in His control. And still more settlers continued to come.

What kind of home did many of the homesteaders build?

The Oklahoma Land Rush

The United States government had settled many of the Native American tribes in the Oklahoma territory. Each tribe had a **reservation**, an area of land set aside for its people. Nearly two million acres of land in Oklahoma had not been assigned to any tribe. The government decided to open this land for settlement under the Homestead Act.

On April 22, 1889, the **Oklahoma Land Rush** took place. All along the borders of the unsettled land, people lined up in wagons, on horses, and on foot. Even trains stood waiting to carry homesteaders across the border. At noon, cannons boomed and bugles sounded. The race for the best land was on.

Tens of thousands of people claimed land in Oklahoma in one afternoon. People pushed stakes into the ground and set up hasty tents to prove their claims. These people were called "Boomers." Later, government agents learned that some people had slipped across the borders and claimed land before they were allowed. These people were called "Sooners." Some of the largest cities in present-day Oklahoma began during the Land Rush of '89.

This monument in Oklahoma City reminds citizens today of the land rush that first formed their city.

The Indians Fight Back
Buffalo Hunts and Broken Treaties

Settling the western frontier brought exciting new opportunities for many Americans. Yet for other Americans it brought painful losses. For the American Indians, the taming of the West meant the end of the life they had known for centuries.

The Plains Indians depended on the buffalo. When they killed a buffalo, they used every part of it. Nothing was wasted.

When white Americans moved west, the buffalo herds began to die out. The areas where the animals could graze grew smaller and smaller. Farms and railroads were built on the open grasslands. Hunters came west to kill buffalo and sell their hides to factories back east. Some hunters shot buffalo from the open windows of trains just for sport. They left the bodies to rot in the sun on the plains.

With so few buffalo left, the Plains Indians had to find a new way to live. Once they had been free to follow buffalo herds. But now they were expected to stay on reservations. The government wanted them to become farmers like the white settlers. But many Indians were not interested in changing their way of life.

This graph shows the decrease in the buffalo population during the 1800s.

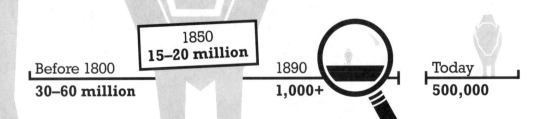

Before 1800
30–60 million

1850
15–20 million

1890
1,000+

Today
500,000

Government officials made many treaties with the Indians. They drew up maps and set up land boundaries. They promised that the white settlers would stay off land set aside as Indian land. But these promises were not kept. Sometimes farmers and ranchers moved onto Indian land. Sometimes gold seekers searched for treasure in territory that belonged to the Indians. When treaties were broken, the Indians fought back.

The Battle of the Little Bighorn

One of the most famous battles happened in 1876, after white Americans entered the Black Hills in search of gold. The Black Hills were on a reservation for the Sioux Indians. Once again a treaty had been broken, and the Sioux were angry. The government sent the United States army to the area. The Sioux joined with two other tribes and prepared for war. Their forces were led by chiefs **Crazy Horse** and **Sitting Bull**.

Colonel **George Custer** led one of the US forces. He was a daring officer, but he was also a proud and reckless man. He had already fought some battles against the Indians. He had attacked and easily defeated a Cheyenne camp some years before. He had killed more than one hundred people, including men, women, and children. He thought this battle would end in the same way.

Chief Sitting Bull

Colonel George Custer

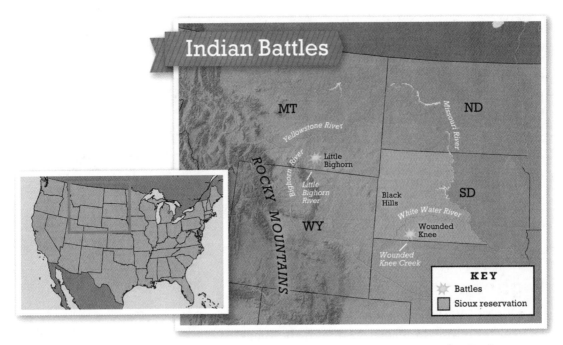

Indian Battles

But Custer was wrong. His men met the Indian warriors at the Little Bighorn River. The Indians had nearly two thousand men. Custer had only about two hundred soldiers with him. He had hoped to attack the Sioux camp at night and take the warriors by surprise. But the Indians found out he was coming. A surprise attack was impossible now. Custer ordered his men to advance toward the camp.

Crazy Horse and his warriors were prepared. Thousands of Sioux rushed out to meet Custer's soldiers. Custer and every one of his men died that day. The battle became known as Custer's Last Stand. But the battle would also be the last great victory for the Indians.

Why was the Battle of the Little Bighorn fought?

The Indians Surrender
Chief Joseph's People Flee

The next year another tribe, the Nez Perce, tried to flee north from Oregon to Canada. They did not want to be kept on a reservation. They traveled many long, dangerous miles. But the US Cavalry caught up with them near the border of Canada. The Nez Perce leader, **Chief Joseph**, agreed to surrender.

"I am tired of fighting," Chief Joseph said. "It is cold and we have no blankets. The little children are freezing to death. My people—some of them have run away to the hills and have no blankets and no food. . . . My heart is sick and sad. From where the sun now stands I will fight no more against the white man."

Chief Joseph

The Nez Perce people were moved to a reservation in Oklahoma. Many of them died there. Chief Joseph traveled to Washington, DC, and spoke with President Hayes about his people. The government finally allowed the Nez Perces to move back to the Northwest. However, the tribe did not live all together. They had to live in two groups in different areas.

The Battle of Wounded Knee

The last major battle between Indians and white men was at **Wounded Knee Creek** in South Dakota. More and more tribes had been forced to live on reservations. The Sioux chief Sitting Bull had been killed.

A group of Sioux had been performing a ceremony called the Ghost Dance. They believed that the Ghost Dance would please the spirits they worshiped. They thought it would give them power over the white man. They hoped it would bring back their old way of life.

The white military leaders did not understand the Ghost Dance. They thought that the Sioux were preparing for war with them. In 1890, US troops at Wounded Knee began firing at a group of Sioux who had been singing and dancing the Ghost Dance. The Sioux returned fire. Only twenty-five white soldiers were killed. But more than 250 Sioux died in the gunfire and cannon blasts. The Indians knew that this defeat was final. They would not try to fight the white men anymore.

In this reenactment of the Battle of Wounded Knee, a line of US troops can be seen approaching the Sioux camp.

The Indians and Injustice

White Americans were guilty of injustice toward the Indians. Although they obeyed God's command to fill and rule the earth, they did not obey His command to love. They did not treat the Indians as people made in the image of God. They did not treat them as people with the same rights as all other Americans. Many treaties were broken because white men wanted Indian land. Indian men, women, and children often suffered cruelty from the American armed forces. Many white settlers feared and hated the Indians because they did not understand Indian ways.

But as time went on, more and more Americans realized they had not treated the Indians justly. Some Americans spoke out against this injustice. Missionaries, writers, and government leaders asked for better treatment of the Indians. Some Indians spoke for themselves. One of the most famous speeches is by the Nez Perce chief Joseph.

Indian artifacts reveal skilled craftsmanship and a love for beauty.

Activity

Comparing Primary Sources

Read the cutting from Chief Joseph's speech during his visit to Washington, DC. Compare Chief Joseph's requests with the first ten amendments in the US Constitution (the Bill of Rights). Was Chief Joseph asking for rights that should have been given to all Americans? Discuss your findings with your classmates.

The US government tried to help make life better for the Indians. Government leaders thought the Indians would have a better life if their culture changed. So the government tried to make the Indians live more like white people did. Congress passed the **Dawes Act**. The Dawes Act allowed individual Indians to own land. But the Indians were used to living in large family groups. They were not used to owning land as white Americans did. Many Indians were not trained as farmers. Land-hungry settlers and gold seekers often cheated the Indians out of their land.

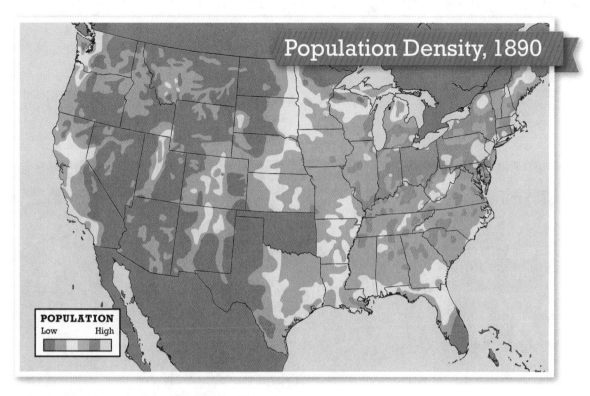

Population Density, 1890

POPULATION
Low   High

The End of the Wild West

By 1890 there was no land left in America that could be called a frontier. Most of the western lands had been opened to settlers or turned into reservations. The "Wild West" was now a thing of the past. But Americans today still love to remember the days when the buffalo roamed and the untamed land stretched for miles, wide and free.

Why did the Dawes Act fail to help the Indians?

4 Busy Cities

Focus

The growth of industry and cities brought opportunities and challenges.

Andrew Carnegie
opens steel plant
1875

1870   **1880**   **1884**   **1890**   **1897**   **1900**
Telegraph lines stretched   First   First subway in
from the Atlantic to the Pacific   skyscraper   United States

A Growing Nation
Businesses Get Bigger

The Civil War taught Americans how to think big. During the war Americans learned how to move thousands of men around the country. They learned how to feed and clothe these men. They learned how to give them the tools they needed to fight. They learned how to raise the money needed to keep everything going. Soldiers learned how to take orders and work together in large groups.

Before the war, Americans worked on farms or in their own shops. Some worked in factories, which were only in the Northeast. After the war, businesses grew. More Americans worked for them instead. Some businesses spread across the entire nation. This growth caused new challenges. Employers needed to make sure that all the workers got paid. Supplies needed to reach the right place. Businesses met these challenges by learning lessons from how things were managed during the Civil War.

Big businesses also looked for new ways to become successful. They learned to produce more goods in less time. People invented machines that did the work of several people. This saved businesses time and money. Businesses could sell more goods with lower prices. Because more people could afford to buy these goods, businesses earned more money.

Some men observed other businesses to learn from them. These men studied how long it took workers to do a task and suggested ways to help the workers do their job better. One of these ways was for workers to always use the same process when doing each task.

Managers counted how many goods workers in a business produced. Such record keeping became an important way to judge how well a business was doing.

Postcard of a leading steel producer in the United States

BETHLEHEM STEEL COMPANY OFFICE AND WORKS, STEELTON, PA.

Changes in Education

Changes in business led to changes in schools. Businesses wanted schools to train men to work in business. This is not what colleges did before the Civil War.

Before the war, colleges focused on training men to be leaders in their communities. Colleges taught about history so that men could learn from the past. Students learned literature to understand important ideas. Colleges taught the languages Greek, Latin, French, and German so students could read what people from other times and places wrote.

Also before the war, people who wanted to work in a business might not go to college. They learned from people who were already in a business. If a person wanted to be a blacksmith, he could work with a blacksmith. The experienced blacksmith would teach him the job. If a person wanted to build carriages for a living, he could work with a carriage builder and learn from him.

But after the war, special colleges were started. These colleges taught men how to be good businessmen. They focused on the things that a business leader needed to know. They did not focus on big ideas. They did not focus on other languages or history.

BEFORE

AFTER

How did the Civil War change businesses in America?

85

Growth of Industry

Railroads were the most important industry after the Civil War. Railroads were used to transport **raw materials** to distant factories. Raw materials are the resources used to make a product. Finished products are called goods. Railroads also transported goods and people across the nation. Goods could be shipped quickly on the railroad, so the prices of goods were lowered.

Describe the difference between the urban Pennsylvania Railroad Station in the early 1900s (above) with the rural Eastland Mill Valley Station in 1894 in California (below).

Telegraph lines were put up along the railroad tracks. By 1870, telegraph lines stretched from the Atlantic to the Pacific. The telegraph allowed a message to be sent instantly between places that were far away, such as California and New York. This was amazing. It took a week or more for a person to travel from New York City, New York, to San Francisco, California.

Other industries grew as the railroad grew. Railroad tracks were made of steel. More railroads meant more business for steel companies. People also found new uses for steel. The first skyscrapers were built at this time. Steel made skyscrapers possible.

Andrew Carnegie became the most important steel manufacturer in the nation. When times were bad, prices for goods dropped. During those times, Carnegie bought what he needed to produce lots of steel. Then when times were good, he could make more steel for less money. People would buy his steel. Carnegie learned the best ways to manufacture steel.

He learned how to manage a large business by observing railroad companies. He also listened to his workers. Most businesses worked their men from sunup to sundown. But Carnegie's men worked eight hours a day. Most businesses paid their workers every month. Carnegie paid his workers every two weeks. The workers liked this. However, the workers did not always think that Carnegie treated them justly. They did not like it when he lowered wages. They did not like that he let workers go when business was slow. Sometimes the workers refused to work unless Carnegie changed the way he treated them.

Oil was another big business after the Civil War. People used oil to light lamps. They also used it to **lubricate** machinery. This helped machine parts move more easily.

Before the war Americans used whale oil. But by the 1850s whalers had to sail further from home to hunt for whales. It took longer to get whale oil. Americans needed to find a replacement for it. People discovered that oil drilled from the ground could replace whale oil. This oil was called **petroleum**. It could be turned into **kerosene** to light lamps. It could also be used to lubricate machines in factories. It could be used on the engines that pulled trains.

Andrew Carnegie

James J. Hill developed a profitable railroad business without any government funds.

John D. Rockefeller

There was a certain process to turn oil into kerosene. People needed to **refine**, or purify, the oil. In the end, whatever separated from the oil was thrown away. People did not know what to do with it.

But one man found uses for the products that formed after oil was refined. He was able to make money selling them. He built much of the equipment needed for his business. This helped him save money because he did not have to pay someone else for equipment.

This man's name was **John D. Rockefeller**. He became the most important man in the oil business. Rockefeller also figured out a better way to turn oil into kerosene. Because Rockefeller could refine oil more cheaply, more Americans could afford his oil. They used it to burn kerosene lights at night.

The growth of industry and business helped make life in America better in many ways. Daily living became more convenient. Andrew Carnegie's steel caused more railroads to be built. More goods and people could be transported. John D. Rockefeller's refined oil caused lamps to burn longer. This meant people could work and read at later hours.

When God made the human race, He blessed them with the ability to rule over His creation. He told man to multiply and fill the earth (Genesis 1:28). Man's intelligence and abilities come from God. This blessing explains why people could make inventions and use resources to help others. It explains why people wanted to connect cities with railroads and string telegraph lines across the nation. All this helped America grow, and it was God's blessing that made this possible.

How did the growth of industry help Americans?

The Wealthy and the Working Class

The growth of business in this time period made certain people very rich. Some wealthy people thought carefully about wise ways to use their wealth. Andrew Carnegie was one of these men. He did not think that the wealthy should hold on to their wealth. When they died their wealth would go to other people. Those people might not use it wisely. Instead Carnegie said that wealthy people should use their wealth to help others while they were alive.

But the world that we live in is a fallen world. Not all people gain their wealth in just ways. Not all wealth is used wisely. During that time in America, some big businesses misused their power. The United States government passed laws that tried to stop businesses from acting unjustly. Some of these laws stopped wrongdoing. But some of these laws also hurt good businesses that were not doing wrong.

Biltmore House and Gardens in Asheville, North Carolina, built by George Vanderbilt in the late 1800s

EMPLOYER

HUMAN RESOURCES

As industries and businesses got larger, workers had to face changes. Workers used to work alongside their employers. Sometimes workers even lived in the same house as their employer. But in large companies the owner might not know many of his workers. Some owners treated their workers simply as resources, or machines, for the company.

But workers did not like being treated like a resource. They thought that company owners made them work too long each day. Workers thought their workplaces were unsafe. They thought they were paid too little. They thought it unfair that the owner would cut their pay when he had more money than he could ever spend.

Over time, however, these workers were better off than Americans who had lived in earlier times. Workers now made more money. They lived in nicer places. They could afford to buy better things. The workers enjoyed a better life because of big business. Their products were well made and cost less money. People with less money could buy nicer things.

But in other ways, these workers also lived in harder times. Working in a factory was difficult and could be dangerous. If a worker was hurt by a machine, he could not work. He would not be able to earn money to live and buy food. The employer did not help him. For this reason many workers lived in fear.

A worker had little power to change things at a company. Workers had an idea. What if all the workers got together and demanded that their company make changes? The workers could say that they would not work unless the company made the changes. This action is called going on **strike**.

Boys gather around an obstacle set up on the railroad track by strikers (Cleveland Car Strike, Ohio, 1899).

Workers on strike united and formed groups called **labor unions**. Unions helped get workers together. They had to work together if a strike was going to be successful.

Unions helped set up strikes. Sometimes unions were successful at making deals with companies. One deal might be for a company to improve the workers' working conditions. Sometimes the deal was to give workers better pay.

Sadly, some union strikes were violent. Sometimes the strikers turned into a mob. They destroyed property and killed people. Men who liked to cause trouble were attracted to the unions. Sometimes company owners hired armed men to break up strikes. These strikebreakers sometimes killed strikers during the fight.

Another problem the unions created came from their own success. When a company had too much power, it could act unjustly toward its workers. Likewise, when a union had too much power, it could act unjustly toward the owners of the company.

Why did workers believe they were treated unjustly?

Cities
Growth of the City

In the years after the Civil War, American cities grew. More people moved to the cities of the United States. Fewer people moved to the **rural** regions of the country. Even in the West, towns sprang up alongside the railroads. Mining towns, oil towns, and meat-packing towns grew. Existing cities, such as New York and Chicago, grew larger.

Many of the new city dwellers were rural Americans looking for work in the cities. Not as many workers were needed on American farms. New machines could reap and harvest the fields. Workers in the city found jobs that paid them more money. They also worked fewer hours. City businesses needed people who could sell items in stores. These businesses needed workers to wait on customers in restaurants. They needed people to work in offices. The cities needed construction workers to build new buildings. Maintenance workers were needed to keep buildings in good repair.

Black Americans moved from the South to American cities elsewhere. These Americans were trying to escape racial discrimination and sharecropping. **Racial discrimination** is treating people unjustly because of the color of their skin.

Immigrants also came to American cities. By the 1880s and 1890s, many people in the cities were immigrants. Over half of the people living in America's largest cities came from other countries. Most of the immigrants who came were from southern and eastern Europe.

Many Americans thought the immigrants looked different. They also lived differently than other Americans. The immigrants worshiped differently. Most Americans were Protestant Christians. But most of the immigrants were Jewish, Roman Catholic, or Eastern Orthodox. Some Christians saw the coming of these immigrants as a great missions opportunity. They printed tracts and Bibles in the immigrants' languages. Christians also tried to help immigrants as they arrived in the United States.

THE BAKER'S DOZEN

City Transportation

In early America people who lived in cities could walk anywhere in the city. The cities were small. People worked near where they lived. They might even work and live in the same building. If employers lived near their workers, both saw how each other lived. Employers could know whether their workers were good people or not.

As the cities grew, people could no longer walk everywhere. They needed new ways to move around a city. At first people used buses and streetcars that were pulled by horses. But horses were messy and smelly. Electric-powered streetcars replaced them in the 1880s. Some cities, like New York and Chicago, used trains to move people around the city. Some tracks were built above the streets. Boston, New York, and Philadelphia built trains that ran underground. An underground railroad is called a **subway**.

Electric-powered streetcars and trains changed how people lived and worked in cities. Businesses stayed in the center of a city. Around this center were factories. Apartments for poor people were built near the factories. These people could not afford to use streetcars or trains to travel to work. The poor needed to live near where they worked. Farther out from the center of the city lived the middle-class people. The wealthier lived on the edges of the city. They could afford to travel farther on trains and streetcars each day to work in the city. Their homes were built in quieter neighborhoods. They liked to live away from all the noise of the city.

The Flatiron Building, named after its shape, was one of the tallest skyscrapers in New York City.

City Buildings Grow Up

Growing cities spread out as more buildings were built. Cities also grew up. Taller buildings were built. In the past, thick stone walls were needed to support the weight of a tall building. The tallest buildings in a city could not rise more than twelve stories. But now steel could be used to support and build skyscrapers. Skyscrapers could rise over thirty stories into the air. Office buildings in the center of cities such as New York and Chicago rose high into the sky.

People needed to find a way to get to the top of these tall buildings. To walk up thirty flights of stairs would have been a lot of work. The invention of the elevator solved this problem. The elevator was a practical way to move for people who lived and worked in tall buildings. With an elevator, people could get to the highest floor quickly and without tiring themselves out.

The Brains by Thomas Nast is a political cartoon of Boss Tweed, a leader who was part of the machine that stole millions of dollars from New York City.

City Problems

The growth of cities also led to challenges. More people meant more crime. More buildings meant more fires. More roads needed to be built and more sewers created.

Immigrants who were unfamiliar with life in America needed help. Often this help came from city machines. "**Machine**" was the name given to a group of people who controlled the way a city ran. The city machine would help people in various ways. But it helped people for bad reasons.

Leaders of a city machine wanted people to vote for the machine's candidates in the next election. The machine wanted power in government so that the machine's members could make money. They did dishonest things if people gave them money. Sometimes city leaders who were part of the machine ignored the fact that gambling was taking place in the city. Or a construction company might give money to machine leaders. The leaders would then give government construction projects to that company. The bosses of the machines were not the kind of virtuous leaders America's founders had wanted to run the nation. These machine leaders were not just, and they did not rule in the fear of God.

Why did America's cities grow?

Life in the City

In cities the poorest Americans lived in housing called tenements. **Tenements** were often old houses and buildings that were divided up into many small rooms. These rooms did not have a good water supply. Tenements were not always built well, and they were often dangerous from overcrowding. Areas in cities that are poor, run-down, and overcrowded like this are known as the slums.

With so many people living close together, it was hard to keep tenements clean. The water supply was often **polluted** by waste. Diseases spread quickly. Also, many bars operated in the slums. Drunkenness was a major problem. Drunkenness often resulted in violence.

The cities did try to solve some of these problems over time. New York City set building standards to make buildings safer. Cities also began to treat sewage systems. The cities knew they needed to keep their water supply clean. Newspapers ran articles that explained the importance of personal cleanliness and good diets.

Tenement housing in New York City

Those who were not poor lived in their own neighborhoods. Some lived within the city. Others lived in suburbs. Suburbs are the areas around the city. Many could not afford to buy a house if they lived in the city. They rented apartments or row houses there. An **apartment** is a set of rooms within a building that a person or family can rent to live in. A **row house** is a house in a row of houses built without any space between them.

Modern-day row houses in Brooklyn, New York City

Apartments and row houses were built better and were much nicer than tenements. By the 1870s they had indoor plumbing with hot and cold water. They also had gas or electric lights. These lights made it easier for people to stay up later and read. Families often read the Bible together. Many of these homes had special spaces set aside for displaying the family Bible. Christian families were expected to have family devotions. Children learned the **catechism**. A catechism is a book of questions and answers that teaches about God and the Bible. Children would learn the correct answers to these questions.

Inside the main salesroom of Hill Brothers Millinery Goods in New York City

Some people chose not to live in the city but in the suburbs. Land was cheaper in the suburbs. More people could afford to buy their own houses there. Many people thought living in the suburbs was healthier than living in the city. The suburbs reminded some people of the small towns that Americans used to live in. Children had more space to play in the suburbs than in the city.

The suburbs were an escape from the city. But they were also close to the city. Men could ride streetcars into the city to work every day.

People also went to the city to shop. Department stores were a new attraction in cities. People used to go from store to store to find what they wished to buy. A department store is a huge store divided into different departments, or sections. One part of the store might sell clothes. Other departments might sell dry goods, toys, or furniture. Department stores were very fancy. They were modeled after palaces. Department stores included restaurants for when people got hungry. There were sitting areas for when people were tired. Department store owners wanted people to stay in the store and shop all day.

Why did people move to suburbs?

Religion

The growth of the city led to some problems. So did the growth of industry. But some Americans did not want to solve these problems. This way of thinking was the result of the writings of a man named **Herbert Spencer**.

Herbert Spencer built on the ideas of Charles Darwin, who taught about evolution. Spencer invented the phrase "survival of the fittest." It meant that the fittest are those that are best suited to survive. He said that this did not just happen with animals. He said it happened in businesses and society. Spencer believed that trying to solve problems allowed the weak and unfit to survive. He said that helping the poor would only hurt everyone else. Making businesses act justly allowed the weak to survive and weakened society. These types of views are called **Social Darwinism**.

Social Darwinism did not fit with Christian beliefs. Christians helped those in need. They knew that sometimes sin kept people poor. The sin of drunkenness wasted people's money. Drunkenness also made people unfit for work. So Christians preached the gospel. They warned people about their sins. They also tried to help new Christians in their struggle against sin.

Groups like the Young Men's Christian Association and Young Women's Christian Association built gymnasiums and study halls. Cities provided many temptations. Christians wanted places to escape the temptations.

The Young Men's Christian Association (YMCA) was established to provide safe, low-cost housing for young people. It focused on teaching good citizenship in a Christian environment.

Groups like the Salvation Army opened soup kitchens for those needing food. They opened schools to help train those without jobs. Those who came for help heard the gospel preached.

American Christians had a long history of helping those in need. But the help that each person needed most was salvation from sin. What benefit would there be to improving society if a person suffered in hell for all eternity?

But by the late 1800s, some pastors in the United States dismissed the idea of hell. They said God was kind. They said He would not judge anyone's sin. They also denied that Jesus is God. They said Jesus did not rise from the dead. They said science made these claims impossible. They no longer believed the Bible as God's Word. They said the men who wrote the Bible had many good ideas that people could still learn from.

Some pastors also said that the Bible had mistakes that must be rejected. These pastors claimed to be Christian. But they had made up a new religion. The new religion was called **liberalism** or modernism. It had a new gospel, or message, that was not of the Bible. This new gospel was called the **Social Gospel**.

The Social Gospel had a different view of salvation. This new gospel said that society should be improved. The progress of society was salvation.

Many Christians wanted to see society improved. But they did not think improvement of society was the gospel. They agreed that drunkenness should be opposed. They agreed that workers should be treated fairly. But they did not think this made America Christian. Fixing society was good. But it was not salvation.

B. B. Warfield

What: professor, Bible teacher

When: 1851–1921

Where: Princeton Seminary

Benjamin Breckinridge Warfield was a professor at Princeton Seminary. He taught there from 1887 until 1921. Warfield was an important Bible teacher. He knew more about the Bible and theology than most other men. Some people said the Bible had errors in it. Warfield defended the Bible against such teachings. Warfield's writings about the Bible are still very helpful. Christians still study them today.

True Christians opposed liberalism. They believed that Jesus is God. They believed the Bible is the Word of God. Some Christians said that liberals should not be pastors in churches. They said liberals should not teach in schools.

Princeton Theological Seminary, located in New Jersey, was founded in 1812 and is the second largest seminary in the United States.

One of the most important schools for training pastors at this time was Princeton Seminary. The professors at Princeton wrote articles that defended the Bible. They taught the Bible is God's Word. They also defended the Bible's teaching about Jesus and salvation.

But some Christians did not want to fight with the liberals. These Christians thought they could all get along. They thought it was cruel to force liberal pastors to leave their churches. They also would not force liberal teachers to leave their schools. They were willing to tolerate false teachers.

Later on the liberals gained control of the churches. Then the liberals forced the Christians out. Earlier the Christians had allowed false teachers of liberalism. But when the false teachers gained control, they did not accept Christians.

What does every person need salvation from?

People used catalogs to order goods, which could be shipped to the buyers. These pages show a sewing machine and a kitchen stove in a 1907 Sears, Roebuck & Company catalog.

Rural America

As America grew, many Americans still lived and worked in rural areas such as small towns and farms. At first, rural Americans welcomed changes. They thought the changes would help their farms and towns prosper.

But these benefits did not always come. Businesses in the city often got and shipped goods more cheaply than businesses in small towns. A person in a small town might order an item from a city business. The item would be shipped to him by train. This helped shoppers. They had more choices. They could also buy their goods for less money. Businesses in small towns could not compete with the large city businesses.

The farmers also faced trouble. They faced more competition with each other. Railroads made it possible for farmers to ship their crops to more places. Progress in industry made it possible for farmers to grow more food to sell. Since there were many crops, they became cheaper. This was good for people buying the food. But it was bad for farmers who did not get as much business. Some people bought more from certain farmers. If farmers had borrowed money to buy seed or equipment, they needed business. They needed to make enough money to pay their debts.

Farmers had many expenses. Farmers had to pay for the railroad to transport farm goods. Farmers also had to pay for warehouses, buildings for storing goods. A building where farmers stored grain was called a grange. The farmers were called grangers.

Farmers wanted to change laws to favor themselves. They created the Granger movement. The farmers wanted the government to force railroads and warehouses to charge less money from farmers. They also wanted the government to print more paper money. But these were not good ideas for helping the nation as a whole. Most of these ideas did not become law.

Rural Americans also distrusted some of the improvements that city people wanted. The farmers took care of their own roads. But city people who traveled on these roads complained. They said country roads were not good enough for long-distance travel. They wanted hard-surface roads. The farmers did not understand why they needed to pay more for the roads that other people wanted.

Many farmers also resisted people's attempts to change the one-room schoolhouse. People wanted to divide it into grades. But many rural Americans did not want this. They did not want people to tell them what to teach in their schools. They wanted to remain in control of what their children learned. They were concerned about some of the new ideas taught in the schools. Rural Americans wanted schools to focus on reading, writing, and math.

American life was not all work and school. Americans now had more time to spend outside of work. They also had more time to spend outside of church. This was true in both the city and the country. Sometimes activities for entertainment replaced church. Sometimes they replaced volunteer work. Many of these activities were not wrong. But some Christians were concerned that they replaced better things.

Some Christians decided to set up retreat centers, which were similar to camps. These retreat centers were places to enjoy fun activities. But the Bible and God were not left out. Christians could go to retreat centers to go hiking or boating. People might attend a concert there. The retreat centers offered Bible studies and sermons and also held prayer meetings.

Chautauqua Hall of Philosophy, an open-air lecture hall, was a retreat for Christians.

Conclusion

America grew during the late 1800s. The businesses founded during this time laid a foundation for American prosperity, or success. American cities became places of opportunity. But cities were also places of crime and corruption. American businesses were not always just in their actions.

Christians faced challenges from false teachers. These teachers wanted to change the Christian faith. But Christians still made many opportunities to help those in need. They had many opportunities to spread the gospel.

This was a time period of challenges. It was also a time of opportunities. God blessed Americans with the ability to grow and expand their nation. But Americans needed to be careful that their growth was done in a way that pleased God.

What changes in schools were rural Americans concerned about?

Shoe Box Diorama

A diorama is a small three-dimensional scene that represents a place or an event. Choose a scene you would like to make. Turn a shoe box on its side. Use your imagination to create a background inside. Glue paper objects to the bottom of the box in front of the background. Add an interesting title or caption.

5 All That Glitters

Focus

The Gilded Age was a time of growth and necessary reform in many areas of American culture.

Glitter and Gold

"All that glitters is not gold" is a saying that comes from a line in a play by William Shakespeare. People use it to describe the difference between the way something looks and its true value. A rock might glitter like gold does. But if it is not really gold, it has no great value. We could use this saying to describe American culture in the late 1800s.

In many ways, life in America at that time appeared to "glitter." Large cities bustled with activity. New inventions had brought big changes to business. Work was being done much faster. Factories could produce more goods than ever before. Success in business had made some Americans very wealthy.

But as you read this chapter, you will notice that not everything about America's "glitter" was good. The late 1800s in America are often called the **Gilded Age**. Something that is "gilded" has a thin covering that looks like gold, but it is not real gold. Not everything about the American way of life was pleasing to God. Not all that glittered was gold.

People from Far Away

Immigrants poured into the United States during the Gilded Age. Millions of people came from other countries between 1870 and 1900. Immigrants hoped to find a better life in America. Some were looking for good jobs, and many hoped to become wealthy. Some came to find land for sale at a good price. Some came to escape famine. Others were looking for freedom of religion. Both the East and the West Coasts of America became landing places for immigrants.

Immigrants from Europe

Most of the immigrants who arrived on the East Coast came from Europe. People came from countries such as Germany, England, Ireland, Sweden, Norway, Austria-Hungary, and Russia. Some immigrants moved out west, and some stayed in the eastern cities.

All the new people in America brought changes to its culture. If you walked along the streets of a large city, you might hear several different European lan-

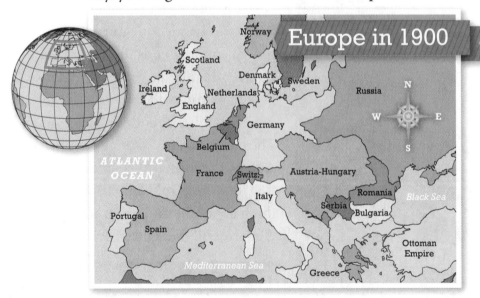

Europe in 1900

guages. You might see shops selling European foods. People from the same country often settled near each other. You might walk through a neighborhood where nearly every home held a Swedish or an Irish family.

The US government saw that it needed an immigrant station. To keep America safe, the government wanted to know who was coming into the country. The station would also be a place where new immigrants could find help. When immigrants first arrived on ships, some needed doctors. Some did not know any English. Many needed help finding relatives already living in America.

On New Year's Day 1892, the US government opened the station on **Ellis Island** in New York Harbor. Annie Moore was the first immigrant to be received at the new station. Annie was an Irish teenager coming to America with her two younger brothers. The three children were soon able to join their parents already living in New York City.

Several years earlier the country of France had sent America a gift. It was a huge statue of a lady lifting a torch. This statue had been placed on an island near Ellis Island. The Statue of Liberty reminded new immigrants sailing into the harbor of the freedom they hoped to find in a new land.

The Statue of Liberty welcomes immigrants.

Chinese immigrants selling goods in Chinatown, San Francisco, California

Immigrants from Asia

Most of the immigrants who arrived on the West Coast were from China. Many of them came to work in the gold mines. Later many more came to help build the railroad. The largest community of Chinese immigrants was in San Francisco, California. The community came to be known as Chinatown.

Chinese immigrants were not always treated justly. They were hard workers. They were often willing to work for less pay than Americans and European immigrants. Other workers did not like to compete with the Chinese for jobs. The Chinese also had different beliefs, ate different food, and dressed differently from Americans. They were often looked down upon for being different.

The US government would not allow most Chinese people to become citizens. In 1882, the government passed an even stricter law against the Chinese. The **Chinese Exclusion Act** said that no more Chinese from the working class could enter the country. Only teachers, students, merchants, and officials could come to America. Any other Chinese would have to wait at least ten years to come.

Why did the United States need an immigrant station?

Bright Ideas
The Typewriter

While America welcomed new people to its shores, it also welcomed many new ideas. Several important inventions were created during the Gilded Age. In the early 1870s, a gun company began producing a new invention by **Christopher Sholes**. It was not a gun. It was the first modern typewriter. Sholes was a newspaper publisher. He knew how long it took a person to set type by hand on a printing press. He wanted to find a better way. Sholes worked to improve typing machines designed by others. He tried some different ways of arranging the letter keys. He finally settled on the order we use on electronic devices today. The first six letters from left to right were Q-W-E-R-T-Y. We now call this arrangement the QWERTY keyboard.

Christopher Sholes

The first Sholes typewriters did not sell well. But slowly the new idea caught on. Soon the typewriter would change the printing industry forever.

In 1873 Christopher Sholes and Carlos Glidden invented the first successful typewriter with a QWERTY keyboard, which is still in use today.

An early Bell telephone

Alexander Graham Bell

The Telephone

Alexander Graham Bell was an immigrant from Scotland. He became a teacher for the deaf in Boston. Both his mother and his wife had problems with their hearing. Bell was interested in machines that sent messages and sounds. He had worked with the telegraph, a machine that sent messages in a code of dots and dashes. But he wanted to find a way to **transmit**, or send, the human voice over wires.

Bell is given credit for inventing the first telephone. He was not the first to experiment with the telephone. But he was the first to get a patent for his invention. Bell's telephone did not transmit the voice very clearly. The person speaking had to shout to be heard at the other end of the line. But Bell and other inventors found ways to improve the telephone. By the mid-1880s, thousands of Americans had telephones in their homes or businesses.

The Light Bulb and the Phonograph

Thomas Edison was a telegraph operator who loved to try new things. He was good at his telegraph work. But he was also interested in doing experiments. Sometimes he spent time on them while at work. This made some of his employers angry, and he lost several jobs. While still a young man, he quit his job to spend all his time inventing.

Electric lamp made by Thomas Edison

Edison set up his own lab in Menlo Park, New Jersey. He invented many things. He improved the telegraph until it could send four messages at a time. He also found a way to improve Bell's telephone. Working on these two machines led Edison to a new idea. He invented a **phonograph**. The phonograph was the first machine to record the human voice and play it back. Edison also found a way to make a light bulb that burned longer and cost less than ever before. Electric lighting soon became more common than gas lighting.

Thomas Edison and his phonograph

The Shoe Laster

Jan Matzeliger came to the United States from South America. He found work in a shoe factory. At that time shoes were very expensive. The upper part of a shoe had to be sewn to the sole by hand. This process was called lasting. The best workers could only last about fifty pairs of shoes a day. Matzeliger wanted to make a lasting machine that would do the work faster. He watched the way the lasters did their work. Then he built a machine that copied the movement of their hands. Within a few years, his lasting machine could last 700 pairs of shoes a day. It greatly helped bring down the price of shoes. Nearly anyone could now afford to buy them.

A later version of Edison's phonograph

Jan Matzeliger

Lasting machine

Jan Matzeliger died shortly after inventing the shoe laster. He had been a faithful church attender. At his death he left a large part of the money from his invention to his church.

New inventions changed the way people lived. Often the changes made life better. Some people looked at the progress being made and gave praise to God. Other people believed that human minds could solve all the world's problems. They began to put their faith in science and invention instead of in God. Thomas Edison openly rejected the God of the Bible. Alexander Graham Bell was an agnostic, one who does not believe we can know if there is a God. These men did not recognize God as their Creator. But without realizing it, they were ruling over His world as He told people to do. God used them to make important discoveries. Sadly, they did not give glory to the one who gave them their gifted minds.

What invention first transmitted the human voice?

Men of Means

During the late 1800s, some Americans had more wealth than ever before. Andrew Carnegie had earned a fortune in the steel business. John D. Rockefeller had earned his wealth in the oil industry. Cornelius Vanderbilt had become rich through the railroad and through shipping. All of these men were worth millions of dollars.

Cornelius Vanderbilt

Many wealthy men of the Gilded Age had not been rich all their lives. Some of them had been born into poor families. But all of them had learned how to work hard, earn money, invest that money, and make even more. They knew when to save their money and when to take risks with it. They noticed when new inventions and new ways of doing business brought changes. They had a talent for investing. They chose investments that would bring them a profit. They avoided those that would end in a loss.

These wealthy men were not only good businessmen. They also gave a great deal of money away. Andrew Carnegie believed that it was better to die poor than to leave wealth behind. He wanted to do good with his money while he was still alive. He wanted to see his wealth being used to help other people.

Carnegie Library in Houston, Texas, is one of many libraries in America built with money from Andrew Carnegie.

Carnegie believed that people should be educated. He gave much of his money to build libraries. During his life, he helped pay for more than 2,500 libraries. He also gave money to schools and colleges. He bought organs for hundreds of churches. At the time of his death, he had given away more than 350 million dollars.

John D. Rockefeller had been taught to give money away when he was a little boy. He too gave away hundreds of millions during his life. Much of his money went to medical research. He also gave millions of dollars to support schools.

Many other wealthy men gave generously. Churches, hospitals, museums, and opera houses received gifts from rich businessmen.

Some people admired these wealthy men and wanted to be like them. "Rags-to-riches" stories became very popular in the late 1800s. Some Americans thought that if they only worked hard enough and used money well, they could enjoy fabulous riches.

But not everyone thought the millionaires were good men. Many thought that these men had too much money. Some did not admire the way the men ran their businesses. Some believed that they had used other people for their own selfish purposes. Some thought wealthy employers expected too much from their workers and did not pay them enough.

Americans were learning how **capitalism** works. In a system of capitalism, the government does not own a country's goods and businesses. The people of that country do. Everyone is free to earn money and to use it as he likes. People are free to start businesses. They are free to buy and sell goods. They may choose to invest money and try to earn more.

With a system of capitalism, some people will be wealthier than others. People with less money often covet the wealth of others. And the wealthy often look down on the poor. People with wealth sometimes forget God's command to be generous. They can focus too much on enjoying wealth and forget to be thankful to God.

People with or without wealth can forget what God expects of them. God expects all people to work hard and to trust Him. He expects people to be content with what He provides. He expects people to do good with the money He gives them.

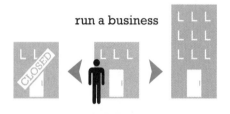

In **CAPITALISM** individuals have the freedom to choose how they

LESS   MORE

run a business

invest their money

work and earn money

buy goods

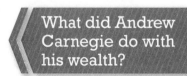

sell goods

What did Andrew Carnegie do with his wealth?

The Arts and the Press

During the Gilded Age art, music, and writing flourished. Wealthy Americans wanted to fill their houses with beautiful things. Many gave dinners and parties in their homes. They wanted their guests to see tasteful art on the walls and enjoy the best music of the day. They wanted to show off their own libraries filled with books. Their wealth made them give more attention to the finer things of life.

Art

One of the most popular forms of art was the **portrait**. A portrait is a picture of a person. Wealthy families would pay an artist to paint a portrait of a family member. A portrait was a way to preserve the memory of a husband, wife, or child. Portraits were costly and took time to create. The person being painted had to sit still for hours while the artist worked. But a beautiful painting to hang in the home was worth the trouble.

John Singer Sargent was one of the most successful portrait painters. He was an American, but he spent much of his life in Europe. He studied the work of the great masters of his day. He tried to capture the thoughts and feelings of the people he painted. He painted several famous Americans, such as John D. Rockefeller and President Theodore Roosevelt.

Child in a Straw Hat (above) by Mary Cassatt and *Lady Agnew of Lochnaw* (left) by John Singer Sargent

Snap the Whip by Winslow Homer

Mary Cassatt grew up in Pennsylvania. Early in life she traveled to Europe and took drawing and music lessons. She later studied art in Philadelphia and in Paris, France. Some of her best-known works are her paintings of mothers and children.

Winslow Homer was another well-known artist of the Gilded Age. He worked in Boston and New York City. Later he moved to the Maine coast. He was known for painting scenes from everyday life. Children at school and at play, country life, and coastal scenes are common in his work.

Louis Tiffany worked in many forms of art. He became best known for his stained-glass objects. His mosaics and lampshades decorated the rooms of many wealthy homes.

A Tiffany poppy table lamp with a stained-glass lampshade

121

Antonín Dvořák

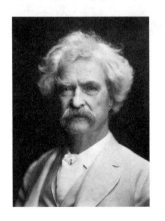

Scott Joplin

Music

Americans enjoyed different styles of music in the Gilded Age. A composer named **Edward MacDowell** wrote classical piano music. Perhaps his best-known piece is "To a Wild Rose." A composer from Hungary named **Antonín Dvořák** spent several years teaching music in America. He wrote a symphony called *From the New World*. This work was first performed in Carnegie Hall, New York's newly built concert hall. The audience cheered wildly at each break in the music. The symphony is one of the most lasting musical works from its time.

Marching music was also popular in this period. **John Philip Sousa** wrote several of his marches in the 1890s. "The Stars and Stripes Forever" is still one of America's best-loved songs.

At the very end of the 1800s, a new form of music called **ragtime** became popular. Ragtime mixed classical music with African American music styles. A black composer named **Scott Joplin** wrote many ragtime songs.

Writing

The Gilded Age is named after a book with the same name. One of the book's writers was **Mark Twain**. He also wrote novels about the adventures of two young boys, Tom Sawyer and Huckleberry Finn. Works by **Louisa May Alcott** rose to fame during this time as well. Her novels *Little Women* and *Little Men* are still widely read today.

Mark Twain

A poet named **Emily Dickinson** wrote hundreds of poems in her lifetime. But few people knew about them until after her death in 1886. Today they are thought to be some of the greatest American poetry ever written.

Newspapers

The press had a great deal of power in the Gilded Age. People believed what they read in the newspapers. But the newspapers did not always print only facts. Two New York newspapers became famous for mixing fiction with the news. Their owners, **Joseph Pulitzer** and **William Randolph Hearst**, each tried to sell the most papers. They made their news stories as exciting as possible. But this meant that they often stretched the truth. Sometimes people were hurt by false reports about them in the papers.

Some benefits came from the press. Newspapers helped raise money for important causes. Pulitzer used his paper to raise more than $100,000 toward a stand for the Statue of Liberty. Newspapers also gave their readers humor. The first comic strips were published in newspapers in 1896.

William Randolph Hearst and a page from the *New York Journal* publishing the sinking of the USS *Maine*

Joseph Pulitzer, American journalist and publisher, and a page from the *New York World* headlining the sinking of the *Titanic*

Why did the arts flourish during the Gilded Age?

Advertisement for Buffalo Bill's Wild West Rough Riders

Leisure Time

Many Americans now had something that had been hard to find in years past. They had leisure time. They also had more money to spend on entertainment. Americans in the Gilded Age found many ways to relax and enjoy themselves. America's big cities now had theaters and opera houses. People crowded into them to watch plays, concerts, operas, and shows. A type of theater called **vaudeville** became popular. Vaudeville shows were made up of short acts. Acrobats, clowns, dancers, jugglers, and trained animals all had a part in a vaudeville show.

Another popular event to see was Buffalo Bill's Wild West Show. "Buffalo Bill" was a nickname for **William Cody**. Cody had been a buffalo hunter, a cowboy, and a soldier in battles with Indians. He decided to put together a traveling show about life in the West. His show presented the West as an exciting adventure. It had gunfights, cowboy stunts, and staged battles between whites and Indians. Cody's show was not always truthful about western life. But it drew crowds.

A favorite performer in the Wild West Show was **Annie Oakley**, a female gunslinger. Oakley had never actually lived out west. But she had trained herself to be an expert at shooting guns. She amazed the crowds with her good aim. She could snuff out candles, hit moving targets, and split cards in two with her rifle.

Annie Oakley holding an L. C. Smith shotgun

Steeple Chase Swimming Pool,
Coney Island, N. Y.

America's first amusement park was developed on the coast near New York City. Coney Island began as a vacation spot in the mid-1800s. Over time it became a large park with a variety of rides, games, and side-shows. Soon after the Ferris wheel was introduced in Chicago, Coney Island had one too. It also had the first roller coaster. The rides and shows were cheap enough that even the working-class people could afford them. The first hot dogs were made and sold at Coney Island. People liked to eat them along with a brand-new fizzy drink called Coca-Cola®.

Public parks had also become popular places to spend free time. Big cities had parks designed by men with an eye for the landscape. Trees, benches, walk-ways, and roads made parks pleasant places. People went to parks to rest, read, stroll, or drive a carriage. Public parks were free for people of any social class to enjoy.

A 1919 post card of the swimming pool at Steeple Chase Park, one of the largest amusement parks on Coney Island

"High wheelers" (above) were dangerous because they often tipped the rider forward, landing him on his head. Safety bicycles (below) had two equal-sized wheels and were safer to ride.

Several new sports began during the Gilded Age. Many people played sports. Others went to watch sporting events. Baseball, basketball, and boxing all became popular sports to watch.

The bicycle also became common around this time. Its design changed from one large and one small wheel to two wheels of the same size. This change made bicycles safer to ride. Even women began enjoying bicycle rides. They found bicycling to be a fun and healthy way to exercise. Some wore a new style of dress for riding called the "bloomer costume." Bloomers were not the fashion for very long. But for a short time they helped women ride bikes without getting a long skirt caught in the chain.

Not all Americans joined in every new form of entertainment. Some Christians thought that there were dangers to guard against. A pastor named A. C. Dixon preached a sermon about Coney Island in a New York City church. He warned that some of its shows and activities were immoral. He believed they might draw Christian young people into sin.

Christians in the late 1800s had to make choices about entertainment just as Christians do today. Rest and pleasure are gifts from God. But God did not mean for us to enjoy them in sinful ways. He meant for us to enjoy them only in ways that honor Him.

Why did some Christians choose not to join in some forms of entertainment?

Making Changes
Settlement Houses

Not everyone in America was wealthy during the Gilded Age. Many people had middle-class incomes. And many Americans living in tenement housing were very poor.

A young woman in Chicago formed a plan to help immigrants in these poor living conditions. **Jane Addams** started Hull-House in 1889. Hull-House was one of several **settlement houses** in big cities. It was a settlement house especially for women. At Hull-House, immigrant women could get nursing care, food, and clothing for their families. They could take classes in English, cooking, art, sewing, and American government. They could also attend concerts and plays and visit a library. Hull-House even offered childcare for immigrant children. It was a safe place for immigrant women to find the help they needed for life in a new country.

Jane Addams

Hull-House

Child-Labor Reform

Many immigrant children were not able to go to school. Instead they had to help support their families. By the year 1900, more than one million children and teens worked in factories.

People began to realize that national laws about child labor would help this situation. Labor unions and reform workers began asking for these laws to be put in place. They wanted limits on the number of hours a child could work. They wanted laws to decide at what age a child could begin working. Some states already had these laws. But many Americans felt that there needed to be national laws about child labor.

Children working in a mill in Macon, Georgia, in 1909

Rights for Women

During the Gilded Age, life for women in America was changing. Many women worked outside the home, especially in factories. More and more women received an education. More women than ever before were concerned about their rights. Most states did not allow women to vote. But women were American citizens.

Elizabeth Cady Stanton   Susan B. Anthony

Many women thought that they should have a say in their government just as men did.

Elizabeth Cady Stanton and **Susan B. Anthony** spoke out the most openly for women's rights. However, both of them also openly rejected verses in God's Word about women. Many other women who loved God and respected the Bible believed that they should be able to vote. The need for women's **suffrage**, or voting rights, was slowly becoming more accepted.

Studying Your Family History

Talk to an older person in your family who remembers things from long ago. Look at old family photos, letters, diaries, or scrapbooks. Did any of your ancestors come to America from another country? What are some interesting or funny stories from your family's past? Share what you learned with someone else.

Health and Nutrition

Disease was a major problem in the late 1800s, especially in large cities. Tenement housing was only one reason for this. Another was a lack of knowledge about nutrition. People did not know which foods had the vitamins and minerals they needed. They also did not have proper ways to keep foods from spoiling. People were just beginning to understand that germs and bacteria could make them sick. Scientists were trying new ways to kill bacteria in meats and dairy foods.

One important change was a way of treating milk. Farmers would bring raw milk into cities to sell. But this milk carried harmful bacteria. The milk needed special treatment before being sold. This treatment was called **pasteurization**. Milk was heated to almost boiling. The heat would kill the bacteria. Then the milk was cooled quickly to keep new bacteria from growing.

Drinking pasteurized milk kept people from getting certain diseases. Tuberculosis, diphtheria, and typhoid could all be caused by drinking raw milk. The change in treating milk helped people live healthier lives.

A French chemist named Louis Pasteur discovered how to kill bacteria in milk in the 1860s. The process was named after him.

How did Jane Addams help immigrants?

Falsehood and Faith

During the Gilded Age, true faith in God and His Word was often mocked or questioned. Charles Darwin's teachings about evolution had been widely accepted. Some people who called themselves Christians no longer believed key Bible truths. They thought the Bible was not God's Word. They doubted whether Jesus was the Son of God. They did not believe that a loving God would send anyone to hell.

Dwight L. Moody

D. L. Moody came to Boston at the age of seventeen to work in his uncle's shoe store. He began going to the church his uncle attended. One day Moody's Sunday school teacher visited him at the shoe store. He spoke with Moody about Christ. Moody became a Christian that day.

Ira Sankey

What: singer and composer of gospel songs

When: the late 1800s

Where: the United States and Great Britain

Ira Sankey began traveling with D. L. Moody in the 1870s. Sankey's singing played an important part in Moody's meetings. He led music before the preaching and helped prepare people to hear God's Word. During his life Sankey wrote music for more than 1,000 gospel songs. His most famous song was "The Ninety and Nine." The song uses Jesus' parable of the lost sheep to tell how He rescues people lost in their sins.

Illustration of Dwight L. Moody and Ira Sankey during a revival in New York on October 24, 1875

Moody moved to Chicago to work in another shoe store. He began to help with a Sunday school. Soon he started a Sunday school of his own. He decided that God wanted him to do this kind of work full-time.

Moody left the shoe business. He worked for several years as a missionary in the city of Chicago. Then he began traveling and holding special meetings in other cities. He had made friends in England during a trip there for his wife's health. They invited him to come and preach in the city of London.

Moody used some methods from the business world to get the word out about his meetings. He put up signs and placed ads in newspapers. He believed he should use the press as a tool for spreading the truth. To many Christians this was a new idea.

The people's response to Moody's preaching was much like the Great Awakening in the 1700s. Large crowds came to his meetings. God used him to win thousands of people to Christ during the Gilded Age.

The End of a Century

The 1800s had come to an end. America had more people, more opportunities, and more wealth than ever before. But America also had many problems. Some of its people lived in slums. Many children worked instead of going to school. Some people trusted in science to solve life's problems. Some looked for happiness in entertainment and in things money could buy. Many rejected the Christian faith that their parents had taught them. The Gilded Age had been filled with glitter. But not all of that glitter was gold.

What did God use D. L. Moody to do?

6 America Expands

Focus
Trade and war made the United States want to expand.

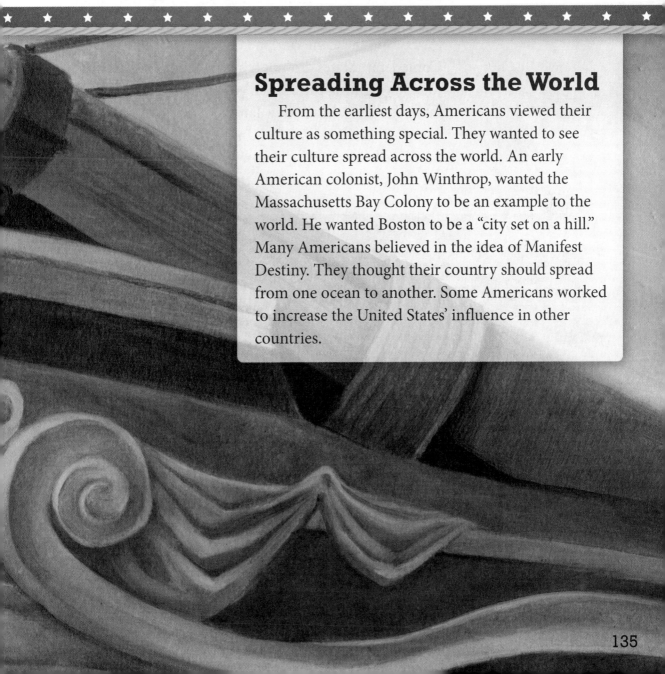

William McKinley
becomes president
1897

Spanish-American War
1898

1895   1896

1900

1904   1905

Gold is discovered
in Alaska

US takes over building
of Panama Canal

Spreading Across the World

From the earliest days, Americans viewed their culture as something special. They wanted to see their culture spread across the world. An early American colonist, John Winthrop, wanted the Massachusetts Bay Colony to be an example to the world. He wanted Boston to be a "city set on a hill." Many Americans believed in the idea of Manifest Destiny. They thought their country should spread from one ocean to another. Some Americans worked to increase the United States' influence in other countries.

The United States and the World After the Civil War

For many years, America had much room to grow. First, the nation spread into the Louisiana Territory. Then Oregon Territory, Texas, and the Southwest all became part of the United States. After 1853 the United States stopped expanding in North America.

During the Civil War, the United States and the Confederate States did not try to expand. They were too busy fighting each other. Neither side seemed interested in claiming new lands.

After the Civil War, the United States began looking for more territory. The country stretched from sea to sea, yet some Americans thought it should grow more.

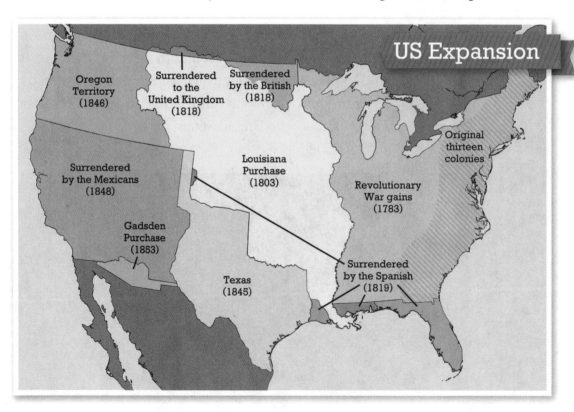

US Expansion

Oregon Territory (1846)

Surrendered to the United Kingdom (1818)

Surrendered by the British (1818)

Original thirteen colonies

Surrendered by the Mexicans (1848)

Louisiana Purchase (1803)

Revolutionary War gains (1783)

Gadsden Purchase (1853)

Surrendered by the Spanish (1819)

Texas (1845)

One man who believed America should grow more was **William Seward**. President Lincoln had made him Secretary of State.

Alaska

While Andrew Johnson was president, Seward bought Alaska, a very cold land in the northwestern tip of North America. Alaska was far from where most Americans lived. Some people joked and called it "Seward's Folly" or "Seward's Icebox." But Seward was wiser than people thought. He had bought the land from Russia. By purchasing Alaska, he kept Russia from controlling land in North America. He also gained rich fishing grounds. Later, Americans would discover gold in Alaska.

Some Americans thought the Caribbean Islands should be part of the United States. When Ulysses S. Grant was president, he asked the Senate to make a treaty with the people of Santo Domingo (now the Dominican Republic). The treaty would add this island to the United States. Grant wanted to put a US naval base in Santo Domingo. He wanted the island to be a place for black Americans to escape harsh treatment in the South. One powerful Republican senator spoke out for black Americans. He thought the United States should do more to protect them. It should not encourage them to move away.

The Caribbean

Reasons for US Expansion

Americans had varying reasons for wanting to expand. Sometimes their reasons worked together.

Many Americans were Christians. They hoped more people around the world would hear about Jesus.

Some Americans wanted to make money. They believed the United States should influence or even control faraway lands. Then traders could make more money for American businesses. Factories in places like Massachusetts could sell goods to people outside the United States. America could sell goods to the Pacific Islands.

Some Americans were afraid other countries would become more powerful than the United States. Nations such as the United Kingdom and France claimed many lands throughout the world. Some Americans thought their country should have more lands too.

Most Americans believed that their government was the best. They thought they should spread the American way of life around the world.

By the end of the 1800s, many Americans wanted the United States to expand. But only some wanted to practice **imperialism**, or the control of foreign lands. Many hoped the United States could help other nations and itself.

The ocean liner *Imperator*, when launched in 1912, was the largest passenger ship in the world.

Another Reason to Claim Land

Traveling around the world became easier in the late 1800s. To get to most places, people had to travel by ship. For most of human history, ships moved in one of two ways. Ships sailed with the wind or people rowed them. After the Civil War many ships had steam engines.

Although steamships were good, they had their own problems. The biggest was that steamships needed coal. Ship captains needed to know they could stop at ports that had coal available.

Captains had to plan their trips carefully. A ship going from New York to London could carry enough coal to go there and back. If the captain wanted to take more people or goods, he could take less coal. Once the ship arrived in England, more coal could be bought for the return trip.

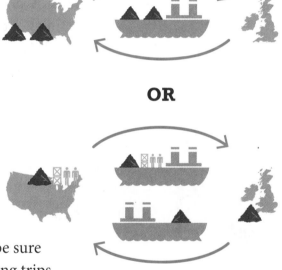

OR

Some trips made captains more concerned. A trip from San Francisco to China covered thousands of miles of ocean. American captains needed to be sure they could purchase coal during these long trips.

Some Americans wanted the United States to have an island in the middle of the Pacific. They planned for coal to be stored there. Then steamships on the way to Asia and US military ships would be sure to have a place to refuel.

> Why did Americans want the United States to influence or control faraway lands?

Traveling with Maps

To find their way across vast oceans, ship captains need good maps. Lines divide these maps. Mapmakers put lines on maps to help people measure distance. Lines of **latitude** run from side to side. They measure the distance between a location and the equator. Lines of **longitude** run up and down. They measure the distance between a location and the prime meridian.

Most maps have a key. The key explains symbols the map uses. Some maps also have a compass rose. It shows the cardinal directions—which way is north, south, east, or west. Most maps have a scale too. Sometimes one inch on a map means 1,000 miles. A map scale is a line that compares distances on a map to distances in the real world.

Some maps are easy to read. They have only a few symbols on their key. Some maps have much information. All maps can help us understand history.

Which lines on a map show how far north or south of the equator a place is?

Read a Road Map

A road map helps you get to your destination. For this activity you will plan a road trip using a road map.

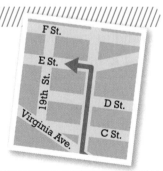

140

Cuba
Spain's Most Important Colony

Of all the islands in the Caribbean, Cuba was the most important. It was the largest. Ever since Columbus discovered the island, Spain claimed Cuba. By the late 1800s, Spain was no longer a powerful nation. It now had very few colonies. It no longer had a powerful navy. Other nations such as the United Kingdom were far more powerful than Spain. Even the United States, a much younger nation, was stronger. For the people of Spain, Cuba was a happy reminder of when their nation was the biggest and best.

Fortress guarding the entrance to Havana Bay in Cuba

Many Cubans did not like being owned by Spain. For many years Cubans wanted independence. Three different times after the American Civil War, Cubans fought to drive out the Spanish. The first war lasted ten years. The next one lasted only one year. Then in 1895 Cubans began to fight again. By this time all of Spain's main colonies in North and South America had been free for many years. Many Cubans wanted Cuba to be free too.

The War in Cuba

Once the Cubans began their fight, the Spanish acted quickly. They had already fought two wars with the Cubans. Spain did not want to lose its last major land area in the Americas. Spain sent over many troops and tried different commanders.

Americans grew concerned about the fighting in Cuba for many reasons. Some Americans owned businesses in Cuba. They feared the war might harm their companies. Cuba exported sugar to the United States. Sugar buyers in the United States were afraid Cuba would not be able to provide enough. The war was destroying the sugarcane fields and killing many of the fieldworkers.

Group of refugees in Cuba

Many Americans took sides with the Cubans. These Americans remembered their own country's fight for freedom from England. They did not like to see other human beings treated without care. They heard that the Spanish forced Cubans to live in camps. Cubans in these camps did not receive enough food or medicine. Most Americans in the 1890s were Protestants. They wondered if the Spanish people's Catholic religion made them cruel. Some Americans wanted to send missionaries to Cuba to spread the news of Jesus' love.

A few Americans wanted to take over Cuba. They feared that the Cubans might become independent.

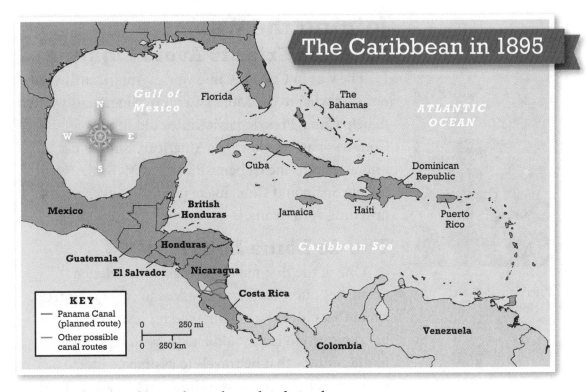

The Caribbean in 1895

Gulf of Mexico
Florida
The Bahamas
ATLANTIC OCEAN
Cuba
Dominican Republic
Mexico
British Honduras
Jamaica
Haiti
Puerto Rico
Honduras
Caribbean Sea
Guatemala
El Salvador
Nicaragua
Costa Rica
Venezuela
Colombia

KEY
— Panama Canal (planned route)
— Other possible canal routes

0 — 250 mi
0 — 250 km

These Americans knew that other islands in the Caribbean had not been at peace after becoming independent. They thought America should take over Cuba and make it into a state. Then the United States could control more of the Caribbean Sea.

The United States wanted to be nearby to keep enemies from controlling a future canal. Some countries wanted to build a canal as a shortcut through Central America.

Many Americans grew concerned about the war in Cuba. But few wanted the United States to go to war. At first, most hoped that President William McKinley could talk to the Spanish government and the Cuban rebels. The Americans hoped he could bring about peace.

Why were Americans concerned about the fighting in Cuba?

Joining the War
America Tries to Avoid Fighting

President William McKinley

The war in Cuba became worse. Americans were not sure what to do. More and more Americans wanted to help Cuba. President McKinley did not agree. Congress passed a law that Americans should not give military aid to the Cubans. President McKinley wanted to help Spain and Cuba make peace. But events kept upsetting Americans.

The de Lôme Letter

One of the first major problems was a letter. Countries often send ambassadors to other countries. An **ambassador** is a person who represents the nation he comes from. He should have a good reputation in the country that he travels to as ambassador. The Spanish ambassador to the United States was named Enrique Dupuy de Lôme.

In early 1898, de Lôme made a mistake. He wrote a letter to his friend in Cuba. In the letter, he spoke rudely of President McKinley. Ambassador de Lôme thought that only his friend would read his letter. Instead, some of the Cuban rebels stole the letter. They sent a copy to the United States.

Ambassador de Lôme was in trouble. Soon newspapers across America published the letter. Americans read that the Spanish ambassador insulted their president. They were furious. Because of his letter, de Lôme returned to Spain. Now many Americans were angry at Spain for having such a rude ambassador.

The USS *Maine*

Another problem came less than a week after Americans first read the de Lôme letter. Now they had a new reason to be upset with Spain. On February 15, 1898, the USS *Maine* blew up in the harbor of Havana, Cuba.

The *Maine* was in Cuba to protect Americans. After the war for Cuban independence had begun, some Americans felt at risk. Spain allowed the United States to send a warship to Cuba. The United States wanted to assure Americans that their lives and businesses would be safe.

The explosion of the *Maine* was a great mystery. To this day no one is sure why the ship exploded. In 1898 many Americans thought they knew why. They knew the Spanish had been treating the Cubans badly. They knew the Spanish ambassador had insulted their president. Many Americans believed the Spanish had blown up the *Maine*.

The USS *Maine* entering the harbor of Havana

The *San Francisco Call* newspaper announced the sinking of the USS *Maine*.

Journalism

Most Americans learned of the de Lôme letter and the sinking of the *Maine* from newspapers. During the late 1800s newspapers became popular. In big cities like New York there were two or three important papers. Newspaper publishers printed a morning paper and an afternoon paper. When there was an important story, they might also publish an evening paper. There were no radio or television stations, and there was no Internet. People read newspapers to find out what was happening in the world. The gathering and presenting of news is called **journalism**.

Newspapers at this time did not always print the truth. To sell copies, the publishers might make stories sound especially bad. William R. Hearst was one of these publishers. He liked to report on bad news and not good. More people would buy papers with bad stories. Stories printed mainly to excite people were called yellow journalism.

Newspapers that published yellow journalism told only one side of the story about problems in Cuba. They usually told how bad the Spanish were. After the de Lôme letter and the sinking of the *Maine*, these papers sold many copies. Many Americans felt that something must be done to stop the Spanish.

Congress and the President Decide

Although many Americans were upset, they did not have enough cause to go to war. The US government is set up so that no one person or group of people can declare war. The president is the commander in chief of the military. That means that he is in charge of directing a war. But even he cannot begin one. Instead, Congress must declare war.

Many congressmen did not want war. They knew that American soldiers would probably die. The army was not ready to fight. They did not know how to get enough soldiers to Cuba. They feared that a war would hurt American businesses. Many in Congress were not surprised about the de Lôme letter. They knew that Spain did not like President McKinley. Congress was not sure about declaring war.

Finally, one congressman changed that. A senator named Redfield Proctor visited Cuba. He was a businessman from Vermont. Senator Proctor was not an emotional man. When he spoke to the Senate, he did not seem sad or upset. Instead, he listed all the bad things he had seen in Cuba. He talked about the suffering of the Cuban people. He described the camps they were forced to live in. Senator Proctor's report encouraged Congress to favor war.

Both Congress and the American people were now in support of a war against Spain. President McKinley finally agreed. He asked Congress to permit the American military to help the Cubans. The United States declared war on Spain. In April 1898 the US Navy began a blockade of Cuba. The Spanish-American War began.

Senator Redfield Proctor

What was one reason Americans wanted to fight Spain?

The Spanish-American War
Preparations

Although the United States had declared war, it was not fully ready to fight. The US Navy was prepared. It had been improving its ships since the Civil War. The navy's fleet, or group of warships, was one of the best in the world. The US Army, however, was not as prepared. After the Civil War the army did not have any major wars to fight. For several decades it fought American Indians in the West. These wars required only small groups of well-trained soldiers.

Theodore Roosevelt as a Rough Rider

The US Army needed to be improved. Attacking the Spanish army in Cuba would take a larger army than the United States had. The army would need to train. It needed a way to get down to Cuba. Many Americans volunteered to fight for Cuba. Probably the most famous volunteer was Theodore Roosevelt. He was serving as Assistant Secretary of the Navy. Then he left that job to join a volunteer cavalry unit called the Rough Riders.

Naval Warfare

As the US Army prepared for war, the US Navy began the fighting. The Spanish navy had two fleets. One was in the Atlantic and the other in the Pacific. Many Americans feared that the Spanish fleets might attack cities in the United States. The American

Secretary of the Navy wanted both fleets to be destroyed.

In the Pacific the United States had a small fleet commanded by George Dewey. He sailed to Manila Bay in the Philippines. The Philippines was Spain's other large colony. On May 1, 1898, Dewey attacked the Spanish Pacific fleet. The Spanish ships were far older than the American ships. The Spanish commander was not able to withstand the US Navy. All the Spanish ships sank, and none of the American ships did.

Naval battle during the Spanish-American War between the US Navy and the Spanish Pacific fleet at Manila Bay on May 1, 1898

The United States was surprised to hear about the great victory. There had not yet been any battles fought in Cuba. But already the Spanish Pacific fleet was destroyed. Some Americans were worried about the Philippines. Would the United States try to take over these islands? Most Americans, however, were happy. At least America's West Coast would be safe from attack.

The Spanish Atlantic fleet was harder to fight. It was newer and faster than the Pacific fleet. Would Spanish ships try to attack America's cities on the East Coast? In late May the US Navy spotted the Spanish Atlantic fleet in a harbor in Cuba. The Spanish fleet was too well placed for the US fleet to fight. Instead, US ships blockaded the harbor. The Spanish ships could not easily leave. If they tried, they would have to fight their way out.

The Rough Riders charging San Juan Hill during the Spanish-American War in 1898

Land War

With the Spanish fleets out of the way, the American army began to fight in Cuba. The most important city to take was called Santiago de Cuba. It was located on the southern coast of Cuba. The city was protected by a number of hills. In early July, the US Army fought to capture the hills. The Battle of San Juan Hill is the most famous. Theodore Roosevelt helped lead the Rough Riders in this battle. He and his fellow soldiers became famous for charging up the hill to drive off the Spanish army.

After the American victory at San Juan Hill, the city of Santiago de Cuba was still under Spanish control. Its harbor had the Spanish fleet. But soon after the battle, the fleet tried to leave the harbor. The US Navy destroyed Spain's Atlantic fleet. Now the hills were taken, and the Spanish fleet was gone. Santiago de Cuba had few defenses left. For two more weeks the Spanish forces held out. Finally on July 17, the Spanish in Santiago de Cuba surrendered to US forces.

Wrapping Up the War

American forces did not move on to Cuba's capital, Havana. Instead, they moved to a smaller Spanish-owned island, Puerto Rico. American forces did not have great success there. They captured about half of the island by mid-August. At that point the United States and Spain agreed to a ceasefire. They would stop fighting. The Spanish accepted US control of Cuba, Puerto Rico, the Philippines, and Guam.

Who won military fame for fighting at the Battle of San Juan Hill?

The Aftermath
Peace with Spain

American and Spanish officials met in Paris, France. They began to work out a peace treaty. In December 1898 both sides agreed to a deal in the Treaty of Paris. Spain gave up Cuba, the Philippines, Puerto Rico, and Guam. The United States gave Spain twenty million dollars for the Philippines. Spain kept its colonies in Africa. After this war, Spain no longer had territory in the Americas or Asia.

The United States took over Spain's colonies. It promised that Cuba would have independence soon. It also said that the Philippines would someday become independent.

The Treaty of Paris showed a change in world powers. Spain could no longer be considered a major force in the world. The United States clearly had become one of the important countries. America now had several lands overseas. Other nations had to listen to America.

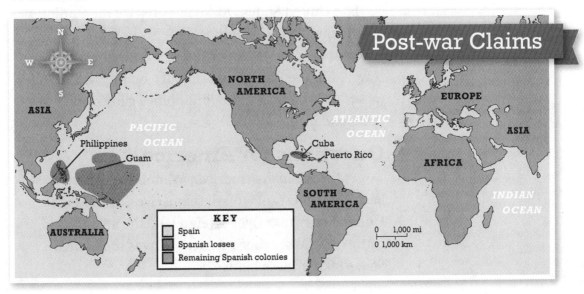

Post-war Claims

War with the Filipinos

The peace treaty was not accepted everywhere. In the Philippines, many native Filipinos were angry. They thought the United States was fighting to set them free from Spanish rule. They did not want to become an American colony.

The United States fought for several years against Filipino forces. Although they were not as well arranged or armed as the Spanish, the Filipino soldiers were hard to defeat. By 1903 the United States had made peace with the Philippines.

Filipino soldiers fought for their independence from Spain.

The United States worked to prepare the Philippines for independence. Filipinos were given more self-government. American businesses and missionaries traveled to the Philippines. Finally, on July 4, 1946 (after World War II), the Philippines gained full independence.

Questions for America

As the Spanish-American War ended, Americans had many questions to ask themselves. Should the United States take over foreign lands? Can a free country control other peoples? Why is the United States taking these lands?

During the middle of the war, the United States gained the islands of Hawaii located between the United States and the Philippines. The United States needed to protect shipping to the Philippines from the Spanish during the war. But several famous Americans spoke out against taking other lands. Among these were Grover Cleveland, Andrew Carnegie, and Mark Twain.

Many people did not think the United States should take over the Philippines. President McKinley promised that the United States would not control the Philippines forever. Even so, many Americans thought the United States should be freeing other countries, not making an empire.

Through the Treaty of Paris with Spain, the United States took over different lands. The Constitution says that the Senate must approve all treaties. The Senate approved the treaty by only one vote. Americans were not united in support of taking new lands.

Other Results of the War

The United States gained new lands and power because of the war. However, afterward America had to deal with new problems. One major problem was diseases. More soldiers' lives had been taken by **malaria** and **yellow fever** than by the war. American army doctors began working to end these diseases. A Cuban doctor had researched malaria. Through his work US Army doctors learned that mosquitoes spread the disease. This was also true of yellow fever. Draining wet areas helped get rid of mosquitoes. Then fewer people became ill from the diseases.

The Spanish-American War led to the completion of the Panama Canal. The United States realized how useful a canal would be. Ships could sail from the Atlantic to the Pacific more quickly. In 1904 the United States took over the digging of the canal from the Caribbean Sea to the Pacific Ocean.

Building the Panama Canal

What: US Army pathologist and bacteriologist

When: 1851–1902

Where: Washington, DC

Walter Reed spent most of his life investigating diseases. For twenty-seven years he worked for the United States Army. He treated many people with wounds and diseases. Reed is most famous for proving that mosquitoes spread yellow fever. Other doctors and researchers helped, but Reed did the most work in showing how the disease spread. Because of his work the builders of the Panama Canal did not have to worry about getting yellow fever from the many mosquitoes. The United States' largest military medical center is named after Reed in honor of his work.

Conclusion

During the late 1800s, the United States changed a great deal. One big change was America's move toward control of foreign lands. Some Americans wanted their nation to expand. But others did not. They did not want to see the world's major free country control other peoples. The war in Cuba led America to take over lands such as Hawaii, Puerto Rico, and the Philippines. Most Americans, even those against imperialism, wanted Spain to stop mistreating Cubans. In time the United States ended up controlling islands across the globe.

Why did some Americans not want the United States to control other lands?

7 Progress and Problems

Focus

Progressive Americans thought science could solve America's problems.

Wright brothers' first
successful flight
1903

1900   **1904** **1905**   **1909** **1910**
National Child Labor   NAACP founded
Committee formed

New Problems in America
American Progress

In the year 1800 the United States elected its third president. The Mississippi River formed the western border of the United States. Americans imported most manufactured goods. But foreign navies stopped American ships as they sailed on the seas. At this time, the United States was not one of the powerful nations of the world.

Many things can change in one hundred years. And much had changed by 1900. The United States had more wealth than any other nation in the world. Nations around the world imported American goods. The US Navy was becoming the world's most powerful navy. New inventions made life better. Also, medicine improved. Americans now lived longer than ever. They also had more free time to enjoy sports, concerts, and other activities. This was true not only of rich people but also of many ordinary Americans. The word *progress* described life in America between 1900 and 1917.

Problems with Business

Even with progress, some Americans thought their country had problems to solve. The big businesses that made the United States a wealthy nation were powerful. The leaders of these businesses became much wealthier than anyone else in the country. Some did not think it was good for these men to have so much wealth and power. Some people were also concerned that big businesses would hurt small businesses. These people did not want to see small businesses disappear. Americans valued the growth of their nation. But they also valued equality.

Americans were also concerned about conflict between business owners and their workers. Sometimes workers would go on strike. At times the conflicts between the strikers and the guards hired by the businessmen became violent. This violence worried people.

Political cartoon showing wealthy men using people to get their wealth

Problems for the Poor

Americans also wanted to help the poor. The tenements were bad places to live in. Some Americans thought that children who grew up in them might not learn to be good workers. They might not practice the skills needed to get good jobs. They might follow bad influences and not have the character to do good work.

Journalists Expose Problems

Journalists, or newspaper reporters, made people aware of problems in the nation. Many Americans were living comfortable lives. But they read about suffering in the newspapers. They read about children who worked in dangerous conditions. They read about dishonesty in the government.

Often journalists exposed real problems. Sometimes they went out of their way to get a story. One reporter, using the name Nellie Bly, pretended to be insane, so she could report on the awful conditions in an insane asylum. But often these journalists sensationalized the news. They stretched the truth to make their stories more interesting. Newspapers also made business leaders look like villains. Some business leaders were villains. Many were not. These journalists were called **muckrakers** by people who did not like them. Muck refers to mud and manure. Muckrakers wrote news stories that focused on bad news and sin. Some people did not like this. They wanted journalists to write about good things instead. Others said people needed to know about the filth. This way there would be progress in cleaning it up.

PROGRESSIVE FLY SWATTER

FLY

IT'S SCIENTIFIC!

Problems for Farmers

American farmers had been concerned about their role in a changing America for many decades. The prices for food kept going down. Some farmers lost their farms. They began to work on other farms that were larger. Some moved to work in mines or factories. They thought rich people had become too powerful. They wanted more power returned to the ordinary people. People who had this ambition were called Populists.

The farmers were not powerful enough to bring about change. So they joined with other Americans. These Americans were also concerned that businesses had become too big and powerful. Dishonesty in government concerned them. They wanted to end poverty. These people who thought the country had problems and needed to make progress were known as the Progressives. They had ideas to make that progress happen. These beliefs were known as Progressivism.

The Progressives often identified real problems. But sometimes they made problems even bigger. Some of their ideas worked. But often their ideas did not work. Sometimes the Progressives tried to correct society by controlling other Americans' lives. Many Americans disliked this control. They thought the Progressives' ideas hurt the nation. Americans today still debate the ideas of the Progressives.

Besides the growth of their nation, what did Americans also value?

From Providence to Progress

Before the Progressives, Americans had different ideas about how the world worked. In the 1800s pastors were some of the most important leaders in America. They were better educated than most Americans. Many Americans did not attend college in the 1800s. But the leading pastors had gone to college. After college they studied in seminary. A seminary is a school that trains pastors.

Pastors were some of the most respected leaders because they taught the Bible. Many Americans believed in God in the 1800s. They believed the Bible was God's Word. They wanted to know what God said about their problems. Like the Progressives, earlier generations wanted to fix problems in the United States. But they believed that God's Word helped them find the solutions. For this reason they turned to pastors for help.

These Americans believed God rules over all. Nothing happens apart from God's plan or permission. This truth is called God's **providence**. Good things are blessings from God. Bad things, like the Civil War, might be judgments of God. Sometimes God allows bad things to happen to teach people to trust Him more.

Belief in providence began to change after the Civil War. People began to wonder whether pastors could give people wise advice. Pastors did not agree among themselves about the Bible's teachings on slavery. The pastors could not stop the Civil War. Darwin's theory of evolution also made God seem less necessary. Darwin taught that the world progressed the way it did because of nature. God was not involved.

Scientists replaced pastors for many Americans. Americans turned to scientists to fix their problems. Social scientists became important authorities on American life. A **social scientist** studies societies. He might take surveys about different groups of people. These surveys help him learn about people. Or he might do experiments with groups of people. For example, in Chicago social scientists mapped the city to reveal how crowded or uncrowded different parts of the city were. They also mapped where wealthy people and poor people lived. They mapped what countries people had originally come from. Over time they mapped how long people in certain neighborhoods had lived in their homes. They thought these maps could show connections between city problems and the places where those problems showed up.

The social scientists promised they could give good advice. They said their advice was better than the advice of a pastor or an elected official. Pastors and officials disagreed with each other. Social scientists

believed that science could settle disagreements. Science could show how to solve problems in the United States. Many Americans thought science gave better answers than the Bible. But science could not solve America's problems. The scientists' research sometimes led to wrong conclusions. The information they collected sometimes had errors. Their experiments were sometimes flawed. Science could not guarantee right answers. The Progressives found that many of the improvements were not as successful as they had hoped. Science had not given them wisdom.

Even worse, the Progressives created injustices. They did not agree with the Bible's teaching about justice. They did not treat other people as being made in God's image. They thought that justice was accomplished when people lived according to the Progressives' plan. They thought this plan was right because it was based on science. They pressed for their ideas to be turned into law. They wanted the government to force people to live by the Progressives' scientific ideas. This led to injustice. For example, the governments of some states prevented certain people from having babies. Scientists said these people were stupid and should not be allowed to have children because their children would probably be stupid as well.

But God is real. His providence is real. And His Word really does give wisdom about how society should work. Fallen people disagree about what the Bible says. They might twist what the Bible says to help them get their way. But the Bible still gives people God's wisdom. The leaders of a nation need to listen to God in order to make wise decisions.

Who replaced pastors as important authorities on American life?

Progressivism and Society

The Progressives wanted to make the places where people lived cleaner and less crowded. They wanted to be sure drinking water was clean. They wanted to end poverty. They wanted to forbid alcohol because of the problems it caused. Christians especially supported banning alcohol.

Many of the goals of the Progressives were good. Wanting to end drunkenness is good. And some of their plans for fixing problems were good. For example, they wanted the police to learn skills such as fingerprinting. Some of their plans did not really work. But they did not do much harm either. For example, they thought having more city parks would reduce crime. Play would prevent children from getting into trouble. City playgrounds are nice, but they did not solve the problem of crime.

Progressives thought parks such as Bronx Park would reduce crime.

Many Progressives did not look in the Bible for wisdom. As a result they did not see that sin was the main cause of many problems. A new playground cannot solve a sin problem. Also, the Progressives were too convinced of their own ideas. They forgot they were sinners. They forgot they could do wrong. They forgot they too could make mistakes. They did not trust the wisdom of others. They especially did not value the wisdom found in traditions. Some of their ideas broke traditions that really worked. Sadly, untested ideas of the Progressives often did not work.

The Progressives wanted to change the way prisoners were treated. They said prisoners should not be punished. Instead prisons should help change the prisoner. Prisons should help the prisoner become a better person. It is good to help prisoners change. Christians have often tried to help prisoners change. But the idea that prisons are not for punishment is dangerous. Punishment needs to fit the crime.

The Progressives also sought to change the way children were treated at work. Many states passed laws about children who worked. The laws said children had to reach a certain age before they could work. These laws did not allow children to do dangerous work. They also set limits on how long children could work each day. The states also passed laws that required children to attend school.

Many people were hurt at work. Many of the machines at this time were dangerous. A machine could mangle an arm or leg. The injury could make a person unable to work. Progressives wanted businesses to pay hurt workers. They encouraged employers to buy accident insurance so they would have the money to pay the workers.

Many children worked long hours in factories.

Progressives also wanted to change education. In the past, high schools trained students for a specific trade. Now they trained students to go to college. Progressives thought experts in education needed to run the schools. An **expert** is someone who knows much about a specific part of life. Progressives did not think parents and communities should run schools. They also thought all the schools should teach the same things.

Progressives thought public education could solve other problems. They thought immigration was a major problem. People from other countries lived differently from other Americans. Too many immigrants could change the culture in America. Progressives wanted the children of immigrants to be taught in public schools. The public schools could train children with American values. The Progressives did not want private schools. They did not want religious schools. Those schools might not teach what the Progressives wanted to be taught.

What were some of the changes Progressives wanted to make?

Progressivism and Government

Progressivism began in the American cities. Progressives wanted to remove dishonest leaders. They also wanted cities to become cleaner, safer places.

Progressivism spread from the cities to the states. Progressives wanted the states to make new laws. They wanted laws about education. They also wanted laws to improve working conditions. Many states passed these laws. But some states did not.

The Progressives moved their efforts to the national government. They wanted their ideas to be law in the entire nation. They wanted laws to limit **child labor**. They also wanted to make laws for how railroads and other big companies ran their businesses.

Progressives changed the way the government worked. They wanted to make it easier for their ideas to become law. The Progressives wanted the national government to pass certain laws. The Progressives knew that some states might not want these laws passed. And the states had influence in the national government: each state legislature selected two senators for the US Senate. The Founding Fathers had written the Constitution so the states could have a voice in the national government. The Founding Fathers also thought the people should not have too much power. They thought someone might convince many people to support bad ideas. Through the system of checks and balances, the Senate would keep this from happening.

Progressives did not want the states to have the power to choose senators. Progressives said the state legislatures were dishonest and elected dishonest senators. This was not true. But the Progressives got a constitutional amendment passed. It said senators would be chosen directly by the people instead of by the state legislatures. The states lost influence over the laws Congress passed. One of the checks and balances of the Constitution disappeared.

Progressives suggested new ideas about voting. They did not want the political parties to choose who ran for office. They wanted the people to choose who ran from each party. This way of choosing candidates is called a **direct primary**. Progressives also said that people's votes should be secret. They did not want party leaders to know how a person voted.

The Progressives also wanted to see experts do more in government. The Progressives said the executive branch should create boards of experts to create the policies of government. Progressives thought the experts would make better policies than legislatures would. Experts would look at information from science. They would make the best decisions.

But these experts did not work the way Progressives wanted. Science could not provide all the answers the Progressives needed. The experts did not always make wise decisions. They did, however, make the executive branch stronger.

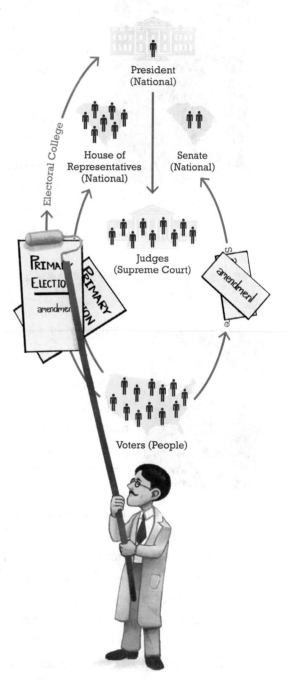

President Theodore Roosevelt

Theodore Roosevelt was president from 1901 to 1909. He supported many Progressive ideas. He set up boards of experts. He also had them make rules for businesses. He told them they should accept his rules or something worse might happen. He said the Socialists might take over. The Socialists thought the government should own the factories for all people. The money a factory made would go to everyone. The Socialist Party had more popularity in the Progressive Era than in any other time in American history.

William Howard Taft followed Roosevelt as president. Taft had served under Roosevelt. Many people thought Taft would be like Roosevelt. Taft did

William Howard Taft

What: lawyer, judge, secretary of war, president, teacher

When: 1857–1930

Where: Ohio

William Howard Taft served his country in many important roles. As a young man he worked as a lawyer. He was later appointed to serve as a judge on an important court. After the United States won the Spanish-American War, he served as governor of the Philippines for four years. After this, President Theodore Roosevelt asked him to serve as secretary of war. Taft did well at all these jobs. Roosevelt wanted Taft to become the next president, and Taft did. But the Republicans were divided between Progressives and conservatives. Taft found himself caught between these two groups. He did not please either one. After he served as president, Taft taught law at Yale University. Later he was appointed chief justice of the Supreme Court. This was the job that Taft had always wanted. He loved being chief justice. Taft spent most of his life serving his country in important roles.

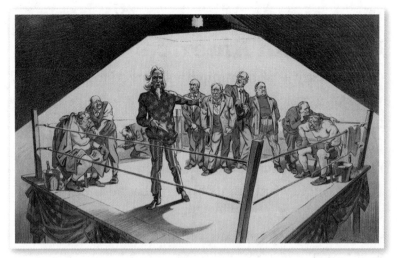

Udo J. Keppler's political cartoon depicting a boxing match between Theodore Roosevelt and William Taft, illustrating the upcoming presidential election

favor some Progressive ideas, but he also saw that businesses were important. They made the nation prosperous. He also thought some Progressive policies broke the law.

Taft moved away from Progressivism while he was president. But Roosevelt became more Progressive. In the 1912 election, Roosevelt challenged Taft. Roosevelt wanted to be president again. The Republicans chose Taft to run for president. Roosevelt left the Republican party. He started his own party called the Progressive Party. The Democratic Party had two competing groups. One group wanted a limited national government and strong state governments. The other group, made up of labor groups and immigrant groups, supported many Progressive ideas. Woodrow Wilson was the Democratic candidate for president. He kept the Democratic Party together by saying he supported both of its competing groups. Meanwhile, the Republican Party divided. This split helped Woodrow Wilson win the election. He followed Taft as the next president of the United States.

President Woodrow Wilson

Why did Progressives trust boards of experts?

Progressivism and Ethnic Groups in America

Progressives and immigrants worked together. They worked to make city life better. They also helped to make workers safer. But the Progressives also thought immigrants caused many problems. They thought immigrants introduced bad habits into American life. They thought immigrants brought crime and other evils with them.

The Progressives thought immigrants were a problem. They attempted two solutions. First, they tried to pass laws. These laws would not let as many immigrants come to the United States. These laws were passed for a brief time in the 1920s. Second, they tried to change public schools. They wanted the schools to teach immigrants how to be like Americans.

School for immigrant children in Boston, Massachusetts

Immigration changes cultures. **Culture** is the customs, beliefs, arts, and institutions of a group of people. Americans valued their culture. They were concerned immigrants might harm the culture they loved. Love for one's own culture can be good.

Love for one's own culture can also be twisted for evil. People have often treated immigrants unjustly. They have not asked why immigrants love their own cultures. They have not asked whether those cultures have good things they can learn from.

Scientists during the Progressive Era arranged people into races. They said some races were superior to others. Racism had already had a long and sad history in the United States. But now it had science backing it.

Segregated drinking fountain in Halifax, North Carolina

Before the Progressive Era, black Americans had suffered unjust treatment. But this treatment grew worse in the Progressive Era. The Progressives used government to keep black Americans below white Americans. Many Southern states passed laws about what black Americans could and could not do. These laws did not allow many black citizens to vote. The laws also said that white and black Americans must stay separated. This is called **segregation**. Many Northern communities also practiced segregation. Black and white Americans could not attend the same schools. They could not live in the same neighborhoods. They could not eat at the same restaurants.

Booker T. Washington (left) and W. E. B. Du Bois (right)

Black Americans disagreed about how to deal with segregation. Booker T. Washington was a freed slave who worked hard to gain an education. He led the Tuskegee Institute. It was a school to train black Americans to be teachers and to work in various other jobs. Washington wanted black Americans to develop schools. He wanted them to gain education. He wanted them to start their own businesses. He wanted to show that black people could succeed in many ways. He also worked to gain support from white Americans. He wanted to bring about the end of segregation gradually. He thought pushing to end segregation right away would do more harm than good for black Americans.

W. E. B. Du Bois had a different idea. He was the first black American to earn a PhD. A PhD is the highest degree that is earned at a college. He wanted black leaders to earn PhD degrees. He wanted to end segregation right away. He founded the National Association for the Advancement of Colored People (NAACP) to aid in this cause.

What injustices did black people face in this era?

Automobiles and Airplanes

The United States changed in other ways during the Progressive Era. The biggest change was the development of the automobile.

Automobiles were very expensive. Only wealthy people could afford them. Automobiles had other problems too. Some ran on steam engines. But steam engines sometimes exploded. This made these automobiles dangerous. Others ran on batteries. But a battery-powered car could not be driven long distances.

Henry Ford

Henry Ford made the automobile that most people bought. Ford did two things. He built an automobile that ran on gasoline. These automobiles could travel farther than cars that used batteries. Ford also built automobiles that ordinary people could afford.

He did this by combining many ideas of manufacturers before him. He used **interchangeable parts**. These identical parts could fit on any of Ford's cars. All the parts could be made and sent to the factory. Each part could be fitted on any of the cars being built. He also used an **assembly line**. An assembly line is a process in which each worker does only part of the total job instead of doing the total job alone. Each person does his task and then moves to the next piece. The car would move down the line from one person to the next.

Assembly lines benefited businesses and people by allowing goods to be made more quickly, which caused prices to go down.

Orville Wright

Wilbur Wright

The automobile changed American life. As more people bought automobiles, they could travel farther from home. People could more easily live in a suburb and work in a city. People from the country could travel into the city more often. Some pastors were concerned that more country folk were learning city sins. Pastors noticed that young people began to follow city fashions. The young people stopped following the traditional ways of their parents.

Ford also changed the way businesses thought about making goods. Before Ford, people thought an automobile would always cost lots of money. Cars were for rich people. But Ford showed he could make more money by selling more automobiles to more people for less money. Soon other companies followed the assembly-line strategy with goods for people's houses.

The Wright brothers' first successful flight at Kill Devil Hills, North Carolina

Ford also paid his workers almost twice as much as other factory workers. He knew that by paying his workers well, they could afford to buy the products they were making. Other manufacturers followed Ford's example.

Airplanes were another great invention of this time. Before this time people had used hot air balloons to ascend into the sky. Gliders had also been invented. But there was no airplane that could fly on its own power and be directed by a pilot. Two brothers, Wilbur and Orville Wright, successfully built such a plane. In December 1903 they made the first successful flight on an airplane. The first flight lasted only twelve seconds. Later that day they flew for almost an entire minute.

Over the next several years, people looked for ways to use the airplane. The military began making planes that could be used in fighting. The US Post Office began using airplanes to transport mail.

How did the automobile change American life?

Make a Paper Glider

Use resources to identify ways to fold paper to make a glider. Use the design of your choice to fold a sheet of paper to make the glider. Use colored markers to decorate your glider before you test fly it. Make necessary changes to how you launch your glider to improve the distance and direction it flies.

Art, Literature, and Religion

Workers complained that working on the assembly lines was dull. They did the same task over and over. But they made more money than before. Now they could afford to buy better things. But some people said that Americans spent too much and saved too little. Modern Americans did not seem as careful about how they spent their money as previous generations.

But these new purchases had many benefits. Americans could drive to work in automobiles. American women could use a refrigerator to keep food from spoiling. Americans could be entertained by going to watch a baseball game, a circus, or a motion picture. Or they might stay home and listen to music on a phonograph.

Children might enjoy curling up with a good book. Edward Stratemeyer hired groups of authors to write series of children's books. These series included The Bobbsey Twins, Tom Swift, and later, the Hardy Boys, and Nancy Drew. Other popular books of the period were *The Virginian* by Owen Wister and the classic Westerns by Zane Grey.

Americans were not as excited about some art produced at this time. Artists developed new styles of art. Americans thought the art was ugly. They thought the artists were breaking all the rules. They did not think breaking all rules was good.

Popular children's books
during the Progressive Era

Many Americans also did not like what was being taught in their colleges. The Bible used to be the source of truth for Americans. Now science was the source of truth for many Americans. Christian ideas were dismissed as old-fashioned. College teachers claimed they did not need the Bible. They had science.

Christians were concerned that Christianity might become unpopular. Liberal Christians were willing to change Christianity. They thought they could remove the parts modern people did not like. They thought they could save Christianity by doing this. But instead they lost Christianity. They created a new false religion.

Bible-believing evangelists who traveled the country pointed out many problems in America. They told people that schools were teaching evolution. They said evolution was a major danger to the Christian faith. They warned people about the changes in colleges. They said the colleges often turned young people away from God. The evangelists were not opposed to education. But some said Christians needed their own colleges. These colleges should be places where Christian young people would not lose their faith.

The evangelists also warned that many other people were also being drawn away from God. The enjoyments and comforts of modern life drew them away. People were distracted from following God. They could watch motion pictures. They could spend time at amusement parks. They could go to musical plays. Often these entertainments were immoral. The evangelists urged people to turn from their sins. They told them how to find salvation in Christ.

Many Americans attended the evangelists' meetings. Christians were often strengthened in their beliefs. Unbelievers often trusted Christ. Their lives were transformed by the gospel.

The Progressive Era was a time of great change in the United States. Some of this change brought great good. There were many benefits in refrigerators, automobiles, and public parks. It was also good that Americans were concerned with helping the poor and others in need. It was even good that scientists were working to solve problems. Scientific discoveries were helpful in many ways. The work of Christian evangelists in spreading the gospel was also good for America.

Much of this change, however, was not good. Important parts of American society, like colleges, turned away from God and the Bible. Even though this was not true of most Americans, it was true of many important Americans. These people placed too much faith in science. They were so confident in science that they used the power of government to force Americans to follow some of their ideas. Sadly, this control led to injustices toward many Americans.

The Progressive Era remained a time of progress and problems.

What drew people away from God during the Progressive Era?

8 The Great War

Focus

America played a key role in ending World War I.

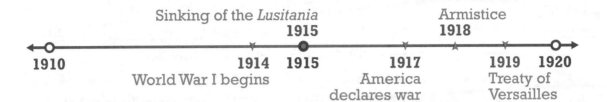

Sinking of the *Lusitania*
1915

Armistice
1918

1910

1914 **1915**
World War I begins

1917
America
declares war

1919 **1920**
Treaty of
Versailles

The World Goes to War

In the early 1900s most Americans were focused on daily life, progress, and change in their own country. Woodrow Wilson had been elected president in 1912. Business in America was good. Many people had worked hard to improve their lives. Most Americans had a job and enough to eat. Life in America was not perfect, but for most it was peaceful and prosperous.

However, trouble was brewing in other parts of the world. People in Europe had strong feelings of pride in their countries. Nations were hungry for more power. They wanted to expand and become empires. Some countries had built powerful armies and navies. Unrest between nations was beginning to develop. Choices in other countries would soon affect all Americans—and all the world.

Europe's Dominoes

Several countries in Europe had made alliances. An **alliance** is an agreement between nations to help fight each other's battles. Great Britain, France, and Russia had made one of these alliances. It was called the **Triple Entente**. Germany, Austria-Hungary, and Italy had formed another alliance. Theirs was called the **Triple Alliance**. These alliances put Europe in a dangerous situation. If one nation in an alliance went to war, the other nations in that alliance would have to join it. A member of the Triple Alliance might declare war on a member of the Triple Entente. A "domino effect" would suddenly begin. The war would not be between only two nations. Many nations would be at war with each other. In 1914 this is exactly what happened.

The War Begins

In June of that year, the Austrian archduke was traveling in Bosnia. Archduke Francis Ferdinand was the heir to the throne of Austria-Hungary. A young man from a **terrorist** group fired shots into the archduke's car as it drove by. Both Ferdinand and his wife were killed.

Archduke Francis Ferdinand of Austria and his wife, the Archduchess of Hohenberg, in 1914

The terrorist group came from the small country of Serbia. Austria-Hungary blamed the country for the killings and declared war on Serbia. The country of Russia took Serbia's side. Russia quickly began moving its army to help Serbia.

Because of the alliances, other countries jumped into action. Germany declared war on Russia. France took Russia's side. Britain had hoped to stay out of the conflict. But the British grew angry when Germany invaded Belgium, a neutral country. Britain joined France and Russia in the war. Italy decided to withdraw from the Triple Alliance. Italy would join forces with Russia, Serbia, France, and Britain the next year.

Germany and Austria-Hungary's side was called the **Central Powers**. Other countries would soon join them. The Triple Entente countries called themselves the **Allies**. They too would be joined by others, including the United States.

Within weeks, it seemed that the entire world was at war. The war was to last nearly five years. At the time of the fighting, people called it the Great War. Later it became known as **World War I**.

What caused the "domino effect" in Europe at the start of World War I?

French soldiers leaving Paris, France

The War in Europe
Into the Trenches

All over Europe excitement about the war ran high. Young men stood in long lines to join their nation's army or navy. Crowds flocked to train stations to see soldiers off to the war. Bands played and people sang patriotic songs at the tops of their voices. Most people thought the war would be over in a few months. They expected their men to be home by Christmas or even before the leaves had fallen.

The hope of a short war soon faded. In the first few battles of the war, thousands of soldiers were killed. The German army hoped to take the French capital city, Paris, but they did not succeed. The French and the British drove them back at the Marne River.

After the opening battles, the two sides settled into trenches along the **Western Front** in France. The war had reached a **stalemate**. Neither side could gain much ground.

In the east the Russian army suffered a terrible defeat by the Germans. But they seized some territory in Austria-Hungary and held on.

The trenches on the Western Front became the soldiers' homes for most of the war. Life in a trench was very unpleasant. Trenches were only about six and a half feet deep and a few feet wide. Rain kept the floor of a trench muddy nearly all the time. Rats and insects were problems. Exploding shells kept the men awake at night.

Between enemy trenches was an area called No Man's Land. Tangles of barbed wire made this area difficult to cross. Soldiers took turns manning the front line of trenches. When not on front-line duty, they would crawl into trenches farther back to support the front line or to rest.

German trenches on the Aisne River in France

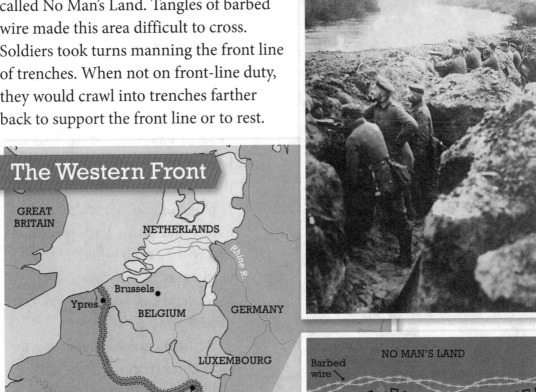

The Western Front

GREAT BRITAIN

NETHERLANDS

Rhine R.

Brussels

Ypres

BELGIUM

GERMANY

LUXEMBOURG

Paris

Marne R.

Verdun

Seine R.

Rhine R.

FRANCE

	Germany		German occupation
	Allies		Neutral countries
∿∿∿	trenches		No Man's Land

NO MAN'S LAND

Barbed wire

Row 1: Main trenches

Machine gun

Row 2: Support trenches

Communication trenches

Row 3: Reserve trenches

By Christmas soldiers on both sides of the war were worn out. They had planned to be home with their families for the holiday. Now they realized the war was going to last much longer.

On the Western Front soldiers began singing Christmas carols in their trenches on Christmas Eve. To their surprise, they heard the enemy soldiers in the opposite trenches singing along with them. All along the front, the singing went on.

On Christmas morning few men felt like fighting with men they had just sung with the night before. In many parts of the front, the men declared **truces** with each other. They agreed to stop fighting just for that one day. German, British, and French soldiers climbed out of their trenches. They walked into No Man's Land. They shook hands cautiously. They smiled and wished each other "Merry Christmas." Some shared tins of food, candy, or coffee. It was a day of peace.

Officers quickly put a stop to Christmas truces. Truces made it difficult for the men to start fighting again. Enemy soldiers could not really trust one another. It was dangerous to try to make friends. After the spring of 1915, there were no more truces.

Christmas truce in No Man's Land

New Weapons

The style of fighting in World War I was new and different from any earlier war. Machine guns were better and more powerful than earlier models. The guns used in World War I could fire more than six hundred rounds a minute. If a soldier even raised his head above the top of a trench, he might be blasted with an enemy machine gun.

Armored tanks were first used in World War I.

Gas masks were worn to protect the soldiers from poisonous gas.

Armies began using **tanks**, moving vehicles that could fire shells as they went along. Because of their heavy armor, tanks were very hard to stop. Later in the war, they were big enough to drive across trenches.

Chemical weapons were also first used in this war. Poisonous gases were placed inside shells. When the shells exploded, the gas was released into the air. The gas was difficult to breathe. Sometimes it made soldiers ill, blinded them, or even killed them. Gas masks were invented to help protect soldiers from poisonous gas.

Aircraft were also used in warfare for the first time. The Germans used **zeppelins**, similar to blimps, to drop bombs. Later in the war, airplanes replaced these slower machines. Fighter planes were light and fast and could carry machine guns.

A German zeppelin

What new weapons were used in World War I?

189

America Watches the War
Concerns

All over the United States people eagerly read about the war in newspapers. President Wilson believed that Americans should stay neutral. They should not take sides, and they should not enter the war themselves.

But Americans were concerned. America had more ties to Great Britain than to any other country. Many Americans traced their roots back to England, Scotland, or Ireland. France had helped America during the Revolutionary War. All these countries traded with the United States. Many Americans felt loyal to the Allies for these reasons.

Another reason for concern was Germany's methods of war. Many Americans thought German strategies were unfair. If Germany invaded neutral countries like Belgium, would it try to attack the United States?

Germany also had a policy called **unrestricted submarine warfare**. The strong British navy had cut off shipping from Germany's ports. The Germans started using undersea boats rather than ships. Germans warned that their submarines would attack any ship that came into a war zone. All ships could be attacked, not just warships. Germany placed ads in America's newspapers. These ads told Americans

not to travel on British ships. Americans, however, thought Germany was wrong to do this. Germany's policy took away Americans' freedom to choose their transportation. As a result, many more Americans favored the Allies over the Central Powers. It was hard to be neutral in the conflict.

The Sinking of the *Lusitania*

In 1915 an event took place that shocked and angered Americans. On May 7 a British passenger ship, the *Lusitania*, was sailing from New York to England. Some of the passengers on the ship were Americans. The ship had just come within sight of the coast of Ireland. Too late, the ship's crew realized that a German submarine was nearby. The Germans fired a torpedo at the *Lusitania*. It struck the ship's side. The ship began to sink.

Some passengers were able to scramble into life-boats. Many jumped from the deck and clung to floating cargo. Others were trapped on board the ship. The *Lusitania* sank in less than twenty minutes. More than one thousand people died. Of those who drowned, 128 were Americans.

President Wilson demanded that the Germans stop attacking ships that were not warships. Germany wanted to keep peace with the United States, so it agreed to stop.

An election campaign truck in New York

"He Kept Us Out of War"

America continued to stay out of the war. The American people read in the papers about the Battle of Verdun in France. Hundreds of thousands of men died in the long battle. Then they read of the Battle of the Somme River. It seemed that the war was dragging on and on. Neither side seemed to be able to win.

The sinking of the *Lusitania* had caused more Americans to feel loyal to the Allies. But there was still not a strong belief that Americans should join the war. Many of them hoped that the European countries would be able to make peace soon.

Woodrow Wilson ran for another term as president in 1916. "He kept us out of war," Americans reminded each other. The phrase became the official slogan of Wilson's campaign. President Wilson was elected to a second term.

Why did Americans favor the Allies?

America Goes "Over There"
America Declares War

Early in 1917 the German government broke its promise to the United States. It announced that Germany would begin unrestricted submarine warfare again. Germany knew that this would anger America. But the Germans also believed this was the only way they could win the war.

The German government also sent a telegram to Mexico. The telegram asked Mexico to join the war on Germany's side. Germany feared that war would break out with the United States. It wanted Mexico to fight for them against the Americans. In return Germany offered to give the states of Texas, New Mexico, and Arizona back to Mexico.

British spies found out about this telegram. They sent the message to the United States. Americans were outraged.

President Wilson realized that the time for keeping peace was over. On April 2, 1917, he went before Congress and asked for a declaration of war on Germany. "The world must be made safe for democracy," the president said in his speech.

President Woodrow Wilson addressing Congress

Four days later, the United States declared war. Americans began to prepare. The American army was small, but many more men wanted to fight. America used a draft system. In a **draft**, local boards in each state choose men to go into military service. More than four million Americans served in World War I.

A songwriter named George Cohan wrote a song about the American soldiers going to war. "Over There" became very popular, and it was played and sung all over the nation. Its brave lyrics and lively tune made it seem cheerful. "The Yanks are coming," said the song, "and we won't come back till it's over over there!" Many of the men who sang this song never came back. More than 115,000 American soldiers were killed in the war.

George Cohan

Activity

Learning a Wartime Song

Listen to the recording of "Over There." Sing along as your teacher plays the song again. Think about why this song was inspiring to many Americans during World War I.

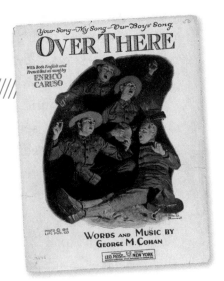

American Attitudes

The war brought out strong patriotic feelings in most Americans. Some still opposed going to war. But the most common attitude among Americans was eagerness to help the war effort.

President Wilson formed a special committee to give Americans information. Posters and ads helped make people excited about supporting the United States. Information like this is called **propaganda**. It is designed to make people think or feel a certain way.

War propaganda also gave many Americans negative attitudes toward all Germans. Posters called the German people "Huns." The Huns were an ancient tribe known for their cruelty in war. The name was used to promote fear and hatred of the enemy.

American schools stopped teaching German. Foods with German names were given new ones. People called hamburgers "Liberty Burgers." They called sauerkraut "Liberty Cabbage." They even renamed dachshund dogs "Liberty Pups." German Americans became fearful. Others often treated them with unjust cruelty. Sometimes they were accused of being spies. Many worked hard to prove their loyalty to America.

Propaganda poster advertising liberty bonds, which people bought from the government to help the war effort

Was it right for Americans to hate all Germans?

Helping the War at Home
Helping by Working

Changes came to America as the soldiers trained and left for war. With so many men leaving the country, many jobs were left with no one to do them. Often women took over these jobs. More women than ever before took jobs outside their homes during World War I. Women did farm work, delivered mail, and worked as clerks in stores and offices. Some worked on railroads or drove trucks and ambulances.

Colt's Patent Fire Arms Plant in Hartford, Connecticut, where women inspected automatic pistol parts

A Red Cross nurse during World War I

Some women worked directly with the war effort. Many went overseas to work as nurses. But there were war jobs to do at home too. Volunteers rolled bandages or knit warm socks for soldiers. Women built weapons and shells in factories. The navy even allowed women to enlist. The position they held was known as yeoman, but people called them **yeomanettes**. Yeomanettes did mostly office jobs such as translating, operating telegraphs, and sending messages.

Some women were glad to go back to their household work after the war. But many others realized they had been able to earn more money than ever before. They continued to work after the war ended.

Helping by Saving

Another change on the home front was the need for Americans to save money and food. A country at war must pay for many new expenses. The more citizens can save, the more resources can be used to help the war effort.

By this time many Americans owned cars. One way they could help was by saving gas. The nation's fuel was needed to move war goods from place to place. The government urged people to walk more instead of drive. Many Americans planned for one day a week to be a "gasless" day. They would try to go for an entire day without driving their cars.

Propaganda poster advertising for help in the war effort

President Wilson asked a man named Herbert Hoover to take charge of the Food Administration. Hoover asked Americans to help save food. They could volunteer to have "meatless days" and "wheatless days." In this way, more meat and grain could be shipped overseas to feed the soldiers. The Food Administration published recipes for foods that could be prepared without sugar or without meat. Americans also planted gardens and grew their own vegetables and fruits. They called these "Victory Gardens."

Schoolchildren raised cabbage and other vegetables in Victory Gardens to help the war effort

Propaganda poster advertising a war bond that could be bought to support the Allies during World War I

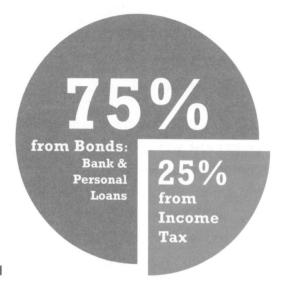

Americans raised over $30 billion for the war effort.

75% from Bonds: Bank & Personal Loans

25% from Income Tax

Helping by Paying

Just before World War I broke out, Americans had begun to pay **income tax**. Income taxes were an important resource the government used to pay for the war.

Americans also paid for the war in more direct ways. Americans could buy war bonds. Buying a war bond was like loaning money to the government. Someone who bought a war bond could get his money back later on. Since the government paid interest on war bonds, he got back more than what he had paid.

Even children helped. The government set up a special program for them. They could buy War Savings Stamps for twenty-five cents each. Posters encouraged children to "help Uncle Sam" by buying these stamps.

Name three ways Americans at home helped in the war.

Americans in the War
Doughboys in Europe

The first American soldiers arrived in France in the fall of 1917. Their commander was **John J. Pershing**. They had been named the **American Expeditionary Force**. But people called them **doughboys**. Some people believe this nickname came from the buttons on their uniforms. Many thought the buttons looked like lumps of bread dough. Others think the name was used because American soldiers made their own food in camp.

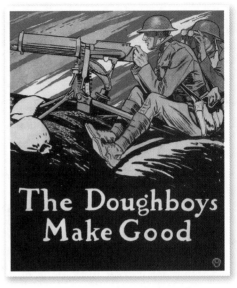

This magazine cover by illustrator Edward Penfield celebrated the American soldiers who brought new hope to the Allies during the war.

The coming of the Americans brought hope to the Allies. Their soldiers were tired. They had lost thousands of men in recent battles. Russia had withdrawn from the war. The Allies were in desperate need of help.

American forces were given their own section of the Western Front to defend. This map shows some places where Americans gained ground for the Allies.

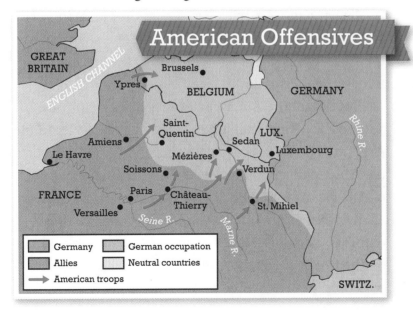

199

African American soldiers wearing the Cross of War medal return home from Europe after World War I. More than 350,000 African Americans served as soldiers.

The Cross of War medal was awarded by France to American soldiers for their support during the war.

Americans played a key role in saving Paris, the French capital. The Germans tried several times to break through the Allied line and capture Paris. Americans pushed the Germans back across the Marne River at the town of Château-Thierry. Americans also held back the Germans in Belleau Wood. This was the last major effort by the Germans to get to Paris.

The greatest American attack on the Germans was at Saint-Mihiel. With help from the French, Americans used guns, tanks, and planes to crush the German forces in only two days.

But not all the American efforts were victorious. Some heavy American losses came during battles in the Argonne Forest. In one battle only about one-third of the American troops survived. Hundreds of thousands of Americans were killed or wounded in other battles.

Another surprising killer during the war was an outbreak of sickness. A flu virus spread among soldiers on the front. Then it spread to people at home. Millions of people around the world died of the flu.

Fighter pilots who shot down enemy planes were called "flying aces." They were heroes after the war. Captain Eddie Rickenbacker was the top American ace. He won twenty-six victories over other planes.

Most fighter planes in World War I were biplanes. They had two long wings, one above the other.

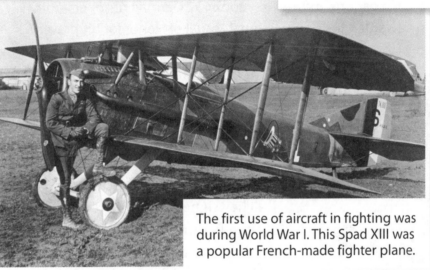

The first use of aircraft in fighting was during World War I. This Spad XIII was a popular French-made fighter plane.

The Spad XIII carried two machine guns. The pilot controlled them from the cockpit. A fight in the air between two planes was called a dogfight.

This plane had a single 200-horsepower engine. It could fly at speeds of up to 135 miles per hour.

Sergeant Alvin York

What: American soldier

When: World War I

Where: Argonne Forest, France

A Christian from Tennessee, Alvin York at first did not believe he should fight in the war. When he was drafted he tried to refuse. But the draft board would not accept his refusal. After further study of the Bible, York decided it was his duty to serve his country. In one battle he led a group of seven men in a daring capture. They took 132 German prisoners. York was awarded the Congressional Medal of Honor for his bravery.

The *Bismarck Tribune* newspaper announcing the war's end

The War Ends

The fighting finally ended on November 11, 1918. At 11:00 in the morning, Germany stopped firing its guns. German leaders met with the Allied commander, **Ferdinand Foch**. They signed an **armistice**, an agreement to stop fighting.

November 11 became known as Armistice Day. It was celebrated as a holiday every year. Today we still celebrate a holiday on November 11. But now on that day we honor all Americans who have served in our country's armed forces. We call it **Veterans Day**. Other countries call it Remembrance Day.

What key role did Americans play in the war?

Making Peace
President Wilson's Goals

It seemed as though the world had gone crazy with happiness. In the Allied nations people filled the streets, singing, shouting, and dancing. Cheers rose from the crowds. People laughed and wept at the same time. Church bells rang, and many gave thanks to God. The long, terrible war was finally over.

But peace could not be made in one day. The making of the peace treaty was a long process that took several months.

President Wilson went to France to meet with the other Allied leaders. He had certain goals for the meetings. He had made a list of fourteen points he wanted to see put in place. The most important point was his plan for a League of Nations. The League would help keep peace in the future by talking through problems, not by fighting wars.

But not all the other leaders agreed with Wilson. They thought his idea for a League of Nations would never work. Some of them wanted to see Germany punished more harshly than Wilson did.

Celebration at the White House at the end of World War I

The Treaty of Versailles

After much talking and arguing, the leaders reached an agreement in June 1919. The peace treaty was called the **Treaty of Versailles**.

The treaty did include a League of Nations. But the treaty was harder on Germany than Wilson had wanted it to be. It blamed the war entirely on Germany. It took away Germany's landholdings overseas. Germany also lost some land in Europe. Germany had to pay France and Great Britain for their war costs. The huge sum was more than the country could afford.

The "Big Four" were the top Allied leaders: Woodrow Wilson from the United States, David Lloyd George from Britain, Vittorio Orlando from Italy, and Georges Clemenceau from France.

President Wilson urged Congress to sign the treaty. He did not like every part of the treaty. But he wanted the League of Nations badly enough to sign it anyway. However, Congress did not agree that the United States should join a League of Nations. Wilson fell out of favor with the American people for his strong views about the League. In the end the United States never signed the treaty, and they never joined the League. Later while Warren Harding was president, the United States worked out its own treaty with Germany.

Painting by John Singer Sargent that portrays the result of a gas attack during the Great War

The War to End All Wars?

Many people called World War I "the war to end all wars." The world hoped there would never be another war like the Great War. Along the Western Front in France, fields of crosses were a silent reminder of the millions of young men who had died. Many American husbands, fathers, brothers, and sons never returned. Others came home disabled in some way for the rest of their lives.

Many historians believe that the war could have been avoided. Countries had rushed into war with no effort to work out differences in another way. The harshness of the peace treaty also caused problems. The treaty sought to punish Germany rather than working with it for a lasting peace.

The French commander Ferdinand Foch did not believe all wars had ended. After the Treaty of Versailles was signed, he said, "This is not peace. It is an armistice for twenty years." Foch believed that the bitter feelings about the treaty would result in another world war. Twenty years later his words would prove to be true.

What did Wilson want most from the peace treaty?

9 Enjoying the Peace

Focus

In the 1920s Americans tried to move on from the war and get back to business.

Women's suffrage
1920

Scopes trial
1925

Stock market crashes
1929

1920
Prohibition begins

1925
Charles Lindbergh flies
solo across the Atlantic

1927

1930

Returning to Normal
Restarting Life

Americans had fought in World War I for only a little over a year and a half. However, every part of American life had been affected by the war. With the fighting over, Americans wanted to go back to how life had been before the war.

The Business of America

The Republican presidents of the 1920s were exactly what America wanted after the war. The first president, Warren G. Harding, said he wanted a "return to normalcy." Most Americans agreed. Sixty percent of voters voted for Harding and his running mate, Calvin Coolidge. However, after two years as president, Harding died. Coolidge became the next president. Americans loved him. Coolidge said that America should mainly focus on business. President Wilson had said that America needed to make the world safe for democracy. Americans were happy to have a president like Coolidge who did not want the country to be involved in other nations' problems.

Businesses in America

Now the country no longer needed to worry about other nations. Instead, Americans got back to work. Soldiers returning from the military rejoined the work force. During the war, factories focused on making things necessary for the war. Factories made airplanes and bombs instead of cars and radios. Now that the war was over, factories could begin making goods for **civilians** again.

American businesses also did well around the world. Factories in Europe had been making military products too. Most European countries had spent much money to fight the war. They had lost many men in battle and from disease. The American businesses were able to return to normal faster than other countries. Fewer US soldiers had died. Americans were able to begin selling their products around the world.

Many American businesses shared the money they made with **stockholders** or shareholders. Some companies were owned by just one person or family. Others were owned by many people. Each person owned a small part of the company. These parts were

Activity

Learning About Banking

Have you ever visited a bank? Discuss the employees of a bank and what they do. Set up a bank in your classroom. Learn to fill out a deposit slip and write a check. Practice setting up a checking or savings account and make a withdrawal or deposit.

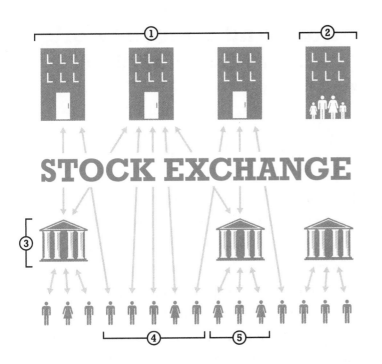

① Many businesses sell small parts of their company through the stock exchange.

② Some businesses are owned by individual families.

③ Banks often use people's money to buy stocks.

④ Stockholders buy stock in a business through the stock exchange.

⑤ Many people put their money in banks.

called stock. When a company made money, it usually gave part to its stockholders. During the 1920s some individuals bought stocks. If they wanted all their money back, they could sell their stocks in the stock exchange. The most important stock exchange was on **Wall Street** in New York City.

Not all Americans bought stocks. Some were concerned that if they owned stocks in a company that did not succeed, they would lose all their money. These people often **deposited** their money in banks. This means that they left their money in a bank to keep it safe. Even then it was not always safe. Many banks used people's money to buy stocks. The people who kept money in the bank would receive a small amount of the money earned from stocks. The money that banks give to their depositors is called **interest**.

What did President Harding want for America after the war?

209

Inventions and Everyday Life
The Roaring Twenties: 1920–1929

Many people called this decade "The Roaring Twenties." America's factories were roaring again. In people's houses new inventions were also whirring, *vrooming*, and swishing. The Twenties were full of new noises.

One invention that changed lives was the washing machine. For thousands of years people washed their clothes by hand. After soaking the clothes in soapy water, the person scrubbed each item on a ridged wooden or metal frame. The person often had scraped knuckles and dry skin after washing the clothes. The washing machine changed all that. Now dirty clothes could be tossed into a

Ads from the early 1900s for new inventions that would make housecleaning easier

210

machine with some soap. The machine did all the hard work. The clean clothes could be pulled out and hung to dry.

The vacuum was another invention that helped housework. Before the vacuum, wooden and tile floors were swept with a broom. Even the most diligent sweeper found it difficult to get everything off the floor. Since rugs were hard to clean, they had to be taken outside and beaten. Many people owned specially made rug beaters. Vacuums could get dirt off rugs much more quickly and thoroughly than beating the carpet could. For Americans with electricity, the vacuum was an exciting tool to buy.

Some other inventions helped household life for Americans. For toast, most people tried to hold a piece of bread near the fire to delicately brown it. If it stayed too long or got too close, the toast burned. The electric toaster allowed Americans to enjoy nearly perfect toast every time. While the toaster did not completely change life for Americans, it helped make life easier. Other new inventions like the steam iron and the electric stove also became part of everyday life for many Americans.

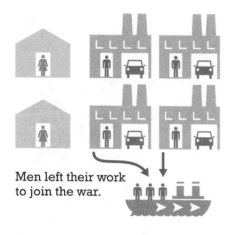

Men left their work to join the war.

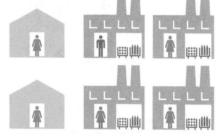

Women began working in factories to support the troops.

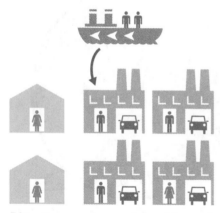

After the war, men returned to work and most women returned home.

How did inventions change life in the Twenties?

Working Life

After the end of World War I, people tried to get back to normal. During the war many men had left to fight. Once they returned, they went back to their jobs. Fairly soon after the war, business began doing well. Most men found work. In the cities men often worked in offices. Some worked in factories. These factories made things like washing machines and vacuums that Americans wanted. Many factories also made cars. Henry Ford kept making cars, and other companies did as well. People bought many Fords, Chevrolets, Oldsmobiles, and other brands also. In rural areas, many Americans farmed. Others ran small stores. Most American men found little difficulty in getting a job.

World War I had changed working life for American women. Many women who had taken men's jobs during the war were young single women. These women often married returning soldiers and returned to housework. Even with the new inventions, there was much housework that needed to be done. During the 1920s most Americans thought that women should be housewives. But some women continued to work outside their homes. Women were often nurses, teachers, secretaries, or telephone operators. America was gradually changing.

Leisure in the Twenties
The Radio

Another change in American life was the invention of the radio. Although it was invented before World War I, it did not come into common use until after the Twenties. Over the decade, millions of Americans bought radio sets. Soon most major cities had their own radio stations.

Americans used the radio as a source of information and entertainment. News programs told what was happening in the world. Preachers' sermons were broadcast every week. Radio programs aired funny or scary stories. Some of them were written just for children. Others were for their parents. Some programs broadcast performances of famous pieces of classical music or plays. In the evening families gathered around their radios to listen to the nightly programs.

Parents and children enjoyed listening to the radio together.

The radio helped change American living. It allowed the people to hear news almost as soon as it happened. Americans no longer had to buy a newspaper to know the headlines from the news. Now they could turn on the radio. It also let them hear from people far away. Instead of traveling to hear a famous preacher or political speaker, people could listen to him on their radios. The radio provided a way for Americans to enjoy music, stories, and sports from their own homes.

By the end of the 1920s, some people even had radios that could work in their cars. The radio was part of American life.

George Herman Ruth

Jack Dempsey

Other Entertainment in the Twenties

In their extra leisure time, Americans who had cars often enjoyed going on drives and sightseeing. Some families would plan an outing and pack a picnic lunch. Others stopped by roadside diners to eat. Some Americans took even longer road trips. Although there were no major highways, people could still drive from one state to another.

With added access to world news, some Americans followed celebrities. In the 1920s sports also gained popularity. Many cities had professional baseball teams. **Babe Ruth** was the most famous baseball star. His skill at hitting home runs helped the New York Yankees reach the World Series six times in the decade. They won three of these championships. Some Americans also followed the career of the famous boxer **Jack Dempsey**. Others cheered for the American swimmer **Gertrude Ederle**. In 1926 she became the first woman to swim across the English Channel. In 1927 everyone in America followed the story of **Charles Lindbergh**. He was the first person to fly solo across the Atlantic. He flew from New York to Paris.

Americans also enjoyed listening to music live and attending plays. Large cities often had orchestras that played classical music. Many cities and towns had stages for plays. If there were no professional actors, some people in a town would stage their own play. Sometimes travelling companies of actors would visit and put on plays. Composers like George Gershwin wrote music that combined traditional classical music and modern jazz.

Many Americans also enjoyed going to movie theaters during this time period. For most of the Twenties, only silent films were made. These movies had the actors' lines printed on the film. Theaters had organists or pianists play mood music during the movie. Whether it was a sad or happy scene, the music would match the emotion. At the end of the decade, "talkies" were introduced. These films had the actors' lines and music recorded. Now people could enjoy both the sight and sound of the film.

Gertrude Ederle

Charles Lindbergh

George Gershwin

During the 1920s several novelists wrote famous books. Francis Scott Fitzgerald's book *The Great Gatsby* helped Americans see some problems with the decade. People loved dancing and eating, but they realized they needed more to make life satisfying.

As the 1920s went on, Americans continued to enjoy more and more free time. Much of it was a result of new inventions. The popularity of the radio and movies also helped Americans to become more similar in their way of life. People from different cities all over America could see the same movies and hear many of the same programs. New technology helped unite America in its leisure activities. The Twenties was a wonderful time for many Americans.

What were some things Americans did with their free time?

Not all the fun things from the 1920s were good. Preachers warned that some movies and other entertainment did not encourage goodness. Sometimes people chose to watch baseball rather than meet with their churches.

Changes in the Cities

America changed a lot in the Twenties. One of the biggest changes was that cities continued to grow. In 1920, for the first time, more Americans lived in urban than in rural areas. The growth of urban populations had both good and bad consequences.

The Great Migration

Southern black families moving north helped speed the growth of cities. From Reconstruction on, life was difficult for many Southern blacks. Few jobs were available to them. Most worked as sharecroppers. Some could scarcely afford to feed their families. Racism also made the South unwelcome for many black Americans. Because of all these problems, thousands of blacks moved north.

Sojourner Truth housing project in Detroit, Michigan, in 1942

The black Americans' move into Northern cities took place over many years. Many moved during World War I when there was a large shortage of workers. After the war they stayed in the North. Soon their families also moved. Sometimes only immediate family members came. Often brothers and sisters also moved.

As black Americans migrated from the South, they helped change the culture in Northern cities. The most famous result was in New York City. Many black people moved to an area called Harlem. Some worked to improve the lives of all black Americans. A number wrote novels and poems about the hardships. Others tried to influence politics. This movement is called the Harlem Renaissance.

Most black Americans had much to adapt to when they moved to cities. They often worked in factory jobs. Some worked in car repair shops or in other service industries. These jobs were different from Southern jobs. In the South, most black Americans had been farmers. Still, most found life improved by moving north.

Unwelcome Immigrants

People from other countries also wanted to move to American cities. During the war, few people immigrated to the United States. When the war was over, many tried. People from Europe and East Asia especially wanted to come to America. Unlike Europe, the United States did not suffer physical damage in the war. To people around the world, the United States seemed to be a land of wealth.

James Weldon Johnson

What: author, educator, lawyer, diplomat

When: 1871–1938

Where: Harlem

James Weldon Johnson promoted the Harlem Renaissance through his writing and speaking. Originally from Florida, Johnson represented the United States government in Nicaragua and Venezuela. After that he worked to help improve the lives of black Americans. He also studied spiritual songs and taught at Fisk and New York Universities. Johnson also wrote a book of sermons in verse called *God's Trombones*.

Many recent immigrants from Southern and Eastern Europe and Asia did not quickly fit into American society. They often found English hard to learn. Many lived in big cities. Immigrants often lived in neighborhoods with other people from their home country. This helped them feel at home. Cities like New York and San Francisco had neighborhoods called "Little Italy" or "Chinatown." Some Americans were concerned that these immigrants would never fit into American life.

Little Italy in New York

Soon many people trying to immigrate to the United States learned that they were not welcome. In 1921 and 1924 Congress passed laws. They were designed to slow or stop immigration. These laws tried to get more immigrants from countries like England and Germany. They tried to stop much immigration from places like Italy or China. Congress did not want immigrants who could not adjust easily. It did not want immigrants who would do the same jobs as former soldiers. The immigrants who came from Southern and Eastern Europe and Asia felt unwelcome. They felt they should remain in their own neighborhoods in the cities. Despite this attitude, immigrants worked hard to become Americans.

Crime in the City

Many Americans in the 1920s were concerned that cities were centers of crime and violence. Three events caused people to believe this.

Governor Calvin Coolidge inspecting the troops

Boston Police Strike

In 1919 the police union in Boston held a strike. Problems began the first night that there were no police officers on duty. Criminals looted and vandalized buildings throughout the city. Then the governor of Massachusetts sent in National Guard troops. Even they could not stop the violence right away. This event left some Americans distrustful of unions and cities.

Sacco and Vanzetti

The next year more news from Boston made the situation worse. Two men delivering money to a business near Boston were shot. Soon, two Italian immigrants were arrested for the murders. Nicola Sacco and Bartolomeo Vanzetti were known to be **anarchists**. These people believe that there should be no government. They were eventually tried for the murders. They were found guilty and executed. Many Americans thought the two men were innocent. Some

Bartolomeo Vanzetti and Nicola Sacco

Al Capone

people protested their trials and execution. Many Americans believed that immigrants and cities were unsafe.

Al Capone

Americans often associated cities with **organized crime**. This means many criminals worked together to break the law. In Chicago many criminals did work together. Their leader was named Al Capone. These criminals sold illegal alcohol, helped people gamble, and committed other crimes. During much of the Twenties, Capone represented crime in the cities. Finally, in the early 1930s, Al Capone was arrested.

Although the Twenties was a time of much prosperity, not everything was perfect. Americans had problems, especially in the cities.

Why did Americans not like some immigrants?

Reform and Science

Much in the Twenties seemed new and different. But some older ideas influenced the decade. Before World War I, people had different plans to improve America. Progressives wanted political reform. Prohibitionists wanted to stop people from drinking alcohol. Many Americans believed that people needed to be better Christians. All of these plans for improving America lived on into the Twenties.

Political Reform
Prohibition

In 1919 the Eighteenth Amendment became law. This amendment made making, transporting, or selling any alcoholic beverage illegal. Drinks like beer or wine are alcoholic. This law is sometimes called **Prohibition**. To prohibit is to forbid something. Since the 1800s many Americans wanted Prohibition. They knew that drinking alcohol could lead to drunkenness. Drunkenness often led to injuries or crime. Many Americans hoped that stopping people from drinking would solve the problem of drunkenness and lessen crime in cities.

Government leader pouring out beer in support of Prohibition

Some Americans did not obey the law. They bought alcoholic drinks illegally. Criminals, such as Al Capone, sold the drinks. Selling illegal alcohol earned criminals much money. The Eighteenth Amendment did not work perfectly. Even so, Prohibition did prevent much suffering from drunkenness.

Women's Suffrage

In 1920 different states had different rules for women voters. Most states in the West allowed women to vote whenever men could. In the Midwest women could usually vote for the president. Some states in the East and South never allowed women to vote.

The Nineteenth Amendment passed soon after the war. It promised all women the right to vote. No one could be stopped from voting for being a woman. This change became law in 1920.

Some Americans had wanted women's suffrage since the 1800s. *Suffrage* means "the right to vote." Some people believed that women would be more honest than men were. These people hoped that women would elect better candidates than men did. Other Americans just thought that all citizens should have the right to vote.

Women's suffrage was not like Prohibition. It did not make a sudden change in American life. Women often voted for the same candidates as men did. For the rest of the Twenties, no more changes were made to the Constitution.

Women protesting in front of the White House to support women's suffrage

Changes in Science

While people cared less and less about political reforms, more and more people thought that science would improve life. New ideas helped spread this hope.

Einstein

Albert Einstein

In 1921 Albert Einstein won the Nobel Prize in Physics. This award is given to a person who proves a new idea about how the universe works. Einstein's idea helped scientists understand how light works. He worked on other scientific problems too. Einstein's work gave Americans hope. They began to think that scientists would one day understand how the universe works. They hoped that science could solve most of life's problems. When Einstein visited America many people attended his lectures. Eventually, Einstein moved to the United States.

Medicine

Pharmaceutical bottle from the 1920s for pills

During the 1920s scientists also made discoveries that directly improved peoples' health. In 1922, insulin was discovered by two doctors in Canada. **Insulin** could treat diabetes. Until this discovery most people with diabetes did not live long. Insulin allowed diabetics to have fairly normal lives. In 1923 French and English scientists came up with a new immunization that could prevent **diphtheria**. Diphtheria was a throat infection that killed many people every year. After being immunized, people would be safe from the disease. In 1928 a Scottish doctor discovered **penicillin**, which came from a mold called penicillium. This discovery was perhaps the most important advance in medicine of the decade. The doctor realized that the penicillium mold stopped bacteria from growing. This discovery was not useful for another decade. But modern antibiotics can be traced back to this drug.

Frozen Food

Freezing food well was another important discovery. People already froze food to ship it. But when it was cooked, thawed food usually had little flavor. Sometimes it was dry or mushy. In the 1920s a man named Clarence Birdseye figured out how to solve this problem.

For a while Birdseye lived in the Arctic. There he ate fish that had been frozen. It tasted as good as fresh fish. Birdseye realized that freezing food quickly left better flavor and texture. Slowly frozen food can taste bland.

Birdseye moved to Massachusetts and opened a company selling frozen fish. He did not give up when his business failed. Instead, Birdseye opened another. This time he was successful. Soon Americans were able to buy frozen foods that tasted good. Even in the winter people ate summer vegetables that tasted fresh. People far from the ocean could eat fresh-tasting fish. Birdseye's discovery and hard work helped Americans to have more and better food options.

Over the Twenties, science helped improve life for all Americans. Some began to think that science would continue to solve problems. They hoped that science could answer all questions about the world.

Clarence Birdseye

Magazine ad for Birds Eye frozen foods

What were some old reforms that came back in the Twenties?

John Scopes

Clarence Darrow

Religion in the Twenties
The Scopes Trial
Background

By the Twenties, many scientists taught evolution. This idea states that life evolved or developed from things that were not alive. These scientists believed that all living things come from a single ancestor. Over time small changes over many generations led to all the different forms of life that exist today. In some parts of America, Christians did not want their children to be taught evolution. They believed the Bible's teaching that God created mankind. In 1925 the state of Tennessee made a new law. Teachers must not teach evolution in public schools. A man named John Scopes chose to break the law. He wanted to see if a court would say the law did not follow the Constitution. In 1925 John Scopes was put on trial for teaching evolution. This famous science story is called the Scopes Trial.

The Trial

By the middle of 1925, Scopes was on trial. The famous Democratic politician William Jennings Bryan wanted to help. He supported the government's case against Scopes. Clarence Darrow agreed to defend Scopes. Darrow was famous for defending people who were supposed to be guilty. He also opposed religion. During the trial, Darrow switched his focus. He did not try to prove Scopes was innocent. Instead, he tried to prove that the Bible was full of errors. Even though Scopes was found guilty, Darrow's harsh attacks on the Bible stuck in peoples' memories. Many wondered whether the Bible was wrong and evolution was right.

Religions in Conflict

Leaders in American churches disagreed about how to respond to ideas like evolution. Some leaders thought that Christians should accept these ideas. These leaders were called Modernists. Other leaders thought that these ideas threatened true Christianity. These leaders were called Fundamentalists.

Modernism

Modernists thought Christians had to change some of their ideas. They said modern science showed evolution was true. They claimed that the Bible was wrong about some parts of science and that miracles were impossible. Modernists believed that history showed the Bible made mistakes.

But Modernists did not want to give up on Christianity. They wanted people to come to church. They wanted people to live good lives. They thought the Bible was very important for people to learn how to be good. The Modernists said they wanted to save Christianity. Instead they created a new religion.

Fundamentalism

The Bible is God's Word. It is more trustworthy than modern science or history. Fundamentalists believe that the Bible is completely correct. Something

Billy Sunday

Billy Sunday's baseball card for the Chicago White Stockings

fundamental is something of basic importance. Some teachings in the Bible are fundamental to being a Christian. These teachings are so important that a person cannot be a Christian unless he believes them. Fundamentalists said that these teachings included Creation, Jesus' Resurrection, and His Second Coming.

Fundamentalists said that Modernists were not Christians. Fundamentalists wanted Modernists to leave the schools and churches. But the Modernists would not leave. Many Fundamentalists started new churches and schools. These churches and schools were supposed to be faithful to the Bible.

Fundamentalist Leaders
Billy Sunday

Billy Sunday was the most famous of the Fundamentalist preachers. He grew up in an orphanage in Iowa. Eventually, he became a star baseball player. In the late 1800s he became a Christian. Soon after, he married. Then in the early 1900s, Sunday left baseball to become a preacher.

Rather than being a pastor, Sunday became an evangelist. An **evangelist** is a preacher who travels from city to city. Many people liked Sunday's preaching. He spoke with excitement and gave vivid examples. He marched around the platform and kept people's attention. He wanted people to know Jesus as Savior.

By the 1920s Sunday had preached in many important cities in America. He had met presidents. When Sunday visited a city, thousands of people came to hear him preach. Many churches helped support his ministry.

Over the Twenties, Billy Sunday became less popular. Rather than hearing a sermon, many people preferred listening to the radio or watching a movie. However, Sunday kept preaching the Bible. He always encouraged people to serve God with their lives.

J. Gresham Machen

J. Gresham Machen was the most respected Fundamentalist teacher. He studied at the best schools in the world. In the 1920s Machen taught at Princeton Seminary. He wrote many books to defend the Christian faith. In one book, he defended one of the greatest miracles. He defended the Bible's claim that Jesus was born of a virgin. Gresham looked at all the other explanations that denied this. He showed that none of them explained all the facts. Only the Bible's claim of the virgin birth could be true.

Reverend John Gresham Machen

Machen showed that people could have knowledge and education and still believe the Bible. The Modernists said that Christianity had to change. But Machen showed that Modernism needed to change.

During the 1920s some people said that Christianity must change. They said it would disappear if it did not change. Government leaders and teachers looked down on Fundamentalist Christians. But these Christians still preached the gospel to many Americans. Fundamentalist churches and schools grew. They would be a major force for world missions in coming years.

Why did Fundamentalists start new schools and colleges?

The End of the Twenties
A New President

In 1928 the United States seemed to be doing well. Most Americans had jobs. Factories were busy. Eight years of Republican presidents seemed to have helped the nation. When Americans had to choose a new president, the choice seemed easy for most.

Herbert Hoover was the Republican candidate. During the Twenties he served in the Cabinet as Secretary of Commerce. Many Americans liked Hoover. Al Smith was the Democratic candidate. He was from New York and was a Catholic who opposed Prohibition. Many Americans did not trust Smith. When the votes were counted, Hoover won by almost 60 percent. Americans trusted the Republican Party to keep America doing well.

The Great Bull Market

When President Hoover was sworn into office on March 4, 1929, the United States seemed to be doing better than ever. One sign of prosperity was the record-high prices of stocks on Wall Street. The term for rising stock prices is a **bull market**. Americans thought that the country was in a permanent bull market.

Americans kept the stock market high by buying. Many Americans bought stocks. Even those who did not buy stocks bought other things. The sale of radios, automobiles, and steam irons all helped companies make money. When people did not have enough money to buy something right away, they could still

Herbert Hoover

Al Smith

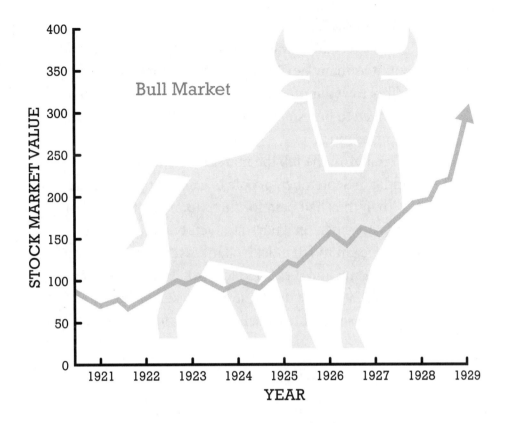

Bull Market

STOCK MARKET VALUE

400
350
300
250
200
150
100
50
0

1921 1922 1923 1924 1925 1926 1927 1928 1929

YEAR

get it. Many companies allowed customers to buy an item by making payments. For example, if a washing machine cost $81.50, a customer could take it home by paying just $21.50. Then for the next six months, the customer paid $10 each month.

In the Twenties a type of business that encouraged people to buy things grew quickly. This business was advertising. Advertising agencies tried to convince people that they needed more things. They suggested that no housewife could be happy without a vacuum cleaner. Every man needed the newest safety razor. People kept buying. Businesses kept making money. Wall Street seemed fine.

The Crash

But everything was not fine. Many Americans had bought as many new things as they wanted. People had borrowed money to buy appliances. Some had borrowed to buy stocks. In early 1929 people stopped buying as much.

Finally, in the fall the market collapsed. In the middle of September, people began selling stocks for less than they had paid for them. Bankers tried to bring prices up. Then on Thursday, October 24, 1929, stock prices began to fall quickly. Bankers tried to bring up prices again, and it seemed to work. But on Tuesday, October 29, prices on the stock market collapsed. Everyone seemed to be selling stocks for very little.

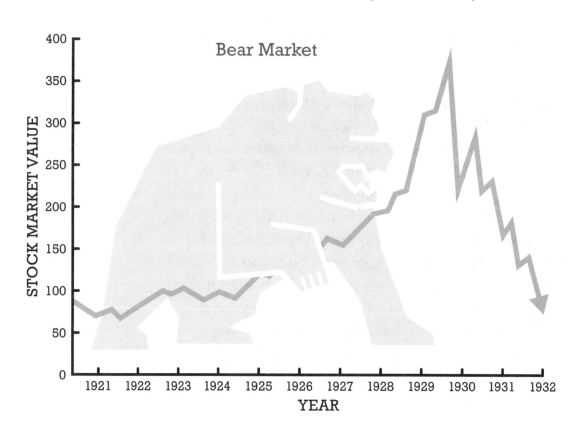

Black Tuesday, the nickname for October 29, 1929, affected all Americans. Many had bought stocks. Now stocks were worth very little. Some banks had bought stocks with their investors' money. These investors lost the money they thought was safe. With less money, people bought fewer things. Factories no longer made as many cars. Workers from factories lost their jobs. Black Tuesday began a hard time in America's history called the **Great Depression**.

Conclusion

The 1920s was a good time for many Americans. The war was over. Life was getting back to normal. However, problems still existed. The biggest problem was that many Americans were confused about whether the Bible was true or not. There were other problems too. Immigrants were not welcomed. Many cities suffered from crime. Many people thought that buying more things would make them happy. The 1930s would help Americans place less value on things and more on people.

What is the day of the stock market crash called?

10 Living Through Hard Times

Focus

Fighting the Great Depression altered American government.

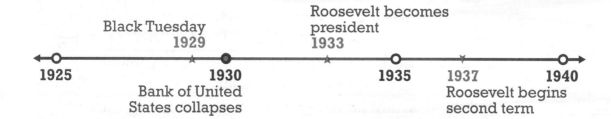

Black Tuesday
1929

Roosevelt becomes president
1933

1925

1930
Bank of United States collapses

1935

1937
Roosevelt begins second term

1940

The Great Depression

Americans knew about stock market crashes and depressions. These downfalls in the economy had happened before. In 1901 the stock market crashed. A year later the American economy began to slow down and remained slow for two years. In 1907 a panic led stocks to fall and banks to fail. The 1920s began with a yearlong depression. These crashes, panics, and depressions were often short, but they could be painful. Somehow the economy always recovered. And it always continued to grow again.

Stock Market Crash

The crash on Black Tuesday in 1929 was the biggest crash in American history. But Americans had many reasons for thinking their economy would keep growing. Many new inventions were being sold at this time. The companies that assembled these inventions made money. Inventions that produced and conveyed electricity sold well. In the 1920s electricity became available in many American homes. A person who had electricity at home would buy other appliances that also used electricity, such as refrigerators and toasters.

Many homes were still without electricity. This meant there were opportunities for power companies and refrigerator companies to grow. People could buy stock in those companies. Their money would help fund the companies to build more products to sell. In return the owners of the stock would share some of these companies' wealth. But the owners would only get money back if the companies succeeded. No one knew which companies would succeed. And no one knew when the growth would come. This risk is part of the reason why stock prices went up and down.

During the 1920s, stock prices mostly went up. This rise in prices led some people to **speculate** on the stock market. Speculating meant that people bought stocks and then sold them as soon as the price went up. These people were not trying to make wise investments. They were trying to get money quick. Sometimes people speculated with borrowed money. These people were

in trouble when the market crashed. Now the stock was worth less than what they had paid for it, and they did not have money to pay back their debts.

The stock market suffered from another problem. Companies that sold stock often withheld information about their company. People who bought stocks needed this information to make wise investments. Sometimes people in the company took advantage of the information that no one else knew. They could make money because they knew things others did not. This type of investment was not just.

Stock exchange in 1908

Problems with the stock market were part of the reasons for the great crash on Black Tuesday. But these problems were not the main reasons for the crash. Many things worked together to bring about the stock market crash of 1929.

Activity

Understanding the Stock Market

Have you heard someone say that stocks closed higher or lower? People invest money in stocks from companies, hoping they will make money. Newspapers and news programs give daily information on how stocks are performing. You will learn how to track how a stock is performing.

stock market crash

tariff on imports

tariff on exports

foreign debtors

bank runs

Responses to the Crash of 1929

Americans did not expect the crash of 1929 to lead to a great depression. A crash meant that stocks quickly lost more than half their value. Stock market prices had risen higher than the companies were worth. A crash was simply bringing the market back to reality. As companies continued to grow, the prices would slowly rise again. And this is what happened after the crash in 1929. No company caved in. No bank failed immediately after. The stock market began to rise again. Most Americans did not own stock. But for many people, life changed drastically and suddenly.

Many people incorrectly think the crash of 1929 caused the Great Depression. But many things happened to bring about the Great Depression. The stock market crash was only one of the causes.

The stock market crash did show that the US economy was struggling. Congress decided that they needed to protect US businesses. They passed the Smoot-Hawley Tariff Act. A tariff is a tax on goods that are shipped into a country. The Smoot-Hawley Tariff was one of the highest ever passed. This tax might have sounded good to the protected businesses. But it caused prices to go up for many Americans. Other countries also raised tariffs on American-made goods, hurting American businesses that sold their goods overseas.

Many of these foreign nations owed the United States money. They had borrowed money during World War I. But their economies were having trouble too. Many of them were not able to pay the United

States the money they owed. The United States needed money, so not getting paid hurt.

Bank Runs

Also, some banks ran out of money. People put their money in banks for safekeeping. But a bank does not keep all the money locked up in a safe. Banks know all

A bank run at the Bank of United States in New York, December 11, 1930

depositors do not usually withdraw all their money from the bank at the same time. So the bank lends the deposited money to other people. Those people pay the loan back with interest. They have to pay the bank the amount of money they borrowed plus some extra. This system is one way banks make money. But if borrowers do not repay their loans, a bank can run out of money and fail. When one bank is in danger of failing, concerned people might rush to the bank to withdraw their money. When many people do this at the same time, the action is called a **bank run**. As a result, the bank loses more money and can fail.

Most banks in the United States at this time were small banks. But in December of 1930, the Bank of United States failed. This was a large bank. Other large banks could have loaned it money to keep it from failing, but they chose not to. Now that a big bank had failed, people were very worried about keeping their money in banks. Because of its name, some people thought the Bank of United States was owned by the United States government. But it was not.

What is a bank run?

Herbert Hoover

Herbert Hoover

Americans had lived through depressions before. They waited depressions out. In a few years life improved. Some people wondered whether depressions could be prevented. Or if they happened, maybe they could be shortened.

Many people thought Herbert Hoover was just the man to help America through the Great Depression. Hoover was an engineer. He was a problem solver. He knew how to handle big projects. During World War I, people in Belgium needed food. Hoover headed efforts to provide food for these people. When the United States entered World War I, Hoover ran the US Food Administration because the American troops needed food. In 1927 the Mississippi River flooded. Hoover organized the relief effort for the US government. He thought energetic, organized action could solve any problems the nation faced.

Now as president, Hoover sprung into action. He called major business leaders to the White House. He asked them not to cut people's wages. He asked them not to lay off their workers. Businesses often cut wages and laid off workers during hard times because the businesses were not making as much money. To stay in business, the businesses needed to cut something. But the businesses agreed not to lay off workers or cut wages.

This decision was helpful to the workers, but it did not help the country out of the Great Depression. The businesses were hurt. They were not making money. Eventually they had to cut the number of hours people worked. This was another way of reducing the amount paid to workers. And as time went on, businesses saw they needed to let workers go or go out of business entirely. Many Americans during this time did not have work. And without work they did not have money to buy the things they needed.

Hoover decided that the American government should not go into debt at this time. He wanted the government to pay its bills without borrowing money. To do this Hoover had to raise taxes. But during a depression people did not have much money. Raising taxes hurt families and businesses. It did not help to overcome the Great Depression.

Hoover acted energetically, but he did the wrong things. He raised tariffs and taxes, taking money out of the economy. During a depression, money needed to be put into the economy.

As time went on, Hoover became very discouraged. He had always been able to take command of a situation. But nothing he did now seemed to make a difference. Instead, life became worse for most Americans. This problem was outside Hoover's control.

President Franklin D. Roosevelt broadcasting from the White House

In 1932 Hoover was up for reelection. He was challenged by Franklin D. Roosevelt. There were not many differences between the candidates. Hoover was a Progressive Republican. Roosevelt was a Progressive Democrat. Their plans for solving the Great Depression were not very different. But Roosevelt spoke positively to the American people. Roosevelt was also a great speaker on the radio. The radio was new to many people. Many public speakers did not know how to speak on the radio. They shouted as though they were talking to large groups of people. But Roosevelt spoke as though he were sitting right next to you. It seemed to many people that he was speaking directly to them. They thought maybe Roosevelt understood them and could help them. And Roosevelt said he would help. He promised the American people a New Deal.

Why did people think Hoover would lead them out of the Great Depression?

The New Deal
Roosevelt, the President-Elect

Roosevelt convinced the American voter. He won the election. But the months between Roosevelt's election and when he actually took office were difficult for Americans. Hoover was still president. But he was a defeated president on his way out. Roosevelt was not yet in office.

Hoover reached out to Roosevelt. He wanted his advice. He wanted to see whether they could work together while waiting for Roosevelt to become president. He thought that together they might agree on solutions for fighting the Great Depression. This was possible. Many of the programs that Roosevelt began as part of his New Deal were based on programs that Hoover had started.

But Roosevelt knew that Hoover was now unpopular. He did not want any connection with unpopular Hoover. He knew he had to be popular in order for his plans to succeed. So he did not respond to Hoover's efforts to reach out. This decision hurt the economy. Businesses did not know what the government might do or might not do. They did not know whether Hoover's actions would be carried on or reversed by Roosevelt. The uncertainty made the Great Depression worse.

Herbert Hoover and Franklin Roosevelt

Roosevelt Diagnoses the Great Depression

Roosevelt did not think the Great Depression was a brief hard time that Americans needed help to get through. He did not think the US economy would continue to grow.

He thought the economy grew when the United States was growing westward and claiming new land. But now the United States had spread from ocean to ocean. There was no more space to grow. Roosevelt thought he knew the problem: Americans produced too much. Farmers produced too much food. Factories produced too many products. When farmers or factories overproduced, prices went down.

For instance, two factories might produce 1,000 items. What happens if only 500 people want those items? More people might buy the item if the price was lower. So the price might go down from $1 to 50¢. If it took 25¢ to make the item, the profit the company made from the item would also drop. If the prices dropped low enough, a company might have to pay its workers less. It also meant they would have less money to spend on finding ways to make better products.

Effects of
OVERPRODUCTION

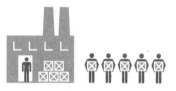

Overproduction drives prices down.

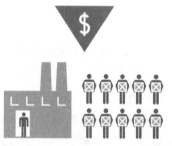

Lower prices lead to higher sales but lower profits.

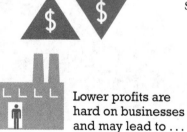

Lower profits are hard on businesses and may lead to ...

lower wages, fewer jobs, and going out of business.

The Farm Bill

Roosevelt thought he could solve this overproduction problem for farmers. He asked Congress to pass a bill that paid farmers to plant less. He thought that if less produce was for sale, then the prices would be higher. If the prices were higher, the farmers would make more money. Higher prices would help the farmers.

But raising food prices hurt Americans who had less money to spend on necessities like food. Also, the bill did not pass until the crops had already been sown. Then the farmers plowed up good fields to get the money for planting less. Americans did not understand why the government was paying farmers to destroy good food. Some Americans were starving.

This policy also hurt the sharecroppers. The owner would get money from the part of the crop the sharecropper sold. But now the owner was being paid not to farm parts of his land. He did not share this money with the sharecropper. In fact, he might no longer need the sharecropper to work his land.

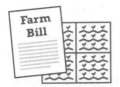

The Farm Bill tried to fix the overproduction of farms.

The government paid farmers to plant less.

Less production meant higher prices & higher profits for the farmers.

Less production also meant fewer jobs and lower wages.

Restoring Confidence in Banks

Roosevelt had to deal with other problems. He wanted to stop bank runs. He also wanted trading on the stock market to be fair.

Roosevelt declared a bank holiday. Banks closed for three days. In that time the panic wore away. The banks reopened, and people did not rush to withdraw all their money.

Congress established the Federal Deposit Insurance Corporation (FDIC). Before, when a bank failed, people would lose all the money they had at that bank. Now the federal government promised that a person would receive up to $5,000 of the money he had placed in the bank. The FDIC helped people trust banks with their money.

WHAT IS THAT BEHIND YOUR BACK?

AUDITOR

TRADER

Congress also passed a law for businesses that sold stock. The law said that businesses had to share information about the money they made and lost. An **auditor** had to check business records. The auditor would make sure the businesses told the truth. This law made trading on the stock market more just. Businesses gave people the information they needed to make wise investments. The law helped prevent people with special knowledge about a business from getting rich quick at other people's expense.

What big problems did Roosevelt try to correct?

246

The New Deal Continued
Unemployment

Unemployment was the most painful problem of the Great Depression. Unemployment means that people who want and need jobs cannot find them. Some people had jobs. But they did not work as many hours as they needed. They were paid for every hour they worked. Fewer hours of work meant less money. These people also had a hard time providing for their families.

For every ten Americans who wanted jobs, two of them could not find work. One historian gives the following illustration. He says the situation was like a football stadium full of 100,000 people being told they all lost their jobs. Then imagine this happening every day for two and a half years. That illustration gives an idea of how many people lost their jobs during the Great Depression.

New Deal Programs

Roosevelt decided the government needed to provide jobs. He thought some Americans would never get jobs otherwise. One of his first programs to give jobs was the Civilian Conservation Corps (CCC). The CCC employed young men for $30 a month. Of that income, $25 was sent back to their families. These men built or repaired national and state parks. They built roads, bridges, and buildings for these parks. They also planted hundreds of trees around the country. When World War II began, the CCC built military bases. As the war continued, the CCC ceased to exist. The young men who had worked with the CCC now joined the military.

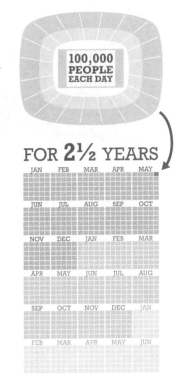

Unemployment During the Great Depression

100,000 PEOPLE EACH DAY

FOR 2½ YEARS

JAN FEB MAR APR MAY
JUN JUL AUG SEP OCT
NOV DEC JAN FEB MAR
APR MAY JUN JUL AUG
SEP OCT NOV DEC JAN
FEB MAR APR MAY JUN

The Civilian Conservation Corps (CCC) working on the soil to control water flow (top) and building a road (right)

Roosevelt created other programs as well. He began the Public Works Administration. He also started the Civil Works Administration. Men working for these groups built schools and hospitals. They worked on roads, bridges, tunnels, and airports.

The National Recovery Administration (NRA) was an important part of the New Deal. Roosevelt wanted workers to have money to buy goods. The NRA said employers had to pay workers a certain amount of money for each hour of work. Roosevelt also wanted to be sure that prices of goods did not fall too low. Businesses could not afford to pay workers more if prices were too low. The law told businesses that they could not lower prices below a certain level.

People liked the CCC. They did not like the NRA. Forbidding competition hurt businesses, and more people lost jobs. Employers had to pay workers more. As a result they kept fewer workers.

The NRA also created other laws. Some of the new laws were used unjustly. One case became famous. The federal government took a chicken butcher business to court. The NRA said businesses could not cut their prices too low. It said that they could not allow the customer to select the chicken he wanted to buy. It said they could not sell sick chickens. The government said the Schechter Poultry Corporation broke these laws. A judge said the business had to pay a fine. The fine was the amount of money one of the workers would earn in a year. And the business owner had to spend three months in jail.

The owner and his workers thought this treatment was unjust. They had tried to obey the laws. But some of the laws were not clear. A person might break a law without knowing it. The owner and his workers took their case to the Supreme Court. The justices on the Supreme Court found some of the rules of the NRA foolish. They laughed when told the customer could not choose the chicken he wanted to buy. The justices thought the NRA did not have the right to make some of the rules. The Supreme Court said the entire NRA was unconstitutional.

Life During the Great Depression

Many people lost all their savings when banks collapsed. Because of the Great Depression many people could no longer pay back the money they had borrowed to buy their houses. They lost their houses. Some Americans now lived in shantytowns. A **shanty** is a house that is pieced together with scraps of metal, wood, and cardboard.

A shantytown in Lancaster, Pennsylvania

Many Americans lost their jobs. Men were often more likely to lose their jobs than women. Women worked in jobs such as teaching school. They might have their wages cut, but schoolteachers were still needed. They kept their jobs. But men who worked in factories often lost their jobs. Many men felt ashamed that they could not support their families.

Of course, having little money meant that people could not afford to buy much to eat. They could not afford new clothes. Many did not want to ask for handouts from the government either. One man said his family ate nothing but bread and water for almost a month before he asked for help from the government.

What was the most painful part of the Great Depression for most Americans?

Roosevelt's Reelection

Roosevelt wanted to be president for another four years. But he faced some big challenges. His New Deal programs had not stopped the Great Depression. Some historians think the New Deal made the Great Depression worse. Other historians disagree.

Historians who liked Roosevelt said his goal was not to end the Great Depression. Roosevelt had another goal. He wanted to change the way government worked. Roosevelt thought America had changed. Rich people lived secure lives because of their money. Roosevelt wanted the government to provide security for the ordinary American.

But historians agree about one thing. The New Deal did not end the Great Depression, and this was a problem. This was what voters wanted to have changed. Roosevelt needed to convince Americans to vote for him anyway.

Roosevelt also faced another problem. The Supreme Court said that many New Deal programs were unconstitutional. He had to shut the programs down.

Unfortunately, Roosevelt had a third problem. Some people thought the government should do more. They thought the poor should get some money from the rich. Since many people had become poor during the Great Depression, some politicians became very popular.

President Franklin Roosevelt giving his presidential campaign speech in Denver, Colorado, on October 12, 1936

Roosevelt solved the last problem. He attacked rich people and businesses. He said people should vote for him instead of the other popular politicians because he would help the poor. Roosevelt's attacks on businesses helped in another way. They allowed him to blame others for the Great Depression.

However, Roosevelt's attacks on businesses made the Great Depression worse. The businesses needed to do well to end the Great Depression. The business owners did not know what Roosevelt might do to them. They did not know what new laws might be passed. It was hard to plan for the future with these fears. Their businesses did not do well.

Roosevelt had another idea for getting reelected. His New Deal agencies appointed work projects to different parts of the country. They gave out money to help with those projects. Roosevelt made sure that the money and the projects went to his supporters. Or he sent them to places where he wanted to gain supporters. Roosevelt had brought the practice of the city machine to the national government. A city "machine" was a group of people who controlled how a city ran. The machine did things for people in exchange for votes. Now the national government would do the same.

THE MACHINE

Roosevelt worked to bring Republicans to his side. At this time the Republicans and Democrats both had Progressives in their parties. Both also had conservatives in their parties. Roosevelt wanted all the Progressives to join the Democratic Party. This would bring more voters to his party.

Roosevelt also passed a popular bill the year before the election. This bill was called the Social Security Act. It was designed to help older people. Many older people had lost their jobs. Some had become too old to work. It was also designed to help others who had lost their jobs. The law said that workers and employers would pay a new tax. The money from the tax would be used to pay money to older people. It was also used to pay something to others without work.

Social Security was the first step toward a welfare state. In a welfare state the government takes responsibility for people's well-being. Roosevelt thought Social Security was the most important of his New Deal programs.

Ida May Fuller receiving the very first pension check from Social Security

Why did Roosevelt struggle to be reelected?

Roosevelt's Second Term

Roosevelt was reelected. His main goal was to make sure the New Deal stayed in place. Roosevelt believed the New Deal should always exist. It would help people during the Great Depression. But he also believed it would help after the Great Depression. He said all Americans needed to be secure. He thought this could only happen with the New Deal.

Roosevelt faced many challenges. He thought the Great Depression might end too soon. He might not be able to put more of the New Deal in place if the Great Depression ended.

Roosevelt also worried that someone else might get rid of the New Deal. A future president might try to end Roosevelt's New Deal. Or the Supreme Court might call the New Deal unconstitutional. The Supreme Court had already stated that some of Roosevelt's programs were unconstitutional.

Roosevelt had a plan. He asked Congress to let him appoint more justices. These justices would support the New Deal. And then the Supreme Court would not declare it unconstitutional.

Roosevelt gave a reason for these changes. But Roosevelt knew the real reason. And Congress knew the real reason. The American people knew the real reason for the law. They knew Roosevelt wanted the Supreme Court to support him.

Nobody liked Roosevelt's plan. It seemed like he was trying to grab too much power. The New Deal had made the executive branch more powerful than before. Even people who supported the New Deal spoke out against the law. Congress did not make Roosevelt's plan a law.

– To Furnish The Supreme Court Practical Assistance –

In the end Roosevelt did not need to worry about the Supreme Court. Four justices turned down the New Deal. Four justices supported it. One moved from one side to the other. In Roosevelt's second term this justice moved to favor the New Deal. Three justices who opposed Roosevelt retired. Another one died. Roosevelt appointed their replacements. The replacements supported the New Deal. Roosevelt did not need to worry about the Supreme Court deciding it to be unconstitutional.

Businesses opposed the New Deal.

The government did not spend enough money.

The New Deal caused uncertainty.

President Roosevelt's attacks on business caused uncertainty.

Roosevelt's second term was difficult. In October 1937 the stock market fell again. The economy had already been struggling. It was a depression in the middle of the Great Depression.

People wanted to know how this could happen. Some people said that depressions were simply a part of life. Nothing could be done to stop them. But this explanation did not help Roosevelt. He claimed the government could solve the problem of the depressions.

Roosevelt said businesses were trying to find ways to shut down the New Deal. He asked the FBI to check into it.

Some supporters of the New Deal had another idea. They said the government needed to spend more money. Only this would end the Great Depression.

Others said that the New Deal caused uncertainty. And Roosevelt's attacks on businesses created uncertainty. This uncertainty led to the new depression. Conservatives agreed with this view. Some people who worked for Roosevelt thought this too.

Roosevelt responded by spending more money. It did not get the economy going. Some supporters of the New Deal said he did not spend enough. Roosevelt also pressured Congress to pass more anti-business laws.

In 1938 the Democrats lost seats in both the House and the Senate. Conservative Democrats and conservative Republicans joined together. They made sure that Roosevelt did not get any more New Deal laws passed.

Conclusion

The New Deal did not end the Great Depression. Roosevelt did not clearly understand the problem. He also had the wrong solution. He thought the problem was that businesses competed too much. He thought they produced too many goods. He thought the economy could not grow as it had in the past.

But the New Deal did change American life. Today Democrats and Republicans debate many things. Many of these debates are about Roosevelt's ideas. Democrats tend to think that Roosevelt's ideas for government were good ideas. Many Republicans think several of Roosevelt's ideas were bad ideas. Learning about Roosevelt and the New Deal is important for American citizens today.

What was Roosevelt worried the Supreme Court might do?

11 At War Again

Focus

Once the United States joined World War II, it fought to restore peace and democracy throughout the world.

The World Before the War
The World During the Great Depression

During the 1930s many nations around the world suffered. People wanted better lives. In some countries men seized power. A person who controls everything in a nation is called a **dictator**. Several countries in Europe were controlled by dictators and their political parties.

Russia

Since 1917 the Communist Party controlled Russia. This country was also called the Soviet Union or the **USSR**, which stands for Union of Soviet Socialist Republics. During the 1930s everyone in the USSR had to obey **Joseph Stalin**. Anyone who made Stalin unhappy could be killed.

Europe Before the War

Legend: Axis Powers / Allies

Joseph Stalin

Benito Mussolini

Stalin threatened the people inside the USSR more than those outside. At one point people from a particular part of the country made him unhappy. Stalin had all their food taken away. Many of the people died of starvation. Stalin also tried to end all religion.

Italy

In 1922 **Benito Mussolini** became prime minister of Italy. He took the title Il Duce, or "the leader." Mussolini called his political party the Fascists. He took that name from ancient Roman history. Mussolini told the Italians that he would make their nation the center of a new Roman Empire. To accomplish his goal, Mussolini left the people of Italy with few freedoms. He also attacked other countries.

Germany

Adolf Hitler became dictator of Germany in the 1930s. His title was the Führer, and his political party was the **Nazis**. Hitler and Mussolini were friends. But Hitler was worse than Mussolini.

Hitler believed that many people had hurt the German nation in the past. He wanted to punish these people. He hated and wanted to destroy the Jewish people. Hitler thought Germans were a superior race and that all others were inferior. He also wanted to fight France and conquer parts of Eastern Europe.

Hitler worked hard to accomplish his goals. He built a large military. He made friends with the leaders of Spain and Japan. He started claiming pieces of European countries that spoke German. By 1939 people around the world worried what Hitler and the other dictators might do.

Adolf Hitler

The Democracies of Europe

Not all of Europe's countries had dictators. Many had strong democracies. In a democracy the citizens are able to vote for the country's leaders. The people are free to choose whichever ruler they want.

The French democracy was troubled. Many French people favored politicians like Hitler. Others liked Communists and Socialists. Although France was a large and powerful country, it struggled to oppose the dictators.

Great Britain had less political trouble. However, the leader of Great Britain, the prime minister, did not think the country was strong enough to stand against Hitler. Some politicians said that he must be stopped. **Winston Churchill** was the most famous of these politicians. Great Britain was preparing to fight Hitler.

Winston Churchill

Many of the smaller countries tried to be ready to fight. They feared Hitler. If he attacked, they felt they would not be able to successfully defend themselves.

Asia

Many Asian countries were part of European empires. However, the two major free countries had some of the same political issues that the European nations had.

Chiang Kai-shek

Mao Zedong

China

China suffered from financial loss, division, and war. Two men claimed to be the leader of the country. **Chiang Kai-shek** supported Western ideas. His wife had even attended high school and college in the United States. The other man, **Mao Zedong**, wanted China to become Communist like Russia. When Japan attacked China in 1937, the Chinese stopped fighting each other. Chiang Kai-shek led the non-Communist Chinese fighters to defend their country.

Hirohito

Tojo Hideki

Japan

Japan had two leaders. Most Japanese people thought that Emperor **Hirohito** was a living god. General and Prime Minister **Tojo Hideki** ran the country. He made most of the country's decisions, but he respected the emperor's wishes. Tojo led Japan to build a huge military. They attacked and conquered parts of China. Japan hoped to control most of East Asia as an empire.

The United States

Back in the United States, most people just wanted peace. President Franklin D. Roosevelt warned that war might come. Americans hoped that China could stay free from Communist rule. Few Americans thought that they needed to fight to protect other nations.

What three European countries had dictators in the 1930s?

Pre-war Expansion

The Battles Begin
Fighting Before the War

Even before World War II officially began, many countries were fighting. In 1935 Italy invaded Ethiopia. Just two years later Japan invaded China. In 1938 Germany took over Austria. The two countries did not fight, but many Austrians wanted their country to be free. Then in 1938 and 1939, even more trouble occurred.

First, Adolf Hitler demanded that Germans in Czechoslovakia be allowed to join Germany. France and Great Britain had promised to help Czechoslovakia. Instead, they let Hitler take pieces of the country. But that was not enough for Hitler. In March 1939 he took over the entire country.

Hitler next wanted to conquer Poland. But the USSR to Poland's east also wanted some of the country.

Even though Hitler and Stalin did not like each other, they made an agreement. They would each take half of Poland.

Americans watched Europe edge closer and closer to another world war. Most Americans hoped that their country would not need to get involved.

War Starts

The democracies in Europe knew war was coming. France and Great Britain warned Hitler that he must not attack Poland. They told him they would fight if he did. But Hitler had already made them back down before in his takeover of Czechoslovakia.

He believed his military could beat them. Hitler had many soldiers. The German air force, or **Luftwaffe**, had new well-built planes. German tanks could move quickly.

On September 1, 1939, German forces attacked Poland. Great Britain and France gave Hitler one day to withdraw. He did not. On September 3, France and Great Britain declared war on Germany. **World War II** had begun.

France and Great Britain could do little to help Poland. The USSR invaded Poland on September 17. By the end of the month, Poland surrendered.

This fast-moving attack became known as **blitzkrieg**, or lightning war, because it was as fast as a bolt of lightning.

Germany did little for the rest of the winter because of bad weather. In the spring of 1940, the Germans began moving again. Very quickly Germany conquered Denmark and Norway. In early May, Germany attacked Belgium, the Netherlands,

Luxembourg, and France. By the end of May, the smaller countries were conquered. On June 22 France surrendered. Italy joined Germany and attacked countries in southeastern Europe. Only Great Britain kept fighting in Europe to stop Hitler. In Asia, Japan continued its harsh war against China.

In September 1940, the Japanese, German, and Italian empires entered into a three-way alliance. It was called the **Axis Powers**. Japan would get to take over the European colonial empires in Asia. Germany and Italy would split the European and African lands. No country seemed able to stop the Axis Powers.

The United States Enters

As war continued across Europe and Asia, Americans feared that the fighting would spread.

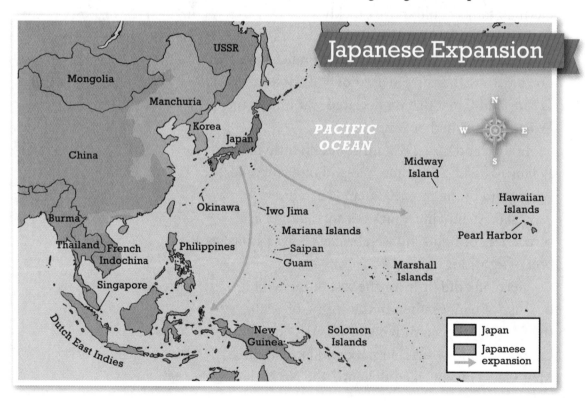

Although few wanted to fight, most Americans began taking sides. A few wanted the Germans to win. They thought Hitler would improve Europe. Most, however, did not like Hitler. They wanted Great Britain to win. Winston Churchill was now the British prime minister. He was a good friend of President Franklin Roosevelt.

Although not officially in the war, America began to help Great Britain. America sent ships to England. In exchange the British allowed the United States to use British military bases. Americans were sympathetic with England when Hitler bombed Britain. They respected the heroism of the British people who refused to surrender. Some Americans went to help Britain.

Americans also sympathized with the Chinese. Some Americans even offered to help them fight against Japan. President Roosevelt worked to stop Japan from getting supplies like gasoline and rubber. The United States refused to trade with Japan.

The USS *West Virginia* was hit with armor-piercing shells during the Japanese attack on Pearl Harbor.

The Japanese decided to get the supplies despite American opposition. They planned a surprise attack on the United States. The American Pacific fleet sat at anchor in Pearl Harbor, Hawaii. On **December 7, 1941**, the Japanese naval and air forces attacked Pearl Harbor. In the surprise attack many Americans died.

The next day Congress declared war on Japan, and the United States was part of World War II. Britain and the other nations fighting the Axis Powers welcomed the United States into their alliance. These countries were called the **Allies**.

What event caused the United States to join World War II?

The European Powers Fight
Germany Before Japan

Once the United States decided to fight, Americans worked hard to ensure success. Japan had attacked the United States. But President Roosevelt believed Germany was a bigger problem.

By this time Hitler had attacked the USSR. Roosevelt told his military leaders to defeat Germany and Italy first. Great Britain and the USSR needed urgent help. Japan would be the second target.

North Africa

To defeat Hitler, the United States needed to get troops into Europe. But Hitler and his followers controlled every landing place. German and Italian armies were even in North Africa. America's first job was to drive the Axis Powers from Africa.

The War in Europe

Axis Powers
Axis control
Neutral countries
Allied advances

As America planned to drive the Axis Powers from Africa, the British fought to stay in Egypt. German troops marched east across North Africa. They wanted the Suez Canal. This strip of water provided a shortcut for Great Britain to its largest colony, India. General Bernard Montgomery fought the Germans in western Egypt. In late 1942 he successfully began pushing them west.

At the same time, American troops under General **George Patton** arrived in North Africa. His troops pushed the Axis forces east. The Germans were trapped between the two Allied armies. A large German army surrendered, and North Africa was freed.

Bernard Montgomery

The Weak Spot in Europe

The Allies next moved to attack Hitler through Italy. The island of Sicily lay halfway between North Africa and Italy. It offered a jumping-off place. In the latter half of 1943, American and British troops moved north from Africa. Allied troops invaded mainland Italy from Sicily in early September. On September 8, 1943, Italy surrendered.

After Italy's surrender, the war continued in Italy. Mussolini escaped to the German forces. Hitler sent many soldiers into Italy, but the Allies began inching up the peninsula. As the Allies advanced, President Roosevelt tried to make good decisions, but his two biggest allies did not like each other.

George Patton

Allies: Great Britain and the USSR

One of America's allies was Great Britain. From the beginning of the war, Great Britain fought Hitler. Led by Winston Churchill, the British refused to surrender. Americans liked Great Britain. It was a democracy. British people were free. Americans had much in common with Great Britain.

America's other ally was not a free land. The USSR's dictator Joseph Stalin allowed his people almost no freedom. But he was fighting to defeat Hitler. President Roosevelt remained friends with the USSR. He knew the Allies needed as much help as possible to defeat Hitler.

The three Allied leaders: (from left) Joseph Stalin, Franklin D. Roosevelt, and Winston Churchill

Several times during the war, all three Allied leaders met. Churchill and Stalin did not like each other. Churchill believed Stalin would enslave people almost as much as Hitler did. President Roosevelt told them to get along. Hitler was attacking both Great Britain and the USSR. Because both countries needed American help, they listened to Roosevelt.

Why did President Roosevelt choose to focus on Germany instead of Japan?

War in the Pacific
Japanese Advances

While the United States moved in Europe and North Africa, Japan advanced in the Pacific. After their surprise attack on Pearl Harbor, the Japanese tried to claim as much land as possible. Within two months they swept into British, Dutch, and American colonies. The Allies tried to resist. But the Japanese were victorious in many places. Hong Kong, the Philippines, Singapore, and the Dutch East Indies (now Indonesia) fell to Japan.

The United States struggled to keep the Philippines free. General **Douglas MacArthur** was in charge of defending the Filipino nation. Finally President Roosevelt told MacArthur to leave. Roosevelt wanted the general safe to continue leading the war elsewhere.

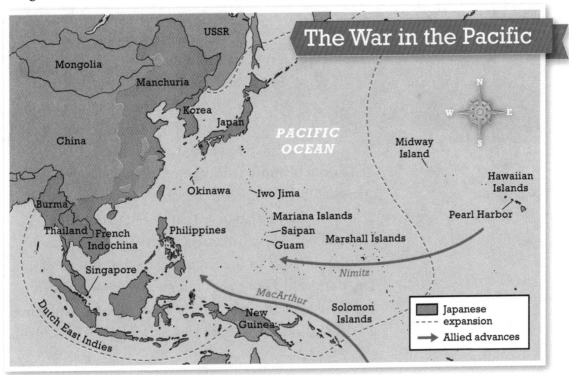

The War in the Pacific

The general promised the Filipino people "I shall return." The Allied troops still in the Philippines were forced to surrender to the Japanese.

For the Allied soldiers who remained, life was hard. The Japanese rounded up American and Filipino soldiers. These soldiers had to march many miles without food or water. Anyone who fell down would usually be killed immediately. The soldiers who survived long enough to reach the prison camp suffered in horrible living conditions. There was not enough food and little or no medicine. Many more soldiers died in the prison camps. Americans eventually heard about this atrocity. They grew angrier at Japan.

The Doolittle Raid

Bomber aboard the USS *Hornet* before launching the Doolittle Raid on Japan on April 18, 1942

Even as the Japanese conquered more and more land, the United States would not give up hope of a final victory. President Roosevelt had told the military to focus on Europe. But one man came up with an additional plan that would prove that the United States was not afraid of Japan.

Colonel Jimmy Doolittle led sixteen crews of five men each on a dangerous misson. They took an aircraft carrier as close to Japan as they dared. Doolittle's pilots dropped bombs on Tokyo, Japan's capital. The planes could not return to the aircraft carrier. It was too far. Their tanks did not have enough fuel for the return flight. Instead, the crews tried to reach safety in China. Of course, much of China was under Japanese control.

The mission was successful. Three men died during the raid, but most of the crews escaped to friendly lands. Eight men were captured by the Japanese. Three of these men were executed. The sixteen planes did little physical damage to Tokyo. But they greatly helped the American cause. The victory encouraged American morale.

The bombing concerned the Japanese. They had believed their homeland was untouchable after Pearl Harbor. Now they feared what the Americans could do. As the Japanese military conquered more lands, the United States found more weaknesses.

Midway and After

The Doolittle Raid helped American spirits, but the Japanese kept advancing. They planned to move east and finally capture Hawaii. To get there Japan needed to capture Midway. This tiny island lies about halfway between North America and Asia, hence its name.

The Battle of Midway was a trap in many ways. Japan planned to trick American aircraft carriers into showing up at Midway. Then the Japanese would surprise them

Create a Secret Code

During World War II some Navajo men made a code that could not be broken. They used it to send radio messages for the American Marines. Make up a written code. Use letters to represent other letters or symbols that stand for letters or words. Write a message. Invite a friend to try to break the code.

with a large fleet. But the United States knew of Japan's plan. American code breakers figured out where the Japanese ships would be. When the battle began in June 1942, the Japanese were the ones surprised.

The Battle of Midway was the turning point of the war in the Pacific. Until then the Japanese empire had been steadily growing. At Midway, Japan lost four aircraft carriers. The United States lost only one. For the rest of the war, the United States pushed back the Japanese advances.

Island hopping became the American strategy for the rest of the war. American forces needed to reach the Japanese islands. There were many occupied islands across the Pacific. The United States did not have enough time or men to conquer each one. Instead, the Americans hopped from one important island to another. They skipped the less important ones.

American forces in the Pacific took two main routes. Admiral Chester Nimitz led the navy across the smaller Pacific Islands. American forces wanted to get close enough to bomb Japan. General MacArthur fought in the large islands north of Australia. His forces steadily drove the Japanese out. Japan's Asian empire was crumbling.

The Code Talkers

What: radio messengers

When: 1939–1945 (during WWII)

Where: American Southwest

During World War II the American military feared that the Japanese might listen to secret transmissions. If the Allies made a code, the Japanese might break it and learn battle strategies. Many Native American Indians joined the military to serve as code talkers. Most were from the Navajo tribe. The code talkers changed military terms into their native languages, which the Japanese were not able to decode. The code talkers helped the American military to win World War II.

What battle was the turning point of the war in the Pacific?

Life on the Home Front
Everyday Life

While soldiers, sailors, airmen, marines, and nurses worked to bring peace around the world, Americans at home adjusted to a different lifestyle.

Rationing

One of the biggest differences was in food selection. The government needed to be sure the armed forces were supplied. It began to **ration** food and other items useful to the war effort. When an item was rationed, each person could buy only a certain amount of it. For example, no matter how much money someone had, the government might limit him to buying five pounds of sugar a month.

To deal with rationing, American cooks invented new recipes and meals. Meat was especially hard to get. To make small amounts last longer, meat was mixed with bread crumbs. Cakes were made with only one egg instead of five. Only people living on farms had easy access to more foods.

World War II poster (top) Children role-playing at a ration store (below)

Entertainment

The war also affected entertainment. Many movies in the theaters opened with short films about the war. Movies showed the Allies as heroes. The Germans, Italians, and Japanese were villains. The Walt Disney Company made short movies about the war. Even cartoon characters could beat the Japanese.

Fighting from the Home Front

But the efforts to help the war were not limited to food and movies. Americans worked hard to support their troops in other ways as well.

Working for War

As in World War I, many women worked during the Second World War. With many men off fighting, women filled in the workforce. Factories stopped making goods like automobiles. Instead they made fighter planes, bombs, and watches with glow-in-the-dark hands. "Rosie the Riveter" came to represent the American working woman.

The United States military tried to find people with special skills who would not necessarily be in combat. Those who had good math skills could become code breakers. Someone who spoke a foreign language might become an interpreter or even a spy. Every American was needed to help.

Congress also passed a draft. Men might be selected at random to join the military. Every man between the ages of eighteen and forty-five was subject to be drafted.

Some men did not believe that fighting was right. These men could support the nation in other ways. Some filled jobs left by men who had joined the military.

Workers assembling 37 mm armor-piercing shells in a converted factory

"Rosie the Riveter" World War II poster

Guarding the Borders

Although fighting never spread to America's civilians, the country needed to beware. Americans offered to safeguard the country.

Many civilians with aircraft took part in the Civil Air Patrol. These pilots often flew along the Atlantic Coast. They looked for German submarines and even sank one at one point in the war. Other pilots patrolled America's southern border.

Children recycling scrap metal to make shells, guns, and tanks

Many Americans helped in other ways. Some served as air-raid wardens. Others sold war bonds. School children supported the war effort by helping in their family's victory gardens and running scrap-metal drives. Most Americans believed the United States was fighting to preserve freedom throughout the world. They supported that fight.

Enemies at Home

Of course, not all Americans trusted each other. A few tried to help America's enemies. Others were suspected because of their family background.

Spies and Saboteurs

Many Americans were concerned about spies. Spies might share information with the enemy. Two men near New York City tried to tell Germany about the location of some American ships. Both men were captured. Americans were concerned that other unfaithful people might threaten their country.

Americans also worried about **saboteurs**. These are people who would do damage to hurt war production. In 1942 a German submarine sneaked eight men into the United States. Their mission was to destroy important factories. Instead, two turned themselves in to the government. The other six were then taken as prisoners. Even though this plot failed, Americans worried that others might succeed. Fortunately, none did.

Nisei

Americans were concerned about Japanese people who were citizens of the United States. Many Americans believed that anyone with a Japanese background was an enemy. Because of the Pearl Harbor attack, some people thought all Japanese were liars. Americans born of Japanese parents who had relocated to the United States were called **Nisei**.

During World War II, Nisei were taken to internment camps.

In February 1942, President Roosevelt signed an order that imprisoned many Nisei. This was not as punishment for any crime. The government merely feared these people because of their family backgrounds. Over 100,000 people were taken from their homes. They were put in **internment** camps. They were given housing and food, but they had little to do.

Many years after World War II, America recognized that it had treated these people wrongly. The government apologized to these people and their families. The United States said it was wrong to judge someone based on his family or appearance.

Why did Roosevelt order many Nisei imprisoned?

D-Day and Beyond
Planning the End

While American civilians tried to support their country and soldiers, the military made plans to end the war. There were two enemies. And the military had come up with two very different strategies.

Germany
D-Day

Dwight D. Eisenhower

Germany sat surrounded by countries that it had conquered. In the East, the USSR slowly pushed Nazi armies westward. The other Allied troops were focused on Italy. But between Italy and Germany were the Alps.

In late 1943 President Roosevelt made General **Dwight D. Eisenhower** the supreme Allied commander in Europe. Eisenhower and his aids developed a strategy. All the Allies (except the USSR) would land troops in a part of France called Normandy. They would first trick the Germans into thinking they were landing somewhere else. The code name for the landing day was D-Day.

American troops landing on the northern coast of France

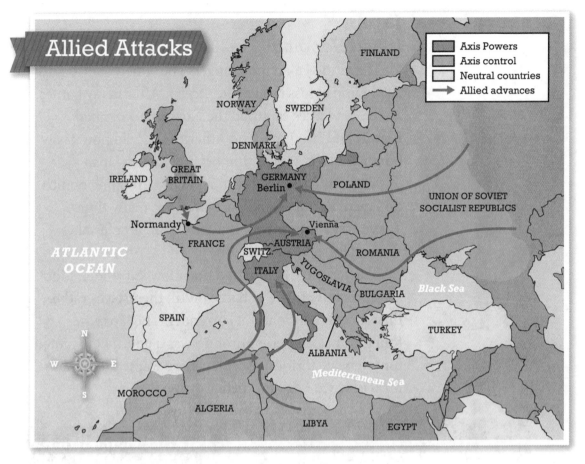

Finally, on June 6, 1944, the Allied liberation of France began. One hundred sixty thousand Allied troops landed on the Normandy beaches. The battle to free Europe was hard. Many men died. But under Eisenhower's leadership, the Allies started to push the Germans back to Germany.

The End of Nazi Germany

It took almost a year to free Europe. Finally, the Allies reached Germany. But before Russian troops reached the heart of Berlin, Adolf Hitler killed himself. On **May 8, 1945**, German leaders surrendered. The war in Europe was over.

Japan

Island Hopping

Defeating Japan took longer. The Allied plan was to island hop across the Pacific Ocean. After many battles, American forces captured the Northern Mariana Islands and Iwo Jima. The Americans could now easily bomb Tokyo and other important cities in Japan.

The United States began regularly dropping bombs on Japan. Factories and ports were hit many times. Tokyo was **firebombed**. But the Japanese refused to surrender.

The Japanese culture did not allow surrender. Most soldiers chose to die in battle or kill themselves rather than face the dishonor of surrender. The Japanese thought that Emperor Hirohito was a god. They wanted him to be victorious. Most Japanese wanted to fight until they won or they died.

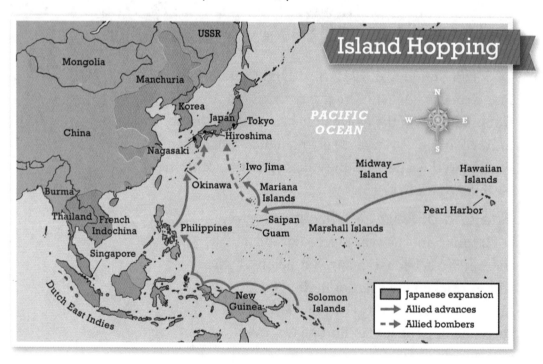

The United States did not want to fight that battle. American soldiers could attack and conquer the Japanese main island. But too many Americans would die. The American military feared that Japanese civilians might fight as well. Then they and more Americans would die. The United States had to use another plan.

The Bomb

The United States had begun working on a new type of bomb. It did not use normal explosives. Instead, it split atoms. The power of an **atom bomb** was far greater than any other weapon in existence.

Soon after Germany's defeat, President Roosevelt died. Harry Truman became president.

The atom bomb that was dropped on Nagasaki was called "Fat Man."

President Truman decided to use the atom bomb on Japan. He believed it would be better for American and Japanese citizens. Fewer American soldiers would die. Also, fewer Japanese citizens would die than in an invasion. The United States and the other Allies asked Japan one last time to surrender. Japan refused.

On August 6, 1945, an American plane dropped the first atom bomb on the Japanese city of **Hiroshima**. Tens of thousands of people died. The Japanese government still would not surrender.

Three days later a second bomb was dropped on **Nagasaki**. Very soon after that bombing, Japan agreed to give up as long as they could keep their emperor. Japan's final surrender was signed on September 2, 1945. The war was completely over.

What country dropped the atom bomb on Japan?

The Aftermath
The World After the War

Even after the war ended, the United States had much work to do. Many nations had suffered from fighting. Millions of people had died. Americans wanted to rebuild the world. Few knew all the problems they would find.

Jews wearing badges of the yellow star of David (left)
Wedding rings Germans removed from their victims (right)

The Holocaust

The worst news for most Americans was learning about the **Holocaust**. Americans knew that Adolf Hitler was a dictator. They knew that he thought Germanic people were the best. After the war, Americans discovered how much evil Hitler had done.

In order to make Germany how he wanted it, Hitler had tried to kill everyone he thought was not good enough. Most of all, he hated the Jews. Hitler killed about six million European Jews. He had them rounded up, shipped in railway cars like animals, and then killed. Some were left alive but were enslaved in Hitler's factories. This murder of Jews and other people is remembered as the Holocaust.

Many people had tried to rescue the Jews. In the Netherlands a courageous woman named Corrie ten Boom and her family hid Jews in their house. Eventually the Nazis captured the ten Booms. Even then, the ten Booms did not tell about the Jewish people hidden in their house.

After the war many Jewish people left Europe. They moved to the land in the Middle East that had been Israel. They reestablished the country in 1948. President Truman encouraged the Jews to set up their own state.

Rebuilding Europe and Japan

Americans also learned of the destruction of Europe and Japan. In order to defeat the Axis Powers, the Allies had bombed cities and factories. Many people had no place to work or live. Countries like Germany and Japan also needed to start new governments.

Dresden, Germany, after the bombing

George Marshall's plan helped many countries rebuild after the war.

The United States wanted to help these countries. American bombs had caused much of the damage. Now American money would rebuild. The United States wanted the world to be filled with healthy countries.

The United States sent money and advisers to help countries rebuild. In Europe the Americans set up the **Marshall Plan** to help rebuild industry. By the early 1950s Western Europe had recovered from much of the physical destruction of the war.

Tokyo Station being rebuilt

The Iron Curtain

But not all of Europe shared in the recovery. Once the fighting of World War II ended, a new type of war began. Joseph Stalin still controlled the USSR. His armies controlled many countries in Eastern Europe. These countries had little freedom. Stalin refused to let them receive American help. Soon he cut them off altogether from Western countries. Winston Churchill said that an "**iron curtain**" had cut Europe in half. For the next forty-five years, the United States fought to prevent Communism from spreading.

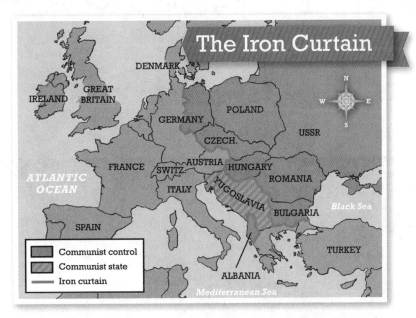

The Iron Curtain

DENMARK
IRELAND
GREAT BRITAIN
GERMANY
POLAND
USSR
CZECH.
FRANCE
SWITZ.
AUSTRIA
HUNGARY
ROMANIA
ITALY
YUGOSLAVIA
BULGARIA
Black Sea
ATLANTIC OCEAN
SPAIN
TURKEY
ALBANIA
Mediterranean Sea

- ▨ Communist control
- ▨ Communist state
- — Iron curtain

Conclusion

In 1945 few Americans thought about problems with Russia. Instead, they celebrated the victory against Germany and Japan. American soldiers flooded home. They left the military, got jobs, got married, and bought houses. Although the world did not have complete peace, Americans began to return to a normal life.

As soldiers and sailors got married and had children, Americans moved to suburbs like this one in Levittown, New York.

Why did Hitler want to destroy the Jews during the Holocaust?

12 The Northeast

Delaware, Pennsylvania
& New Jersey Rhode Island
1787   1790

Maine
1820

1750   1775   1788 1791 1800   1825

Connecticut, Massachusetts, Maryland, Vermont
New Hampshire & New York

Regions of the United States

In what part of the United States do you live? Maybe you live in the chilly Northeast or the dry Southwest. Maybe visiting a beach is an everyday part of your life. Maybe you live on the grassy plains and have never seen the ocean. Perhaps you do not live in the **continental** United States. You might live on one of the Hawaiian Islands or in a US territory.

The United States can be divided into different areas. There are a number of ways to group states. In this book you will read about six different areas called regions. Then you will learn about US territories and commonwealths. Each region is unique. Each has its own history, culture, climate, and wildlife. Each has its own economy and industries. Each has important cities and landmarks. If you are a United States citizen, you will learn many reasons to appreciate the region where you live.

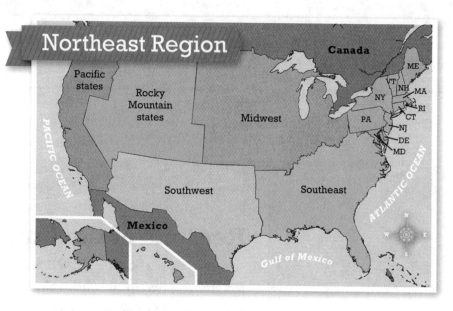

Northeast Region

The Northeast
Shaped by Its Past

There are eleven states in the Northeast region of the United States. How has this part of the country been shaped by its history? Let's remember some important events that took place in the Northeast.

Many different Indian groups once lived in the Northeast. The Wampanoag people met the Pilgrims at Plymouth. God used them and their friend Squanto to help the Pilgrims survive in America. The Narragansetts lived in what is now Rhode Island. An English preacher named Roger Williams bought land from them. He held different beliefs from the Puritans. He wanted to start his own colony. This colony became Rhode Island. Pennsylvania and New York were once home to the Lenape Indians. Perhaps the largest group in the region was the Iroquois. This group was made up of five Indian nations, later joined by a sixth. Iroquois longhouses dotted the Northeastern woods.

As Europeans filled the Northeast, many Iroquois were forced to move west. But their wampum beads and pottery can still be found in museums.

The Northeast was a place of action during the American Revolutionary War. Several events of the war happened in Massachusetts. The city of Boston was home to a number of Patriot leaders. Many colonists did not want the British tax on tea. One night citizens of Boston dumped British tea into the harbor. This event became known as the Boston Tea Party. The Boston Tea Party moved the American colonies closer to war with the British. The first battles of the Revolutionary War were also fought in Massachusetts.

After the war a new country was born. Northeastern states were the earliest to join the United States of America. Delaware was the first colony to become a state. It gained statehood on December 7, 1787. Pennsylvania and New Jersey became states a few days after Delaware.

Boston Tea Party

Liberty Bell

Two important documents were written in the Northeast. The Declaration of Independence was signed in Philadelphia, Pennsylvania, in 1776. The US Constitution was also completed there in 1787.

Some important national landmarks are located in the Northeast. The Liberty Bell in Philadelphia was rung at the first reading of the Declaration of Independence. The Statue of Liberty stands in New York Harbor. For more than a century, the statue has been a symbol of America. It reminds us of America's freedom and opportunity.

The Northeast has an important religious background. Many European settlers in this region in the 1600s were Puritans. They came to America to freely practice their faith. They held strong Christian beliefs. They read and believed the Bible. They met faithfully for worship. They built schools and colleges where young people could study God's Word. They wanted to bring the gospel to the Indians living around them.

This Puritan influence is no longer strong in the Northeast today. One reason for this is that people with different beliefs came to the region. Immigrants from Ireland settled there. They brought Roman Catholic beliefs. Many descendants of Puritans also gave up religious beliefs of any kind. Colleges like Harvard and Yale were once places to get a Christian education. Now they are no longer religious colleges.

What religious group settled in the Northeast in the 1600s?

All Things Bright and Beautiful

The Northeast is home to many beautiful things God created. The plants, flowers, and trees in a region are called its **flora**. The animals and birds that live there are called **fauna**. Some of these flora and fauna are the state flowers, trees, or birds for Northeastern states.

The state tree of Maine is the eastern white pine. This tall, sturdy tree has been used to make ships' masts for hundreds of years. The paper birch, state tree of New Hampshire, supplied the Indians with bark for canoes. Vermont and Rhode Island both chose a type of maple as their state tree. Sap from Vermont's sugar maple trees is used to make maple syrup. Delaware's state tree is the American holly. Holly branches with their pointed leaves and red berries are common at Christmas.

eastern white pine

The mountain laurel is the state flower of Connecticut and Pennsylvania. This pink flowering shrub blooms in the woods and fields in spring. Maryland's flower is the black-eyed Susan. These yellow flowers have dome-shaped black centers. They grow along the roadsides and in fields. Massachusetts chose a small white flower called the mayflower. The ship that brought the first colonists to Massachusetts had the same name.

black-eyed Susan

paper birch

The Northeast is home to a variety of wild animals. Moose are found in the states farthest north. They like the cool climates of Maine, Vermont, and New Hampshire. Moose are the largest type of deer. The Northeast also has many white-tailed deer. This deer is the state animal of New Hampshire and Pennsylvania. Bobcats, foxes, and black bears also live in the Northeast. There are a number of smaller animals like raccoons, rabbits, squirrels, and bats as well.

fox

The state of Connecticut has a sea creature for its state animal. The sperm whale is now rare in the waters off Connecticut's coast. But in the 1800s both Connecticut and Massachusetts had large whaling industries. The sperm whale was useful for its oil.

Birds are plentiful in the Northeast. They live both inland and along the shores. The state bird of Maine and Massachusetts is the black-capped chickadee. You can tell a chickadee by its song: *chick-a-dee-dee-dee!* Finches are also common Northeastern birds. New Hampshire chose the purple finch as its state bird.

goldfinch

New Jersey chose the goldfinch. Pennsylvania's bird is the ruffed grouse. This unusual bird makes a fan shape out of its tail feathers when seeking a mate.

moose

ruffed grouse

Many birds live only along the coasts of the Northeast. Birds like sandpipers, gulls, and plovers might be seen during a walk on a beach. Some loons live year-round in the far north.

The Northeast has many kinds of reptiles and amphibians. Turtles, frogs, and several kinds of snakes can be found. The diamondback terrapin is Maryland's state reptile. This turtle is known for the detailed pattern on its shell. Massachusetts chose the garter snake. This snake is not poisonous. It often finds its way into gardens and backyards.

Some of the Northeastern states have chosen state butterflies. Maryland chose the Baltimore checkerspot. Its wings are checkered with patches of black, orange, and white. Delaware's state butterfly is the tiger swallowtail. It is yellow and black, often with blue spots around the bottom edges of its wings.

Observing wildlife in a region is a good way to see God's creativity. The Northeast offers great variety to appreciate in the creatures God has made.

sandpiper

diamondback terrapin

tiger swallowtail

garter snake

Which state's flora and fauna interest you most?

295

State Trees, Flowers, and Birds of the Northeast

	Tree	Flower	Bird
New Hampshire	paper birch	purple lilac	purple finch
Maine	eastern white pine	pine cone and tassel	black-capped chickadee
Massachusetts	American elm	mayflower	black-capped chickadee
Vermont	sugar maple	red clover	hermit thrush
New York	sugar maple	rose	eastern bluebird
Rhode Island	red maple	violet	Rhode Island red
New Jersey	northern red oak	violet	American goldfinch
Maryland	white oak	black-eyed Susan	Baltimore oriole
Connecticut	white oak	mountain laurel	American robin
Pennsylvania	eastern hemlock	mountain laurel	ruffed grouse
Delaware	American holly	peach blossom	blue hen

The Nature of the Place

New England

The six states in the upper Northeast are often called New England. This area was settled mostly by English colonists. The climate, however, was harsher than that of England. These colonists needed several years to get used to New England's weather.

Maine, Vermont, New Hampshire, and northern Massachusetts have cooler climates than southern New England. Rain falls in these northern states throughout the year. Winters are long with heavy snow. Southern Massachusetts, Connecticut, and Rhode Island are warmer. The eastern areas near the coast are humid. They receive rain but little snow.

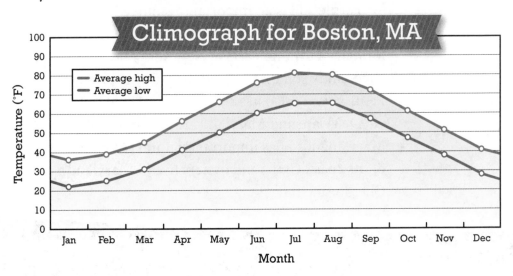

Climograph for Boston, MA

New England has been blessed with a variety of natural resources. It has many natural seaports. Lobster and many kinds of fish are plentiful off its coast. It also has mountains and forests. New England is a good source of granite, slate, and marble. Its forests provide wood for timber and sap for maple syrup.

The Middle Atlantic

The five states in the lower Northeast are called the Middle Atlantic states. They are New York, Pennsylvania, New Jersey, Maryland, and Delaware. The climate of these states is different from New England's. It is affected by both the Atlantic Ocean and the Great Lakes. This area has mostly mild springs, humid summers, and cold winters. New York often receives heavy snow in winter.

New Jersey's humid climate makes it a good place to grow many fruits and vegetables. It is called the Garden State. Its **wetlands**, or bogs, are ideal places to grow cranberries. One of these boggy areas is full of pine trees. It is known as the Pine Barrens.

Fertile soil is an important resource in the Middle Atlantic. New York's river valleys provide grassy land for dairy farming. Parts of New York and Pennsylvania have sandy soil that is good for growing grapes. Pennsylvania also has rich sources of coal.

Delaware and Maryland are rich in forest resources. Maryland also has important natural resources just off its coast. Crabs and oysters live in Maryland's Chesapeake Bay.

Cranberry harvest

Resources and Products of the Northeast

KEY

Coal	Fruit	Marble
Crab	Granite	Oysters
Cranberries	Grapes	Slate
Dairy	Lobster	Trees
Fish	Maple syrup	Vegetables

St. Lawrence R.

Maine

Lake Huron

Vermont

New Hampshire

Lake Ontario

New York

Massachusetts

Lake Erie

Rhode Island

Connecticut

Pennsylvania

ATLANTIC OCEAN

Ohio

New Jersey

Maryland

Delaware

Ohio R.

West Virginia

Virginia

Which Northeastern states are likely to have heavy snow?

Making a Living

A region's industries are the major ways the people make a living. Industries are goods or services produced. Often an area's natural resources create industries. For example, the many maple trees in New England create two industries. They provide maple sugar for the syrup-making industry. Vermont leads the nation in maple syrup production each year. The maple trees create another industry as well. In the fall the leaves change color. New England hillsides are covered with red, orange, and yellow leaves. Tourists come from near and far to see the brightly colored maple leaves. Inns, restaurants, and shops in New England towns profit from the tourism industry all through the fall.

Dairy farming is a major industry in New York and Pennsylvania. These areas have fertile land where cattle can graze. The milk from the cows is used to make cheese, yogurt, ice cream, and other dairy products. The state of New Jersey has many small farms that grow fruits and vegetables to sell. These farms are called **truck farms**.

The beautiful fall trees in New England attract many tourists each year.

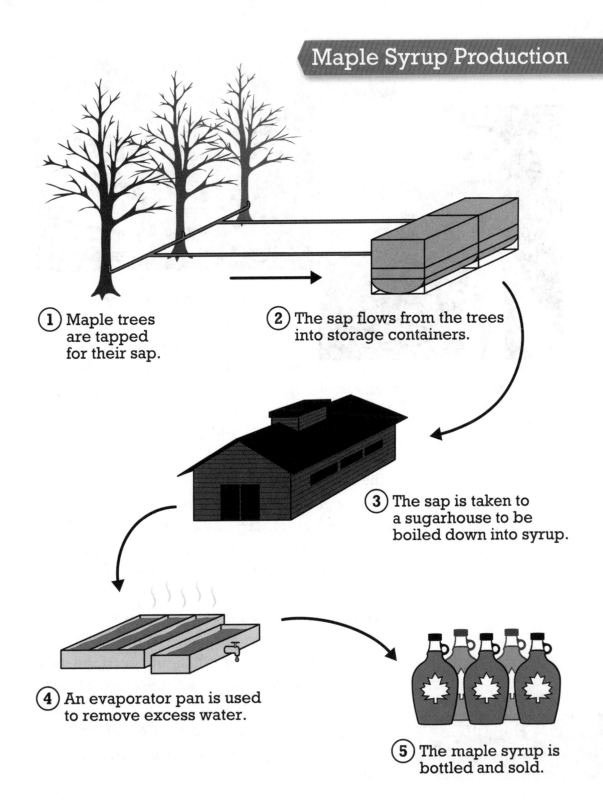

(1) Maple trees are tapped for their sap.

(2) The sap flows from the trees into storage containers.

(3) The sap is taken to a sugarhouse to be boiled down into syrup.

(4) An evaporator pan is used to remove excess water.

(5) The maple syrup is bottled and sold.

Lobster trapping is a large industry in the Northeast.

Manufacturing is another major industry in the Northeast. Many states produce chemicals for medicines, cleaners, and other products. The Northeast also has many service industries. Computer and insurance services are two of the most common.

The states along the Atlantic coast are leaders in the fishing industry. Maine is the top producer of lobsters in the United States. Lobsters are caught in special traps dropped to the sea floor from boats. Chesapeake Bay off the coast of Maryland also has a major fishing industry. It has large catches of clams, oysters, and crabs each year. Cod, haddock, and skates are also caught off the Atlantic coast.

New York City is home to many industries. One of the most important is the money industry. Wall Street in New York is lined with businesses that handle money. The New York Stock Exchange on Wall Street is the largest business of its kind in the world. New York City also has many industries connected with the arts. It is home to major publishers, art galleries, and film and theater companies.

What two industries do New England's maple trees create?

Cities and Sites

The Northeast contains four of America's fifty largest cities. One of these, New York City, is the largest in the country.

New York, New York

New York City in the state of New York has more than eight million people. These people live in an area of just over three hundred square miles. Many people living close together makes a city's population **dense**.

New York City is located in the southeastern part of New York. The city sits at the mouth of the Hudson River and is made up of five counties called **boroughs**. These boroughs are named the Bronx, Manhattan, Queens, Brooklyn, and Staten Island.

New York's streets are busy with traffic. But many people who live in New York do not have cars. Public transportation like subways, buses, and ferries takes people everywhere they need to go.

New York has many famous sites. Visitors come to New York from all over the world. Museums, skyscrapers, and stores are popular places to visit. Some people only want to stroll the streets and feel the excitement of this huge, bustling city.

New York City

Philadelphia, Pennsylvania

Philadelphia, Pennsylvania, is the fifth-largest US city in population. A Quaker named William Penn planned this city and chose its name. Philadelphia means "city of brotherly love." Penn began building Philadelphia in 1682. He wanted it to be a safe place for people of any religion.

Today Philadelphia is a busy city filled with history. Visitors can see Independence Hall, where the Declaration of Independence was signed. The Constitution was also written there. Carpenters' Hall hosted the First Continental Congress in 1774. In Franklin Court visitors can see where Benjamin Franklin once lived. Some of his inventions are on display in the museum there. The house of flag maker Betsy Ross is also a popular place to visit. There is even a food named after Philadelphia. The philly cheese steak is a warm sandwich filled with sliced beef, onions, and cheese.

Franklin Court is an area with museums and historic sites. This photo shows a "ghost structure" where Benjamin Franklin's house once stood.

Boston, Massachusetts

Boston, Massachusetts, is the next largest city in the Northeast. It is the capital of the state. Boston is a center for arts, business, and education. Many people visit the city to enjoy its historical sites. Faneuil Hall and the Old South Meeting House were important meeting spots for Patriots during the Revolutionary War. Paul Revere's house is also open for visits. The African Meeting House is the oldest church for black Americans in the country.

Boston also has a busy seaport. Cruise ships, fishing boats, and large container ships come and go. Many people like to visit the harbor to see a replica of the ship from the Boston Tea Party in 1773.

Baltimore, Maryland

Baltimore, Maryland, is the fourth-largest Northeastern city. Its harbor makes it a center of shipping and tourism in Maryland.

One of the most popular places to visit in Baltimore is Fort McHenry. The British bombarded this fort during the War of 1812. They were unable to conquer it. An American lawyer named Francis Scott Key watched the attack from a ship in Baltimore's harbor. He was glad to see the American flag still flying the next morning. He wrote a poem called "The Star-Spangled Banner." This poem later became America's national anthem.

Fort McHenry

West Quoddy
Head lighthouse

Other Sites in the Northeast

The point farthest east in the continental United States is in Maine. Surprisingly, the spot has the word *west* in its name. A lighthouse on West Quoddy Head marks this far eastern point of the shoreline. The coast there is a rocky slope rather than a sandy beach.

Another important site is Niagara Falls on the west side of New York State. The United States and Canada share this group of waterfalls. It is located on the border between the two countries. Many tourists visit the falls each year. These waterfalls are more than just a beautiful sight. The rushing water produces energy for two nearby power plants.

Mountains are part of the landscape in much of the Northeast. The largest mountain range is the Appalachian Mountains. Many smaller ranges are part of the Appalachians. The Green Mountains in Vermont and the White Mountains in New Hampshire are two of these. The highest peak in the Northeast is Mount Washington in New Hampshire. It is 6,288 feet tall.

The Northeast is filled with places to see. Perhaps you and your family can visit one of the many interesting sites in the Northeast.

Which major city in the Northeast would you most like to visit?

Of the People, By the People, For the People

Regions are made up of states. States are made up of cities and towns. Cities and towns are made up of communities. And every community, city, state, and region is made up of people. The study of the people who live in a certain area is called **demographics**.

To find the demographics of a place, we would count certain groups of people. We could then look at those numbers to draw conclusions. We might count people of a certain age or people with a certain job. For example, more than 25 percent of people living in Cape Cod, Massachusetts, are age sixty-five or older. We can conclude that Cape Cod is a popular place to retire.

Sometimes people's religions are part of a study of demographics. The Northeast has a high percentage of Catholics. Five of its states have more Catholics than Protestant Christians. Many of the European immigrants to this region in the 1800s were Catholics.

New York City has more immigrants than most other US cities. These immigrants come from many different parts of the world. For this reason, New York City also has a wide variety of religions. Large numbers of Jews, Muslims, Buddhists, and Hindus live there. Often immigrants from the same country settle in one neighborhood. They speak their own language. They open their own stores and restaurants.

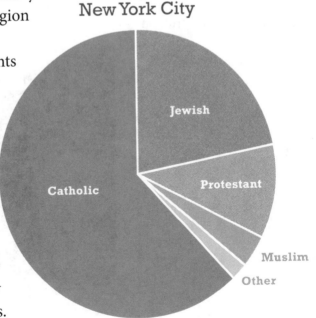

The Religions of New York City

307

On any given day, a resident of New York City would meet people from many different nations on the city sidewalks.

And they keep their own religious beliefs. Christians in New York City live side by side with these people. They can speak of Christ to people from many nations without leaving the city.

In Pennsylvania's Lancaster County, there are groups of people known as the Amish. The Amish have both a particular set of beliefs and a unique way of life. The Amish live very simply. Most are farmers. They rely on windmills to power their equipment. They use horse-drawn buggies for transportation. They wear clothing in plain styles and colors. Most Amish people do not use electricity. They refuse to use many modern inventions. These practices are meant to keep the Amish separate from the world.

Amish transportation

Citizens of the Northeast are under the national government of the United States. But each state has its own government. Cities and towns also have local governments. In each of these governments, the people vote for their leaders. We can draw conclusions about the people in a state or a region by looking at the way its people vote.

In many states, people tend to vote for either Democrats or Republicans most of the time. We call states that tend to vote for Democrats "blue states" and states that tend to vote for Republicans "red states." The Northeast is made up entirely of blue states. It is the most strongly Democratic region in the United States. The table on this page shows the way these eleven states have voted in six national elections.

The Northeast is a place with many things to appreciate. It has beauty, variety, and a wealth of resources. It is a place where people are using God's gifts in helpful ways. Like every region, it is also a place with many needs. It is a place with many people who do not love and honor God. If you live in the Northeast, God has put you there. He can use you. Look for ways to honor God and His Word in the place He has chosen for you to live.

Democrat   Republican

	1992	1996	2000	2004	2008	2012
CT						
DE						
ME						
MD						
MA						
NH						
NJ						
NY						
PA						
RI						
VT						

What are some ways to honor God in the place where you live?

13 The Southeast

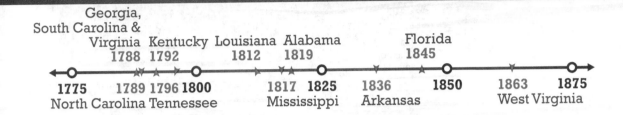

Georgia,
South Carolina &
Virginia   Kentucky Louisiana Alabama   Florida
1788   1792   1812   1819   1845

◄——○————————————○————————————○————————○————————○————○——►
1775   1789 1796 **1800**   1817 **1825**   1836   **1850**   1863   **1875**
North Carolina Tennessee   Mississippi   Arkansas   West Virginia

The Southeast is a unique region of the United States. Its history stretches back to the earliest days of the European colonies and beyond. It has the longest coastline of any region in the continental United States. It is a region of mountains, rivers, fields, and farms. It is also a region of beautiful cities, both old and new.

Shaped by Its Past

The Southeast has a rich history. Various Indian peoples lived in this region. The Natchez lived in what is now Mississippi. They built large mounds as part of their religion. The modern city of Natchez, Mississippi, has preserved some of these mounds for people to see. Another group, the Seminoles, lived in the Florida area. The Seminoles were known for their cypress canoes and their shelters. They built thatched-roof homes without walls and called them **chickees**. The Cherokee, Creek, Choctaw, and Chickasaw tribes also once lived in the Southeast. However, most Indians of the Southeast had to move west under the Indian Removal Act in the 1830s.

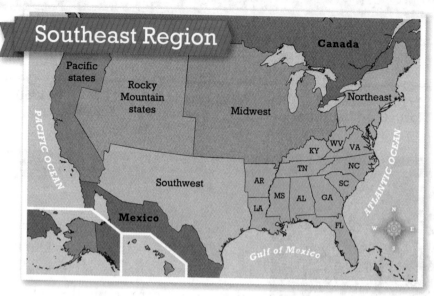

Southeast Region

The first English settlement in America is found in the Southeast. This settlement was called Jamestown. Over time several colonies grew in this region. They were the colonies of Virginia, North Carolina, South Carolina, and Georgia.

These colonies helped the United States become a nation. Americans fought important battles in these colonies. The Revolutionary War ended after the Americans won some of these battles. Many important leaders also came from these colonies. George Washington was one of these leaders. He led the Continental Army during the Revolutionary War. He also became the first president of the United States. Many other presidents came from the Southeast too. Most of these presidents were from Virginia.

The Southeast is also important because it shaped American religion. The first Southern colonists did not come in search of religious freedom. But the Great Awakening changed the South and Southeast. The Southeast became one of the most religious parts of the United States. The Methodist and Baptist churches grew strong in the South. Today the Southeast is one of the most religious regions in the United States.

Southerners built their own distinct culture. Their way of life was different from life in the North. They preferred farming over trade and manufacturing. They thought the life of a farmer was healthier.

Leaders tried to set the example for what Southern life should be. They wanted people to have good manners. They thought men should show gallantry to ladies. They thought Southerners should be polite to all people. They should be caring toward those they rule over.

Hospitality was very important in the Southeast. The people placed great emphasis on doing their duty. They believed in guarding their freedom. They thought a man should own his own land to support himself and his family. Knowledge was also very important to Southern leaders. They valued taking time to read and learn. Even many of those who were not leaders wanted to live a life of leisure.

Typical attire for a Southern gentleman

Hospitality, duty, and knowledge were good goals. But there was a sad part to Southern culture as well. Some of these goals were reached by using something that was not good. Slavery made it possible for Southern leaders to live the life of a gentleman, to own large plantations, and to pursue learning.

Slaves in the South also developed their own way of life. Many of them came from different parts of West Africa. They had different languages, customs, and beliefs. The slaves shared their cultures and ideas with each other. They also learned from the American way of life. The slaves developed their own rich culture from these different sources. Most significantly, many accepted Christianity. Belief in a God who rules over all gave many slaves hope for freedom. Ideas from Scripture often appeared in the songs they wrote. These songs are called spirituals.

A late eighteenth century watercolor painting, *The Old Plantation*, showing a group of African slaves playing instruments during some time off from work

The Civil War changed the Southern way of life. It ended slavery and freed blacks to live and work alongside their former owners. But this new freedom was very difficult for many black Americans. Many Southern whites continued to treat them unjustly. One kind of injustice was called segregation. Segregation separated black and white Americans. Black people could not attend the same schools, eat at the same lunch counters, or drink from the same drinking

A tenth-grade class in 1954 at McKinley Technical High School in Washington, DC, where both black and white students attended together

fountains as whites. Often what was made available to the freed slaves was not as good as what was made available to white people.

Black Americans had their right to vote limited. This injustice led to the great struggle for civil rights. Civil rights shaped the black way of life also. Preachers challenged injustices. Poetry and music talked about the struggles of black Americans. These art forms also celebrated the way of life that black Americans looked forward to living.

The evils of slavery and segregation give some people a low opinion of every part of the Southern way of life. However, this attitude is not a biblical way to think. People are made in God's image. They use God's good creation to make their way of life. We should expect every culture to have good points. But people are also sinners. We should expect every culture to have bad points as well.

What are the strengths of Southeastern culture?

All Things Bright and Beautiful

The Southeast has many marshes and swamps. A **marsh** is an area covered by shallow water in which small plants grow. A **swamp** is an area also covered by water but with larger plants and trees growing in it. The largest swamp in North America is the Okefenokee Swamp. Parts of it are found in Georgia and Florida. The largest combination of swamps and marshes in the United States is in Florida. It is called the Everglades.

Swamps and marshes have certain kinds of plants and animals found nowhere else. In a swamp you might find cypress trees with Spanish moss growing from them. Spanish moss looks like long green beards hanging from a tree's branches. A marsh usually has sweet grass. This humid area is a good place for ferns and orchids to grow. Sometimes swamps and marshes have alligators. Alligators like fresh, calm water. More alligators live in Florida and Louisiana than in any other states. Turtles, herons, and plenty of mosquitoes can also be found in swamps and marshes. Swamp and marsh water is usually full of fish, frogs, toads, and some snakes.

Various animals live in the plains, mountains, and plateaus of the Southeast. Many of these are familiar animals that might live in your backyard, like cardinals, mockingbirds, squirrels, or rabbits. Hawks and eagles also occupy the Southeast. In the forest live deer and black bears.

The Southeast coastline has a variety of birds. The Louisiana state bird is the brown pelican. This bird is easy to spot. It has a pouch under its long bill that stretches to hold fish. It dives from the sky to catch fish in the ocean. Sandpipers, plovers, and gulls are also common shore birds of the Southeast.

The Southeast has many different kinds of trees. In places like Florida or the coast of South Carolina you can find palm trees. In places like West Virginia you will find sugar maples. Some trees have pretty flowers, such as the flowering dogwood and the magnolia. Others, such as pine trees, have needles instead of leaves. These trees have all been adopted as state trees by states in the Southeast.

What is the difference between a marsh and a swamp?

State Trees, Flowers, and Birds of the Southeast

	Tree	Flower	Bird
Alabama	longleaf pine	camellia	yellowhammer
North Carolina		flowering dogwood	cardinal
Virginia	flowering dogwood		
West Virginia	sugar maple	rhododendron	
Kentucky	tulip poplar	goldenrod	
Tennessee		iris	mockingbird
Florida	sabal palmetto	orange blossom	
South Carolina		yellow jessamine	Carolina wren
Georgia	live oak	Cherokee rose	brown thrasher
Arkansas	pine	apple blossom	mockingbird
Mississippi	magnolia	magnolia	
Louisiana	bald cypress		brown pelican

The Nature of the Place

The Southeast has many different kinds of land. Many states in the Southeast region border the Atlantic Ocean and the Gulf of Mexico. Some of this coastland is made up of sandy beaches. Other parts of the coast are marshes or swamps. The flatland stretching up from the coast is called the **coastal plain**. As you move westward away from the Atlantic Ocean, the ground rises. Where the ground rises is called the piedmont. The **piedmont** is the foothills between the coastal plain and the mountains. Many waterfalls can be found in the piedmont.

The main mountains found in the Southeast are part of the Appalachian Mountains. The Appalachian Mountains stretch from Alabama all the way into Canada. The Ozark Mountains are also found in the Southeast. They are found in Arkansas and neighboring states.

Beyond the Appalachian Mountains are the plateaus and plains that make up the western parts of Kentucky, Tennessee, and Arkansas. These plateaus are flat or hilly lands beyond the mountains.

Southeast Lands

The Southeast has several important rivers as well. The most important is the Mississippi River. The Mississippi is the longest river in the United States. It is the fourth-longest river in the world.

The Southeast climate tends to be milder than other regions overall. The summers in the Southeast are hot, but the winters are mild. This is true of the Southwest also. But the Southeast has another special ingredient: rain. This addition means that plants grow well in the Southeast. They get plenty of sun and rain. And the weather is warm enough for them to grow for long parts of the year.

The climate is warmest in the southernmost states and along the coast. The farther to the north and the farther into the mountains, the cooler the climate will be. However, the Southeast also faces dangers from its location and climate. Hurricanes form over warm oceans and often hit the coasts of Southeastern states. Heavy rains can cause flooding even in areas not directly in the path of a hurricane.

Flooding in New Orleans in 2005 due to Hurricane Katrina

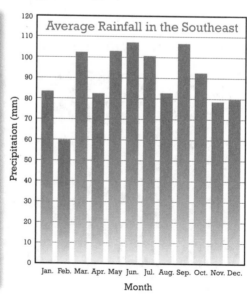

Natural resources can be found all over the Southeast. The coasts of the Southeast are themselves a natural resource. The region has a long coastline with natural harbors. As a result several states have built important ports. These ports are busy places where goods are shipped to and received from countries all over the world.

Cargo ships on the Mississippi River

The rivers of the Southeast, including the Mississippi River, are also important natural resources. Goods can be shipped up and down some of these rivers. Dams built on these rivers create lakes and help control flooding. Dams also allow people to generate power from the water.

The climate and good soil of much of the Southeast are also important natural resources for these states. The long growing season, plentiful rain, and fertile ground found in the Southeast make it an ideal place for agriculture. Trees from the forests can be used to create timber. Not all soil is good for growing things. But it can still be useful. Clay found in the Southeast can be used to make pottery. Stone can be used for gravel and cement.

Some states in the Southeast have abundant coal, oil, or natural gas. People can mine or drill for these resources and use them to provide energy for many Americans.

What is the weather like in the Southeast?

Resources and Products of the Southeast

Iowa
Pennsylvania
Maryland
Illinois
Indiana
Ohio
West Virginia
Virginia
Ohio R.
Missouri R.
Missouri
Kentucky
Mississippi R.
Tennessee
North Carolina
Arkansas
South Carolina
Mississippi
Alabama
Georgia
Louisiana
Florida
ATLANTIC OCEAN
Gulf of Mexico

KEY

Cattle & dairy		Cotton		Oil		Tobacco	
Chicken & eggs		Fish		Peanuts		Trees	
Citrus fruits		Grain		Soybeans		Vegetables	
Clay		Harbor		Stone			
Coal		Hogs		Sugarcane			
Corn		Natural gas		Textiles			

Making a Living

The ocean is important for business in the Southeast. The long coastline has many ports. Norfolk, Virginia; Charleston, South Carolina; Jacksonville and Miami, Florida; Mobile, Alabama; and New Orleans, Louisiana are all major port cities. In the nineteenth century these ports shipped cotton all around the world. Today many different goods are shipped to and from these ports. The long coastline also means that fishing is important for these states.

Agriculture is one of the enduring ways to make a living in the Southeast. Some of the oldest crops are tobacco and cotton. They are still important to Virginia, North Carolina, Tennessee, Georgia, Alabama, Mississippi, and Arkansas. Today apples and soybeans are grown in many places. Peanuts, corn, and grain are also important products. Some states have their own specialties. Florida is well known for its citrus fruits. It grows more of these fruits than any other state. Louisiana grows sugarcane. Some farmers in these states raise dairy and beef cattle. Others raise hogs. Farmers raise chickens both for meat and for eggs.

Florida orange grove

Other industries draw natural resources from the ground. Coal mining is a major industry for West Virginia. Virginia, Tennessee, and Alabama also mine coal. Arkansas, Louisiana, and Alabama all have important oil and natural-gas industries.

Some industries take natural resources and make them into goods to be sold. Virginia, North Carolina, and South Carolina all manufacture textiles. "**Textiles**" refers to cloth. Often this cloth is turned into clothing. Virginia, Georgia, Arkansas, and Louisiana all process food. For instance, milk is pasteurized and bottled to be sold in stores. Yogurt is created from milk. Peanut butter is created from peanuts. Some manufacturers make metal or plastic. Others take that metal and plastic and turn them into cars, planes, and ships. Making automobiles is important to the economies of Alabama and South Carolina. Shipbuilding is important in Virginia.

Textile Manufacturing

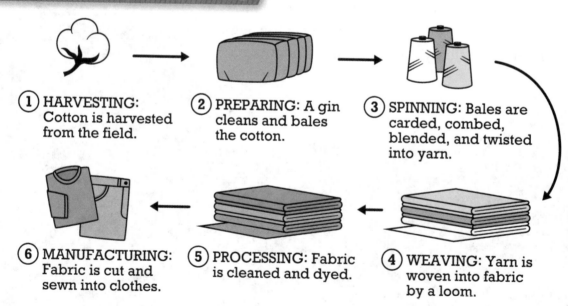

1. HARVESTING: Cotton is harvested from the field.
2. PREPARING: A gin cleans and bales the cotton.
3. SPINNING: Bales are carded, combed, blended, and twisted into yarn.
6. MANUFACTURING: Fabric is cut and sewn into clothes.
5. PROCESSING: Fabric is cleaned and dyed.
4. WEAVING: Yarn is woven into fabric by a loom.

Car plant assembly line (top)
Zinc-coated steel produced
at a steel mill (right)

Tourism is also an important industry for many states. The beaches of the Southern coast attract people on vacation. The beauty of the Appalachian Mountains brings people to camp and hike. Civil War battlefields attract those who love history. Many also come to see the sights of Charleston, Savannah, and New Orleans.

Some industries use more human than natural resources. Charlotte, North Carolina, has become a center for the banking industry. Atlanta, Georgia, is a center for communications. Parts of North Carolina have become known for research. Many government workers live in the area around Washington, DC. NASA hires many people in Florida and Alabama.

Which industry found in the Southeast would you want to work in?

Cities and Sites

The Southeastern United States has many well-known cities. Some of these cities are among the oldest in the United States. Some Southeastern cities are important to the entire nation. Many Southerners prefer living in the country, but cities have always been important to the region.

The United States capital includes the Lincoln Memorial, the Washington Monument, and the Capitol.

Washington, DC

One important city sits between the Northeast and the Southeast. In 1791 people living in Maryland and Virginia gave part of their land to the United States government. The land they gave would become our nation's capital, Washington, DC. The letters *DC* stand for "District of Columbia." The capital is called a **district** because it is not a state, and it is not part of any state. The city of Washington fills up the entire District of Columbia. Washington, DC, is the place where the president lives. Congress meets and makes laws for the country in Washington, DC. The Supreme Court is also located in Washington, DC.

Richmond, Virginia

Virginia was important in the early years of our country. The capital of Virginia is Richmond. Patrick Henry gave his "give me liberty or give me death" speech in Richmond. During the Civil War, Richmond was the capital of the Southern states. Many Civil War battles were fought near or in Richmond. Visitors to Richmond today can visit many historic sites.

Charlotte, North Carolina

Charlotte, North Carolina, is one of the country's most important banking centers. Its history has long been connected with money. Gold mines used to exist around Charlotte. In the early nineteenth century, a mint operated in Charlotte. A **mint** is a place that makes the coins that people use as money.

Charleston, South Carolina

Charleston, South Carolina, is one of the South's oldest towns. It was settled in the late 1600s on the banks of the Ashley River. Its good harbor made Charleston a valuable port city. Because of its importance as a port, Charleston was occupied by the British during the Revolutionary War. Fort Sumter was built in the harbor after the War of 1812. Later it became the tinderbox that set off the Civil War. Today Charleston remains an important city. It is known as a cultural center. Its beautiful houses and parks along the harbor attract many visitors. It also hosts the Spoleto Festival, a festival that celebrates music, drama, and other events. Charleston has been nicknamed the "holy city" because of the many churches and steeples there.

Row houses in Charleston, South Carolina

Madison Square displays a statue of Sgt. William Jasper, a Revolutionary War soldier.

Savannah, Georgia

Savannah, Georgia, is another Southern port city. It is one of the most active ports in the country. The city was founded in the early 1700s by James Oglethorpe. He laid out a special design for the city. The city would be divided into wards, or sections. At the center of each section was a square, or a city park or a garden. North and south of the square were areas for people to live. East and west of the square were shops and other businesses. Originally the city had four of these squares. As the city expanded, it added more. At present the city has twenty-two squares. These park areas within the city make Savannah nice to walk through. They help make tourism an important part of Savannah's economy.

Atlanta, Georgia

Atlanta, Georgia, grew up in the 1830s at the junction of two railroad lines. It was destroyed in the 1860s by the Union army. After the Civil War, Atlanta was rebuilt as a city of the "New South." In the postwar years Atlanta grew into an important economic center. As the home of Martin Luther King Jr., Atlanta also played an important role in the civil rights movement. The civil rights movement was the struggle of black Americans to have equal rights with other Americans. Today Atlanta is home to one of North America's busiest airports. It is also an important financial and telecommunications center.

New Orleans, Louisiana

New Orleans, Louisiana, sits at the **delta** of the Mississippi River. The delta of a river is formed where the river flows into a larger body of water. Louisiana was founded in the early 1700s by French settlers. Americans acquired the city as part of the Louisiana Purchase. It was an important city in the early nineteenth century. Western states could ship goods down the Mississippi River. New Orleans also shipped many goods up the river to the Western states. Its port remains a central part of its economy. Tourism is also another major part of the economy. French buildings and creole food attract many people. **Creole** cooking mixes foods from European, African, Caribbean, and American cultures.

A building in the French Quarter, the oldest, most visited neighborhood in New Orleans, Louisiana

Memphis, Tennessee

Farther up the Mississippi River is Memphis, Tennessee. Memphis sits on a high bank looking over the Mississippi River. It is also the meeting place for five railroads and two major highways. Memphis is an important center for the movement of goods.

Cities are one important way that people have shaped the land around them to be more productive.

Which city in the Southeast would you most like to live in?

Of the People, By the People, For the People

The people of the Southeast are varied. They also share many similarities. The Southeast is a very religious part of the country where many Bible-believing Christians live. The Southeast is often called the Bible Belt. Many people in the Bible Belt are Baptist, Methodist, or Presbyterian. The cities and towns in these states have many churches. Even people who are not Christians are likely to respect the Bible and church. This religious emphasis in Southern life comes from the seeds planted during the Great Awakening.

Some parts of the Southeast are more firmly Roman Catholic. Cities like Miami and New Orleans have many Roman Catholics. This is because of their French or Spanish past.

Politically, the Southeast has been called the Solid South. In recent history the Solid South became solid for Republicans. This will probably change again in the future. People move around the country more than in the past. As cities grow, many people move in with different political opinions. For instance, many people have moved to northern Virginia to work in Washington, DC. Now, northern Virginia tends to be more "blue" than the rest of the state.

People in the Southeastern United States are known for their hospitality. Politeness and good manners are also important. Children are often taught to say, "Yes, sir" and "Yes, ma'am" when speaking to adults. Close

The Solid South

Democrat
Republican

family ties are also an important part of the way of life in this region. People in the Southeast often value tradition. They know there is much wisdom in the way people lived in the past. They do not think problems are solved by changing everything about the way people live.

People who live in the Southeast have a long heritage. Some of these states were the first to enter the United States. Some were among the first to be explored. Slavery and the Civil War are sad parts in the history of this region. Segregation is another sad truth. But there are also happy parts. The Great Awakening was a time of God's blessing. Churches have grown in this part of the country. Strong family and community ties are another good part of Southern life. The Southeast is a region with a rich past and a bright future.

Where did the religious emphasis in the South come from?

14 The Midwest

The states of the Midwest are often called "America's Heartland." They are located in the heart, or the center, of the nation. They are also America's center of agriculture. Many important crops and other food products come from the Midwest. The Midwestern states were settled by many brave, hardworking people. The courage and endurance of Midwestern farm families give this part of the country a special character. These states represent America's "heart."

Shaped by Its Past

The middle section of the United States is famous for its farms and factories. In addition to these things, the history and culture of the Midwest helped to shape the entire country. Twelve states form the Midwest. Before European settlers arrived, American Indian tribes such as the Sauk, Fox, and Dakota lived across the region. Some lived in forests. Others preferred the **prairies**. These grasslands receive little rain and have few trees. During the 1700s European settlers trickled into the area. Eventually most of the tribes were forced farther west.

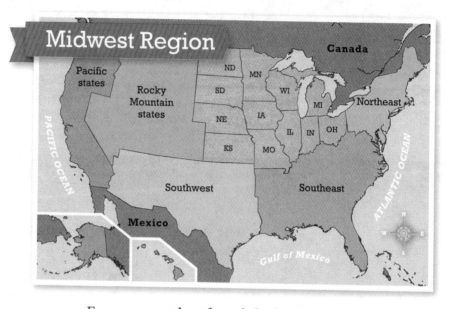

Midwest Region

European settlers found the lands beyond the Appalachian Mountains appealing. They first moved into the Ohio River valley. The Midwest has many rivers. The largest are the Mississippi, the Ohio, and the Missouri. These waterways were the highways for pioneers. During the 1800s Americans poured into the Midwest. Between 1803 and 1889 all twelve Midwestern states joined the Union.

The earliest settlers came from the East Coast. Southerners came from Kentucky into southern Ohio. Pennsylvanians moved through the Ohio River's northeast tributaries. A **tributary** is a river that flows into a larger one. People from New York and other northeastern states also moved west. They often traveled by the Erie Canal and the Great Lakes into the Upper Midwest. Later many immigrants from northern Europe came to the United States. They often ended up in the northern Midwestern states.

Until 1890 most settlers to the Midwest came as farmers. Because of the rich soil and good climate, this area became known as America's Breadbasket. These farmers encouraged improvements that changed America. Better farm equipment allowed bigger farms and more crops. In the western Midwest are fewer rivers. Windmills provide the energy to pump water from **aquifers.** These reserves of water lie deep under the rich soil. Because of these improvements, farms have spread to the high plains of the region.

By the late 1800s most good farmland had been claimed. As a result many later immigrants settled in the cities. Chicago connected the Great Lakes' shipping to the Mississippi River. Chicago became the largest city in the Midwest and the second largest in the United States. Other cities also benefited from their locations on rivers and railroad tracks. Wheat and corn from Midwestern farms could be sent to other parts of the country. Beef cattle could be slaughtered and their meat shipped east.

Windmill in South Dakota

During the 1900s the Midwest kept growing and changing. Farmers wanted improvement in their equipment and crops. Scientists worked with farmers to produce hardier crops and better machines. Foreign immigrants and black Americans moved into the region. Manufacturing of automobiles and farm equipment employed many people. The Midwest produced raw materials and jobs for millions of Americans.

Much of Midwestern culture results from the various groups of people who settled here. Many supported public universities. These centers of learning helped to define the states' culture. The cities provided places for many cultures to mix.

Reaping, threshing, and winnowing is done in one single process by a combine harvester.

During the 1900s Midwestern authors helped shape America. Progressive authors tried to change the nation. They encouraged new attitudes toward politics, business, and religion. One book resulted in cleaner meatpacking plants. Some authors wrote about pioneer life. Laura Ingalls Wilder wrote about growing up in several Midwestern states. Willa Cather wrote about life in the Nebraska prairies. F. Scott Fitzgerald was from Minnesota, but he cared more about life on the East Coast. However, Fitzgerald's Midwestern roots influenced his viewpoint. He told stories about the 1920s. His writings shape how people view that decade even now.

Tractors are built in factories similar to the way cars are built.

The Midwest today still has an important influence on the whole nation. The region's manufacturing companies affect the nation's economy. The blend of cultures in the Midwest also affects all of America. The Midwest continues to attract people of different backgrounds. Many people of Middle Eastern origin have moved to the Midwest. The region also has a growing Hispanic population. Both groups are growing in the country at large. Since so many Americans live in the Midwest, their votes can change the nation as a whole.

What people groups have shaped Midwestern culture?

All Things Bright and Beautiful

The Midwest has a variety of plants and trees. The plains in the eastern part were once covered in **deciduous** forests. Deciduous trees are those that lose their leaves once each year. Although much of the forests are gone now, many trees remain. A common tree is the cottonwood. It grows along creek banks. This tree gets its name from the way it disperses its seeds by wind. They float through the air on a cotton-like material. The northern Midwest region has many evergreen trees. Spruce, hemlock, and pine fill parts of Michigan, Wisconsin, and Minnesota.

The Midwestern states have chosen a wide variety of state flowers. Several of these flowers grow naturally in the wild. The prairies are a good place to find the pasqueflower, the wild prairie rose, and the sunflower. Minnesota's flower, the pink-and-white showy lady's slipper, grows in wet areas or swampy parts of the woods. Other states have chosen the blossoms of shrubs and trees such as the hawthorn and the apple tree.

The Midwest has many kinds of animals. Before settlers arrived, buffalo, wolves, and cougars lived in the Midwest. Black bears, deer, and moose still live in parts of the region. Other mammals include prairie dogs and wolverines. There is also an abundance of beavers, squirrels, rabbits, and mice.

Many birds live in the Midwest. In a **wildlife reserve** in Wisconsin, scientists are protecting the endangered whooping crane. By contrast, songbirds are common throughout the entire region. Midwestern states have chosen some of the most familiar or loved birds as their state birds.

The Midwest has several different kinds of snakes. Some are harmless, like the garter snake and the rat snake. The region also has poisonous snakes like the rattlesnake and the copperhead.

The Midwest is also home to many types of insects. Grasshoppers, crickets, and bees are plentiful on the plains. Moths and butterflies can often be seen flitting among the prairie grasses and wildflowers.

What endangered species are scientists protecting in Wisconsin?

339

State Trees, Flowers, and Birds of the Midwest

	Tree	Flower	Bird
Wisconsin	sugar maple	wood violet	robin
Michigan	eastern white pine	apple blossom	
South Dakota	Black Hills spruce	pasqueflower	ring-necked pheasant
Iowa	bur oak		eastern goldfinch
North Dakota	American elm	wild prairie rose	
Nebraska		goldenrod	
Kansas	cottonwood	sunflower	western meadowlark
Minnesota	red pine	showy lady's slipper	common loon
Illinois	white oak	violet	
Indiana	yellow poplar	peony	
Ohio	Ohio buckeye	scarlet carnation	cardinal
Missouri	flowering dogwood	hawthorn	bluebird

The Nature of the Place
Physical Geography

At first glance the Midwest seems entirely flat. The western areas are covered with prairie, which is mainly flatland. But a closer look reveals that much of the Midwest has gentle slopes. Some areas even have hills or mountains.

Some famous highlands in the Midwest are the Ozark Mountains. These rise in southern Missouri and neighboring states. Their rough terrain makes travel hard. Today people often vacation in the Ozarks. Some enjoy outdoor activities such as hiking, camping, exploring caves, and rafting. Others like visiting places like Branson, Missouri. This city has many theaters that celebrate the traditional culture of the Ozarks.

The Black Hills of South Dakota are another famous highland region. These hills were called *black* because of the trees covering their slopes. The Sioux tribe believed that the hills were sacred. As American settlers moved west, the US government promised the Sioux that they could remain in the hills. But then gold was found. The Sioux were forced off the land.

Mount Rushmore is in Keystone, South Dakota. Each face is about sixty feet tall.

In the Black Hills are two important memorials. Mount Rushmore has the faces of four presidents carved into the rock. Many Americans visit the mountain every year. About ten miles away is an unfinished carving of Crazy Horse. He was a Sioux war chief who fought against American forces. The monument is still slowly being carved into Thunderhead Mountain.

Climate and Weather

Since the Midwest lies in the middle of North America, its weather changes greatly from season to season. The states of the Midwest are far from any oceans. Oceans help keep temperatures from extreme changes. Summers in the Midwest are usually very hot. Winters are cold and snowy. The northern plains and areas around the Great Lakes are regularly buried under many inches of snow. Even fall can be shortened by early snowfalls. Spring is the wildest season of all. Warm and cold days often follow each other. Especially in the southern part of the Midwest, violent weather may result. Sometimes warm air swirls up from the Gulf of Mexico. If it meets cold air from Canada, the region will get severe thunderstorms.

A tornado is a violently spinning air column shaped like a funnel that can spin between 110 miles and 300 miles per hour and stretch from about 250 feet to 2 miles wide.

Many parts of the plains are known for tornadoes. Kansas and Nebraska lie in "Tornado Alley." Because there are few hills in the Midwest to break up the storms, thunderstorms and tornadoes can travel many miles. People in the Midwest plan in advance for tornadoes. Many houses on the plains have storm cellars. These rooms dug into the ground give refuge to people during severe weather. Weathermen are now better able to track storms. They warn people ahead of time to head to their cellars.

Natural Resources

The flatlands that let storms travel far also give the Midwest its vast farms. The Midwest enjoys many natural resources. Huge spreads of **arable** land are the most obvious. Farmers can raise crops on arable land. Each Midwestern state has areas of this good soil and fairly regular rain. As a result, people raise many crops and animals.

Wheat is a kind of grass that is an important source of food worldwide. Wheat seeds are ground to make flour.

Several states also have minerals that can be mined. Minnesota's Mesabi Range is rich with iron ore. Since it is found close to Lake Superior, the ore can easily be shipped for processing.

The northern forests give much wood. Furniture and paper are made from these forests. Minnesota's legendary hero, Paul Bunyan, was famous for logging in the state's woods.

The prairie is cut through with rivers. These rivers running through the Midwest are another great resource. They first provided transportation. Then during the 1800s the rivers were used to power many mills. Now boats travel up and down the rivers. People enjoy fishing and sightseeing on them.

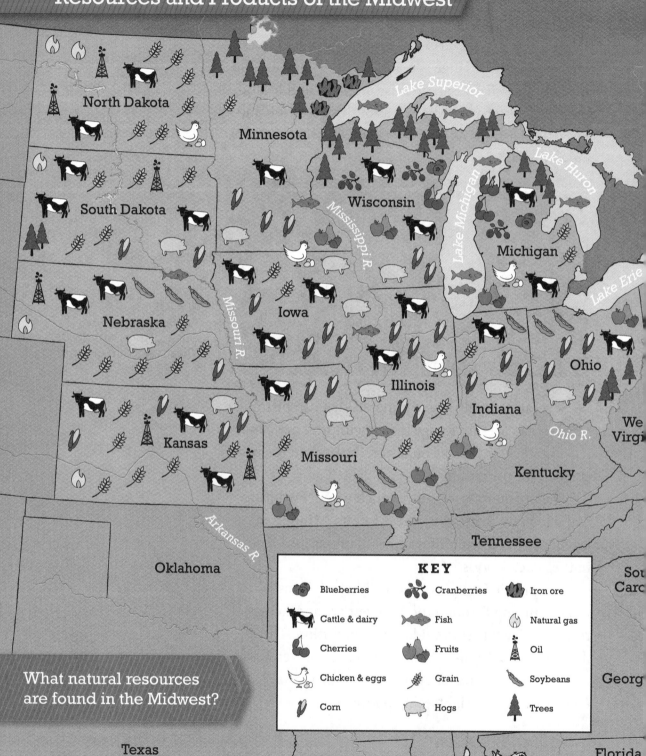

Resources and Products of the Midwest

Lake Superior

Lake Michigan

Lake Huron

Lake Erie

North Dakota

Minnesota

South Dakota

Wisconsin

Michigan

Nebraska

Iowa

Illinois

Ohio

Kansas

Missouri

Indiana

Kentucky

We
Virgi

Oklahoma

Tennessee

Arkansas R.

Missouri R.

Mississippi R.

Ohio R.

Texas

Louisiana

Florida

Georg

Sou
Caro

What natural resources
are found in the Midwest?

KEY

Blueberries	Cranberries	Iron ore
Cattle & dairy	Fish	Natural gas
Cherries	Fruits	Oil
Chicken & eggs	Grain	Soybeans
Corn	Hogs	Trees

Making a Living

The Midwestern states offer a variety of jobs. Most can be divided into one of three categories.

Getting Raw Materials

Some jobs collect raw materials. Agriculture is the most important of these jobs in the Midwest. Much of America's food is grown in this region. Eastern Iowa through Ohio gets enough rain for corn to grow well. They also grow wheat and soybeans and raise hogs or cattle. Western Iowa, where wheat is grown, gets less rain. The states near the Great Lakes have more variety in agriculture. Michigan can grow fruits such as cherries, blueberries, and cranberries.

Soybeans are highly nutritious and are a source of oil and flour.

Some other important industries are logging and oil **extraction**. The forests of Michigan, Wisconsin, and Minnesota offer loggers much wood. North Dakota began drilling for oil in the early 2000s. This oil helps provide many jobs in the state.

Cherry orchards produce a small, round red fruit that is also highly nutritious.

Making Things

During the 1900s the Midwest became a center for manufacturing. Detroit made so many cars it was called "Motor City." Other parts of the Midwest made farm equipment. Companies such as John Deere, International Harvester, and Caterpillar based their factories in the region. By the late 1900s the region produced a wider variety of products. Both Missouri and Kansas have large aviation industries. Indiana produces orthopedic supplies, products that help injured parts of the body to heal.

All the states have food manufacturing industries. Wisconsin is famous for its dairy products. Fans of the Green Bay Packers, Wisconsin's football team, are even called cheeseheads. General Mills, famous for breakfast cereals, is based in Minnesota. Both Kellogg's and Post Foods began in Michigan. Kellogg's later moved to Missouri. The abundant raw materials of the Midwest provide many supplies to manufacture goods.

Dairy Production

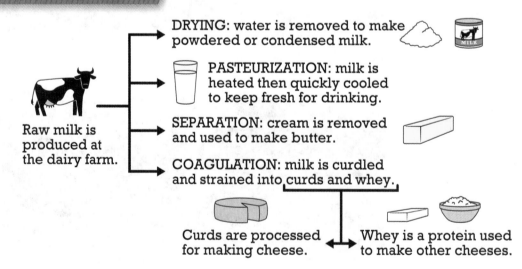

Raw milk is produced at the dairy farm.

DRYING: water is removed to make powdered or condensed milk.

PASTEURIZATION: milk is heated then quickly cooled to keep fresh for drinking.

SEPARATION: cream is removed and used to make butter.

COAGULATION: milk is curdled and strained into curds and whey.

Curds are processed for making cheese.

Whey is a protein used to make other cheeses.

Helping People

Every Midwestern state offers many service industries that provide help for other people. A good example is the Sears company. Founded in the late 1800s, the company sold things people needed. When farmers could not travel to town, they could order from a Sears catalog. In its pages they found clothing, tools, jewelry, and other goods they might need. The company would deliver orders to its customers' houses. Sears eventually built Chicago's tallest building. Other Midwestern service companies that sell goods today are Best Buy and Target. The Midwest has other companies that try to make people's lives better by providing information or other services.

Willis Tower, also known as the Sears tower in Chicago, Illinois, is 108 stories high. It is the second-tallest skyscraper in the United States.

What are some raw materials of the Midwest that provide many supplies to manufacture goods?

Cities and Sites

Chicago, Illinois

Although the Midwest first attracted people to its rich soils, more people now live in its many cities than in the rural areas.

The biggest and most important city in the Midwest is Chicago. Chicago sits at the base of Lake Michigan. This location makes it a center of trade. A canal connects the lake with rivers that flow into the Mississippi.

In 1871 much of Chicago burned. When the city was rebuilt, it became the home of the first skyscrapers in the world. Buildings were made of either stone or metal. No one wanted another fire.

Today the city is famous for buildings such as the Willis Tower and the Hancock Building. From a distance these buildings define Chicago's skyline. A close examination reveals that the buildings are decorated with carved stone. Chicago's buildings are headquarters of companies that do business throughout the United States and the world.

Many tourists visit Chicago every year. It has sports teams, museums, and concerts. Navy Pier, which juts into Lake Michigan, is a popular stop. There is even a Ferris wheel that puts riders high above the lake. Cruises on the lake allow visitors to see the city skyline. Many people choose to look down on the city from the highest buildings.

Navy Pier is Chicago's main tourist attraction. It is 3,300 feet long and is located on the shore of Lake Michigan.

Detroit, Michigan

The Midwest's second most important city, Detroit, was first settled by the French. Eventually, the British claimed this settlement located between Lakes Huron and Ontario. It took over a decade after the War for Independence for the United States to gain the land. Eventually, Detroit became an important part of American culture.

Detroit had times of success and times of difficulty during the 1900s. Henry Ford made cars in the city. This industry helped Detroit grow large and prosperous. For many decades Detroit was the center of all automobile manufacturing in the United States. Since the 1970s, though, the city has not prospered. City and state leaders are working to help Detroit again become a leading city in the region.

Buick assembly line in the 1950s in Detroit, Michigan

Detroit and its suburbs receive many tourists. Some like to see the city's sports teams. Near Detroit is the Henry Ford Museum and Greenfield Village. The Henry Ford Museum shows centuries of American history in one location. It tells about more than cars. Henry Ford collected pieces of American history there. He even moved entire buildings to this museum center.

Minneapolis and Saint Paul, Minnesota

Farther west in the region are Minneapolis and Saint Paul, the largest cities in Minnesota. They sit next to the meeting point of the Minnesota and Mississippi Rivers. Minneapolis first boomed with sawmills and flour mills. Saint Paul is near the Mississippi River. Minneapolis and Saint Paul grew together to become the largest urban area in the United States. This area is called the Twin Cities. Just south of the cities is the Mall of America. This massive shopping center even has an indoor amusement park with a roller coaster. People also visit the many museums and churches in the Twin Cities. The James J. Hill House shows how the very rich lived during the late 1800s.

Saint Louis, Missouri

Located much farther south on the Mississippi is Saint Louis, Missouri, known as the Gateway City. In 1804 the Lewis and Clark Expedition headed into the Louisiana Territory from this city. Many pioneers followed their example. Saint Louis remembers these men and women with the Gateway Arch.

Located on the west bank of the Mississippi River, the Gateway Arch Monument in Saint Louis, Missouri, is 630 feet high, making it the tallest arch in the world.

The John A. Roebling Suspension Bridge crosses the Ohio River from Kentucky to Cincinnati, Ohio.

Cleveland and Cincinnati, Ohio

In Ohio, cities such as Cleveland and Cincinnati also enjoy locations on bodies of water. Cleveland sits at the mouth of the Cuyahoga River on Lake Erie. Like many Midwestern industrial cities, Cleveland struggled during the second half of the 1900s. Many people living there could not find work. Today tourists enjoy visiting its sports arenas and the Botanical Garden.

Cincinnati, at the opposite end of Ohio, sits on the Ohio River. Before Chicago and Saint Louis, Cincinnati was the Midwest's center of trade. Cincinnati is home to America's first professional baseball team, the Red Stockings. People enjoy visiting the city to see its theaters and enjoy Cincinnati's food.

One thing all these Midwestern cities have in common is their location. Successful cities are usually built near water. Many of the cities struggled economically during the late 1900s, but the Midwest is trying to bring in new and better industries.

Beside what natural resource are successful cities usually built?

Of the People, By the People, For the People
Religion

Because the Midwest is a land of immigrants, it has a wide variety of religious beliefs. Most people in the region consider themselves to be Christian. During the 1800s most were Methodist or Baptist. Later, immigrants arriving from Germany and Scandinavia brought Lutheranism with them. The Dutch settlers along the Great Lakes were Dutch Reformed. Immigrants such as the Irish and the Hispanics were often Catholics.

The Islamic Center of America in Dearborn, Michigan, is the oldest mosque in the United States.

The Midwest has many Christian schools and colleges. In the 1900s immigrants came from non-Christian cultures. In the industrial cities there are many Muslims. The largest American mosque is in Dearborn, Michigan. A **mosque** is a place where Muslims hold religious meetings. For many years Americans sent missionaries around the world to spread the good news of Christ. With immigrants coming into America's heartland, Christians can now share God's message with people at home. With many churches and Bible colleges in the Midwest, it is a wonderful place for those who do not know Christ to learn of Him.

Politics

Even the earliest settlers of the Midwest wanted to be represented in their government. When the region was a frontier, the settlers needed protection. They voted for politicians who supported their settlements.

During the middle of the 1800s, the Republican Party began in the Midwest. Many Republicans wanted to stop the spread of slavery. The first Republican president, Abraham Lincoln, was from the Midwest. He grew up in Indiana and lived as an adult in Illinois.

In the 1900s cities grew, and Midwest politics changed. The rural areas often voted for Republicans. But cities, such as Chicago, usually supported Democrats. Today, Midwestern states do not always follow a pattern. Many are **swing states**, voting sometimes Republican and sometimes Democratic. Minnesota has even elected governors who did not belong to either party.

Because of the variety of people who live there and because of its abundant natural resources, the Midwest is a significant region in the United States.

SWING STATE

Why is there a wide variety of religious beliefs in the Midwest?

15 The Southwest

Texas
1845

Oklahoma
1907

1825   1850   1875   1900   1912   1925

New Mexico & Arizona

The Southwest region of the United States is different from any other. Much of the land is desert. The climate is mostly warm and dry. Colorful, rugged landscapes are found there. This region has beaches, mountains, and also the famous Grand Canyon. Like the other regions, the Southwest has a heritage, culture, and people all its own. The Southwest states are Oklahoma, Texas, New Mexico, and Arizona.

Shaped by Its Past

The first people to live in the Southwest were Indians. Some of the earliest Indians were the ancestors of today's Pueblo people. These Ancestral Pueblos often made their homes inside caves in cliffs. Their homes can still be seen today. In an area called Four Corners, visitors can go inside these cliff dwellings. Four Corners is located at the point where the borders of New Mexico, Arizona, Utah, and Colorado meet.

The descendants of the Ancestral Pueblos moved farther south. The Hopis and the Zunis were two of these Pueblo tribes. They were farmers who grew

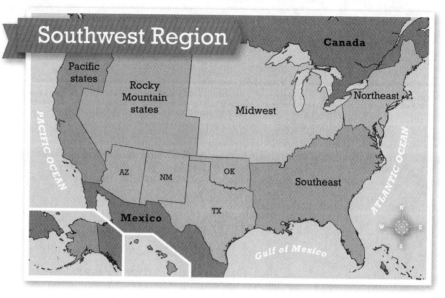

Southwest Region

corn and beans. They made **adobe** bricks from clay and straw. They built homes called pueblos which were made of adobe and stone. The pueblo homes are attached to one another like apartments. Many families live together in a pueblo. *Pueblo* is a Spanish word that means "village" or "town." Today the Hopis live on a reservation in Arizona. Most of the Zuni people live on a reservation in New Mexico.

The Navajo people are another tribe in the Southwest. The Navajos have lived there for hundreds of years. They and the Pueblo tribes have been both friends and enemies. The Navajos made a different kind of shelter from the Pueblos. Their homes, called **hogans**, were dome shaped. Hogans were made of wooden poles, tree bark, and mud. Like the Pueblo tribes, the Navajos were farmers.

The Navajos are the largest tribe in the United States today. Their reservation spreads through parts of Arizona, New Mexico, and Utah. Some of them still live in hogans.

The Spanish were the first Europeans to explore the Southwest. Spanish explorer Francisco Vásquez de **Coronado** traveled north to this region from Mexico. He was hoping to find gold and silver. He never found treasure, but he explored much of New Mexico and parts of Arizona. One of his men was the first white man to explore the Grand Canyon.

Later, Spanish missionaries came to teach the Indians Roman Catholic beliefs. They set up missions in New Mexico, Arizona, and Texas. The most famous of these missions is the Alamo. The Alamo played an important part in Texas history. It was used as a fort when Texans fought for their freedom from Mexico in 1836. They bravely defended the Alamo from the Mexican leader Santa Anna. The Texans were finally defeated. Many of them died in the battle. In a later battle, Sam Houston led the Texans to victory and independence. Tourists can still visit the Alamo in San Antonio, Texas.

The tiny Alamo Mission held back the Mexican army for thirteen days. It now stands as a symbol of the Texans' determination to gain their independence.

Lands in Arizona and New Mexico were purchased from Mexico. Part of Arizona was won during the Mexican-American War.

The Southwest today is still strongly influenced by the Spanish and Mexican cultures. Many cities have Spanish names. A large number of Spanish-speaking people live there. Mexican and Spanish food, architecture, and traditions are common in these states.

You have already learned that Texas was the home of many cattle ranches in the 1800s. The Spanish had been the first to start ranches in the Southwest. As American settlers moved west, more ranches opened. Texas ranchers raised not only longhorn cattle but also sheep, goats, and horses. Texas was the starting point for most of the cattle drives of the 1800s. Both Oklahoma and New Mexico had cattle trails across their land. These cattle drives lasted from the end of the Civil War until the late 1800s. By that time railroads had been built south toward Texas. Cattle could be carried by train rather than being driven along cattle trails.

The Great Depression of the 1930s was a difficult time for many farmers in Oklahoma, New Mexico, and Texas. Millions of acres of land on the plains were damaged by drought and dust storms. The swirling dust clouds ruined crops, homes, and machinery. People and animals died in the storms.

Dust storms, such as this giant dust storm in Goodwell, Oklahoma, in 1937, are caused by drought and poor land use.

It took the farmers years to recover from these losses. Some families even decided to move away from the region. We call this event and the area where it happened the Dust Bowl. Since this time, new methods of farming have been developed to help keep disasters like this from happening again.

Who were the first Europeans to explore the Southwest?

All Things Bright and Beautiful

God has specially designed the flora and fauna of the Southwest to be able to live in a dry climate. Plants and trees must survive without much rain. Many of the state trees and flowers in this region are desert plants.

The palo verde is the state tree of Arizona. The Spanish name means "green stick." The tree is completely green, including its branches and trunk. Its deep roots allow it to pull water up from the ground during dry spells. The tree has pale yellow blossoms in late spring.

The state flowers of Arizona and New Mexico are also desert plants. Arizona's flower is the saguaro cactus blossom. The saguaro is the largest cactus in the United States. It can grow to more than fifty feet tall. Some saguaro cacti live 150 to 200 years. Their creamy white flowers with yellow centers bloom at night during the spring. New Mexico's flower is the yucca blossom. The yucca is known for its sharp, spiky green leaves and stalks of white flowers. Indians used the yucca to make soap and medicines.

saguaro cactus

palo verde

yucca

The Texas state tree is the pecan tree. Texas produces more pecans than any other state except Georgia. Pecan wood is used in flooring and furniture. The Texas state flower is the bluebonnet. These small blue flowers are shaped like a woman's sunbonnet.

The redbud is Oklahoma's state tree. It gets its name from its reddish-pink spring blossoms. Oklahoma's state flower is the dark red Oklahoma rose. Oklahoma also has a state wildflower, the red and yellow Indian blanket.

ringtail

The Southwest has many animals that God designed to survive in deserts. Small mammals like the ringtail, the jackrabbit, and the collared peccary, similar to a pig, live in Arizona and New Mexico. Larger animals such as wolves, mule deer, and black bears are also found in those states.

Many kinds of lizards and snakes also live in the desert areas. One Arizona lizard, the Gila monster, is the largest native lizard in the United States. Most grow to be two feet long and weigh up to five pounds. Southwestern deserts are home to rattlesnakes, sidewinder snakes, and coral snakes.

collared peccary

Some mammals live on the plains. Oklahoma's state animal is the bison, or buffalo. Texas keeps an official

Gila monster

state longhorn herd. The herd is divided among several state parks. Texas is also represented by the armadillo. An armadillo is a small mammal with a long tail and an armor-like shell.

The Southwest is a good place to see many of the unique birds that God has created. Arizona chose the cactus wren as its state bird. This small brown bird builds its nest in cacti. The spines of the cactus protect the baby birds from enemies. New Mexico's state bird is the roadrunner. A roadrunner runs along on the ground more often than it flies. It can run at speeds of fifteen to twenty miles per hour, faster than many humans can run. The roadrunner is not picky about its food and will eat insects, rodents, rattlesnakes, or even eggs.

armadillo

The Southwest has a wide variety of insects. Some of its most unusual are the colorful beetles, moths, and butterflies. Scorpions are commonly found in the deserts of the Southwest. Scorpions move quickly, and some are poisonous. Their stings can be quite painful. One of the largest spiders in the United States is found in Texas and Arizona. The tarantula is a dark, hairy spider that can have a leg span of up to five inches. However, its sting is mild like a bee sting, and it is not likely to attack. Some people keep tarantulas as pets.

roadrunner

scorpion

Name some flora and fauna God has specially designed to live in the desert.

State Trees, Flowers, and Birds of the Southwest

	Tree	Flower	Bird
Arizona	palo verde	saguaro cactus blossom	cactus wren
New Mexico	piñon pine	yucca flower	roadrunner
Oklahoma	redbud	Oklahoma rose	scissor-tailed flycatcher
Texas	pecan	bluebonnet	northern mockingbird

The Nature of the Place

The Southwestern climate varies from place to place. The desert areas are hot with little rainfall. Two major deserts cover portions of Arizona, New Mexico, and Texas. They are the Sonoran and the Chihuahuan Deserts.

Arizona and New Mexico contain mountains, rivers, and canyons. A portion of the Rocky Mountains extends into northern New Mexico. The climate in the mountains can be cool even in summer. Snow falls there in winter. The Colorado River flows down from the north into Arizona and through the Grand Canyon. Rivers in this part of Arizona are an important natural resource. Their water is used to **irrigate** the land for crops. Arizona has other important resources in copper and timber. New Mexico is rich in mineral resources, like uranium, salts, and coal.

Texas borders the Gulf of Mexico. Parts of Texas and Oklahoma are humid because of the warm, moist air from the gulf. Texas is the only Southwestern state with a coast. Unlike the other three states, Texas sometimes experiences hurricanes and tropical storms.

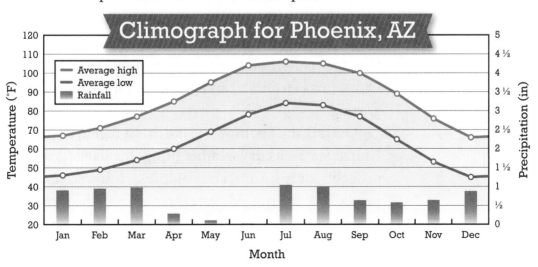

Climograph for Phoenix, AZ

Most of central Texas is made up of plains. Plenty of rivers keep this area well watered. This land is a rich source of soil for farming. In east Texas is a large area called the Piney Woods. Many pines and other hardwood trees make this place a good source of wood. Texas also has resources in oil and natural gas.

The Piney Woods cover 54,400 square miles. It took many men and horses to cut and haul the logs.

Much of Oklahoma lies in the plains. The climate is usually hot in summer, but it is milder in winter than many states farther north. In the spring Oklahoma often experiences tornadoes. The state is shaped like a cooking pan with a long handle. The long, thin portion of the state is called the Panhandle. This part of the state is the highest in elevation. It is usually cooler than the other parts. Some important natural resources are Oklahoma's fertile soil and grassland for farming and grazing.

Overall, the Southwest is the driest region in the United States. Its dry weather brings the dangers of droughts, dust storms, and wildfires. However, many people love the rugged desert scenery and the warm, dry climate.

Resources and Products of the Southwest

KEY

Cattle	Grain	Salts
Coal	Harbor	Trees
Copper	Hogs	Uranium
Corn	Natural gas	
Fruits	Oil	

How is the climate of the Southwest different from that of the other regions?

Oil fields like this one in Saratoga, Texas, in 1908, are areas with many oil wells that bring up petroleum from below the ground.

Today, a pump jack is used to pump oil out of the ground when the pressure is too low for the oil to flow to the surface.

Making a Living

Many different industries bring income into the Southwest. A major industry in all four states is agriculture. Beef cattle are the top livestock product of this region. Grain, wheat, hay, cotton, lettuce, cabbage, peanuts, and pecans are important crops. Texas also has a fishing industry. Shrimp, flounder, and drum are some of the most common fish resources.

Mining is another large industry in the Southwest. Several different metals are mined in the region. One of the most important metals is copper. Copper is often used in wiring and pipes. Arizona is the leading producer of copper in the United States. Oil and natural gas are also important mining industries. In the early 1900s, Texas had several major oil discoveries. An oil boom began. Texas began to make money from the oil business, and people rushed to Texas hoping to become rich. Before long, the state was dotted with oil wells. Texas still leads the nation in oil and natural gas production.

In the cities of the Southwest, a major industry is manufacturing. Factories make computer parts and electronic equipment. Oklahoma produces equipment for air and space travel. Many people of the Southwest work in service industries. In New Mexico, one out of every four jobs is for the federal government.

Another major Southwest industry is tourism. Visitors come from all over the world to see the Grand Canyon in northwestern Arizona. The Grand Canyon is more than 250 miles long. It is about eighteen miles wide at its widest point. Parts of the canyon are more than a mile deep. The canyon was formed as a result of the Flood. Some people come simply to stroll along the canyon rim. They take photos and admire the beauty. Other tourists enjoy hiking, boating, and rafting in the canyon.

Arizona's Painted Desert and Petrified Forest are also popular with tourists. People can drive through the Painted Desert and look out over colorful rocks. Mesas and buttes fill the landscape. A **mesa** is a hill with a flat top. A **butte** is a small hill with steep sides. The Petrified Forest has many fossils of fallen trees. It also has **petroglyphs**, or rock carvings. Scholars believe most of these petroglyphs were carved by the Ancestral Pueblos. Some petroglyphs are more than 1,000 years old.

The Colorado River flows through the Grand Canyon (left). The Painted Desert, located in Arizona, features layers of siltstone, mudstone, and shale, which provide many colors for this area (right).

Tourism is important in New Mexico as well. Tourists come to see the White Sands National Monument. This huge stretch of gypsum sand forms unusual white dunes. Nearby is a military range where the US Army tests missiles and rockets. Tourists also visit Carlsbad Caverns. Evening visitors can watch thousands of bats leave the cave to hunt for food.

Tourism brings money into a region from places outside. Tourism helps support hotels, restaurants, stores, museums, and national parks. Tourism also encourages people in a region to care for their natural resources.

The Tourism Industry

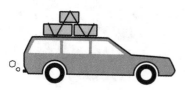

Tourists travel to see new and interesting things.

Tourists need places to eat and sleep while they travel.

Tourist sites have museums and shops to buy souvenirs.

Tourism provides jobs for many people.

What places of interest draw tourists to the Southwest?

Cities and Sites

Four of America's ten largest cities are located in the Southwest. Three of them are found in the region's largest state, Texas. But all four states contain important cities with a wide variety of interesting sites. This section will take a closer look at one city from each state.

Houston, Texas

The largest city in the Southwest is Houston, Texas. It is the fourth-largest city in the nation. Named after Sam Houston, the city is located near Galveston Bay. The bay empties into the Gulf of Mexico. Houston is one of the largest ports in the world. It handles more foreign shipping than any other port in America. Houston is also a leading center of oil and gas production in the United States.

Houston is the home of the Johnson Space Center. Visitors to the center can learn about NASA's space program. They can even experience what zero gravity feels like in space.

San Antonio and Dallas, two other major cities in Texas, are among the top ten US cities in population.

An Apollo Saturn V launch vehicle on display at the Johnson Space Center in Houston, Texas

Phoenix, Arizona

Phoenix is the capital of Arizona. It is America's sixth-largest city. Located on the Gila River, Phoenix was once part of the land where Hohokam Indians lived. This warm, sunny desert area is often called the Valley of the Sun. Little rain falls there. The Hohokam people learned how to direct river water into canals. These canals flowed through the valley and watered the people's crops. Over the years, the well-watered land drew a large population to the area.

The Phoenix Mountains frame the skyline in Phoenix, Arizona.

Modern Phoenix was first settled by pioneers in the late 1800s. Today it is both a manufacturing center and a tourist spot. Aircraft equipment, electronics, and leather goods are a few of its products. Tourists enjoy hiking and biking in the nearby mountains. Phoenix also has several art galleries and museums. Many retired people make Phoenix their home. Its warm, dry climate can be good for their health.

Oklahoma City, Oklahoma

Oklahoma City is the largest city in Oklahoma. Located in the center of the state, the city was formed during the Land Rush of 1889. Ten thousand new settlers staked their claims in what is now the state capital. Today Oklahoma City is important in oil production, food processing, and manufacturing. It is known as the Horse Show Capital of the World. A number of major horse shows are held there each year.

Tragedy came to Oklahoma City in 1995. Men who wanted to show their hatred for the government blew up a federal building with explosives. Today the Oklahoma City National Memorial stands where the building once stood. The memorial is a reminder of those who lost their lives. The memorial includes a quiet pool and a field of empty chairs. It also has a sidewalk where children can draw with chalk.

SkyDance Bridge is a famous landmark of this century. The bridge was completed in 2012. The sculpture on the bridge is shaped like Oklahoma's state bird, the scissor-tailed flycatcher. The bridge is lighted with different colors at night.

SkyDance Bridge in Oklahoma City, Oklahoma, is a 380-foot-long pedestrian bridge that welcomes visitors downtown.

Santa Fe, New Mexico

Santa Fe is the capital of New Mexico. But it was a capital city long before it belonged to the United States. New Mexico was once a province of Spain. Santa Fe became the capital of this Spanish province in 1610. The city has been through several revolts during its long history. It has belonged to the Pueblo Indians, the Spanish, the Mexicans, and finally to the Americans.

Santa Fe today holds many reminders of its history. Pueblo-style buildings and Spanish architecture reflect the different people groups who have lived there. Museums help keep its rich heritage alive for visitors.

A typical adobe building in Santa Fe, New Mexico, can withstand summer rains and winter snows.

The Hoover Dam is located in Black Canyon on the border between Arizona and Nevada.

Other Sites in the Southwest

On the border between Arizona and Nevada is the Hoover Dam. The dam was built during the Great Depression. Builders took five years to finish it. The dam's purpose was to put the water of the Colorado River to use. Hoover Dam provides water to irrigate dry land areas. It also supplies power and controls flooding. It is a National Historic Landmark today.

The highest point in the Southwest is Wheeler Peak in New Mexico. The peak is part of the Sangre de Cristo mountain range. At 13,167 feet, Wheeler Peak is a popular mountain for hikers to climb.

The Southwest has a large number of Indian reservations. Most of these reservations are in Arizona and New Mexico. Many Indians in these areas still create native art such as baskets, pottery, and turquoise jewelry. The Southwest is an excellent place to find Native American arts and crafts for sale.

Which city in the Southwest would you most like to visit?

Of the People, By the People, For the People

The Southwest includes only four states. But these four states are some of the nation's largest in land area. Texas is second largest in land area behind Alaska. Texas is also second largest in population behind California.

However, Arizona, Oklahoma, and New Mexico have smaller populations for states their size. Many states with less land have larger, denser populations. But the people living in these three states are spread out. A large portion of these states is desert or farmland. States like this often have fewer people than states with many big cities and towns.

The main language of the Southwest region is English. But many of its people also speak Spanish. The Southwest has more Spanish-speaking people than any other US region. Many immigrants settle there. Some Spanish-speaking people have come from Mexico or another Latin American country. Others have been born into Spanish-speaking communities in the United States. Many families speak only Spanish in their homes. Children of these families often learn English quickly. They understand more and more as they talk, play, and go to school with English-speaking children. Some public schools in the Southwest have special programs that allow students to learn in Spanish.

Six of the top ten Spanish-speaking US cities are in the Southwest.

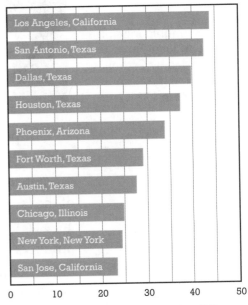

Spanish-speaking population (%)

People of the Southwest do not all agree on politics. Oklahoma is the strongest "red state" in the region. Oklahoma has voted for a Republican for president in nearly every election of the last fifty years. However, Texas, Arizona, and New Mexico are more divided. New Mexico tends to be the most Democratic state of the four.

San Antonio Mission in San Juan, Texas, was founded by Catholics to serve the Nasoni Indians in 1731.

The people of the Southwest have various religious beliefs. The influence of the early Spanish Catholic missionaries is still strong. Roman Catholics are one of the largest religious groups in this region. There are also many Protestant Christians. Texas has large numbers of Muslims and Jews. Another religious group in the Southwest is the Church of Jesus Christ of Latter-day Saints. These people are also known as Mormons. Mormon leader Brigham Young led his followers to Utah in the 1840s. From there the Mormons spread out into several states in the West and Southwest. This area is known as the Mormon Corridor. Much of Arizona is part of this area.

The Southwest has some solid Bible-preaching churches. But these churches are often small. In some areas, believers must drive many miles to go to church. Christians in the Southwest can help each other grow by faithfully attending good churches.

Christians can also reach out to others around them with the good news of Jesus Christ. Some Christians have found a unique way to do this while taking advantage of the beautiful scenery. They have started Christian camps in the Southwest. Children, teens, and adults can visit these camps and enjoy nature and outdoor sports. They can also have a quiet, beautiful place to learn more about God and His Son, Jesus Christ.

If you live in the Southwest, you live in a region God has greatly blessed. It has colorful beauty and interesting landscapes. It has a unique history and many different kinds of people. You can thank God for putting you there. And you can serve Him where you live.

What is a common second language in the Southwest?

16 The Rocky Mountain States

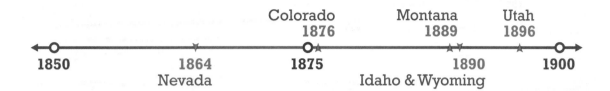

The Rocky Mountains are a major mountain range in the western United States. Six states form the region through which these mountains spread. The Rocky Mountain states are known for their great natural beauty. The mountains have inspired many artists and nature photographers. Every year the region's beauty attracts thousands of visitors.

Shaped by Its Past

The first people to live in the Rocky Mountain region were American Indians. Different Indian groups left behind information about their lives. The Pueblo Indians built their homes of clay on the mountain ledges. They lived in Colorado and nearby states. The Ute Indians gave their name to the state of Utah. The Ute, Shoshone, and Paiute Indians did not live in pueblo houses. They were nomads. **Nomads** move from place to place without setting up permanent homes. The region where these Indians roamed was hot and dry. They had to keep moving to find fresh pasture for their animals.

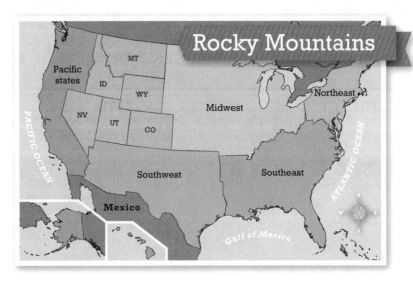

Rocky Mountains

Europeans began to explore this region in the 1700s. The Spanish were the first European explorers to arrive. In 1776 the Spanish investigated what is now Utah and Nevada. In this same year the American colonists wrote the Declaration of Independence.

In 1803 parts of Colorado, Wyoming, and Montana became the property of the United States. This area was called the Louisiana Purchase. Lewis and Clark were the first to explore this land for the United States.

Sacagawea traveled thousands of miles from her home in North Dakota to guide and interpret for the Lewis and Clark expedition to the Pacific Ocean.

Other Americans followed Lewis and Clark. Fur traders soon began to work in this region. Traders and other explorers looked for easier ways to get across the Rocky Mountains. The mountain temperatures grow colder as a person climbs higher. The route that Lewis and Clark took would be too hard for families traveling in wagons. If people were going to travel from the East all the way out to California or Oregon, they needed to find an easier way through the mountains. In 1812 a group of fur traders found the South Pass in Wyoming. A **pass** is a gap between two mountains. Pioneers could now travel to Oregon and California in wagon trains.

Painting by Francis Seth Frost of the Wind River Mountains and the South Pass. Many explorers and pioneers traveled through the South Pass to reach Oregon and California.

Idaho and parts of Montana and Wyoming became US territories in 1846. The lands of Utah and Nevada became territories in 1848. Around this same time Brigham Young led the Mormons across the West to live in Utah.

Throughout the 1800s Americans continued to move to these territories. Before the Civil War, gold and silver were found in Colorado and Nevada. This wealth brought many **prospectors**. By the time the Civil War ended, a railroad crossed the Rocky Mountain region. Americans could now move west on the railroad.

The moving of Americans onto Indian lands brought disagreement. The most famous fight was the Battle of the Little Bighorn. This battlefield is located in Montana. The conflicts with the Indians lasted into the 1890s.

"Custer's Last Stand" at the Battle of the Little Bighorn took place between northern Indian tribes and the United States Cavalry.

Most of the states in the Rocky Mountain region joined the Union in the years between 1889 and 1896. Nevada and Colorado, however, joined earlier. Nevada became a state in 1864, and Colorado joined in 1876.

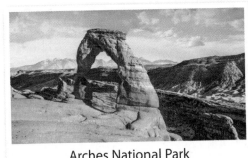
Arches National Park

Many national parks have been created to protect the natural beauty of this region. The first were formed in the years around 1900. Today much of the land in the West is still owned by the government. Few people live on land reserved for national parks. For this reason some Rocky Mountain states, like Wyoming, have small populations. The populations of others, such as Colorado, are large and growing.

Death Valley National Park

Grand Teton National Park

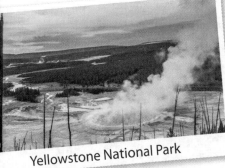
Yellowstone National Park

Sand Dunes National Park

Why did the Ute, Shoshone, and Paiute Indians become nomads?

All Things Bright and Beautiful

The Rocky Mountain region is home to many kinds of trees, plants, and flowers. The most common tree in the mountains is the pine. Several different types of pine and spruce grow there. These trees keep the mountains looking green throughout the year. In the winter they make beautiful scenery when covered with snow. The Nevada state tree is the bristlecone pine. This tree is the longest-living kind of tree in the United States. Some bristlecone pines are thought to be thousands of years old. Other kinds of trees, like the cottonwood and the aspen, add color to the mountainsides, especially in the fall.

Certain types of flowers grow well in the cool mountain climate. The columbine is the Colorado state flower. The most common color is blue with a white center. Another flower often seen in the mountains is the Indian paintbrush. The most common type has the appearance of an artist's brush that has been dipped in paint. The colors of these flowers range from yellow orange to crimson red.

The Rocky Mountain states are filled with many animals. Some large animals live in the mountains like the mountain lion, the black bear, and the grizzly bear. You might also see a bighorn sheep or a pronghorn antelope. Other animals stay more to the flatlands, such as elk, moose, and wolves. Many mule deer also live in these states. Smaller animals abound as well. Jackrabbits, cottontail rabbits, raccoons, foxes, chipmunks, and pika all live in this region. Reptiles to watch out for include the poisonous rattlesnake and the Gila monster. The rivers are full of salmon, trout, and bass.

A wide variety of birds also lives in this area. These may include turkeys, grouse, quail, pheasants, and hummingbirds. More common birds like ducks and mourning doves are also found here. You might even see a majestic bald eagle or a great horned owl. In Utah, seagulls arrive from California every spring and summer.

Which of these animals would you like to learn more about?

State Trees, Flowers, and Birds of the Southwest			
	Tree	Flower	Bird
Wyoming	cottonwood	Indian paintbrush	western meadowlark
Montana	ponderosa pine	bitterroot	
Colorado	Colorado blue spruce	columbine	lark bunting
Utah	quaking aspen	sego lily	California gull
Idaho	western white pine	syringa	mountain bluebird
Nevada	bristlecone pine	sagebrush	

The Nature of the Place

The Rocky Mountain states are named after their most prominent feature: the Rocky Mountains. They are some of the tallest mountains in North America. They are much bigger than the Appalachian Mountains in the eastern United States. Often the Rocky Mountains will have snow on their peaks all year long. Many are so tall and cold that trees cannot grow at the top. The area where no trees grow is called **tundra**. In the tundra only small shrubs, mosses, and grasses grow.

The Rocky Mountain states are not made up of only mountains. To the east of the Rocky Mountains are the Great Plains. These are wide-open flatlands. The eastern parts of Colorado, Wyoming, and Montana are part of the Great Plains. To the west of the Rocky Mountains is a flat area called the Great Basin. The Great Basin is in Nevada and western Utah.

tundra

the Great Plains

the Great Basin

The western **Continental Divide** runs through the Rocky Mountains. On the eastern side of the divide, water flows toward the Mississippi River. On the western side, water flows toward the Pacific Ocean, but not all of it will reach the ocean. The Great Basin gets its name because the water that flows into it never reaches the Pacific. The water either stays in lakes, evaporates, or soaks into the ground. The Great Salt Lake is the largest lake in the Great Basin. It is the largest saltwater lake in North and South America. The climate in the Great Basin is **arid**. That means it is very dry.

The western sides of the Rocky Mountains receive more rain than the eastern sides. Warm, moist air is blocked by the mountains, causing more rain on the western side of the mountains. This rain usually falls before the air crosses the top of the mountain. Therefore, the eastern sides of the mountain are very dry. They are in what is called a **rain shadow**. The Great Plains in the east usually receive their rain from the warm, moist air in the south.

The southern parts of Nevada, Utah, and Colorado can be very hot in the summer. The northern parts of these states along with Wyoming, Montana, and Idaho can be very cold in the winter. They will receive snow. The higher up in the mountains you go, the colder it is. The valley is much warmer.

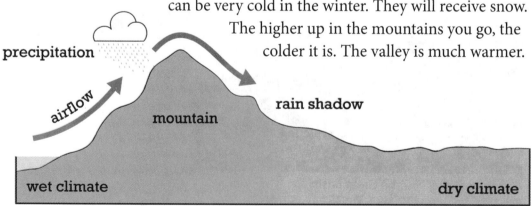

precipitation

airflow

mountain

rain shadow

wet climate

dry climate

A person could go swimming on a hot summer day in the valley and then drive up the mountain for a snowball fight.

The land itself is one of the most important natural resources in these states. The flatlands of Montana and Wyoming support herds of cattle and sheep. And the flatlands in Colorado and Montana have good soil for growing crops such as wheat. Even the natural beauty of the West is a resource to be preserved.

The trees that grow on the mountainsides are also natural resources. They can be used for lumber. Gold, silver, copper, lead, and iron are mined from under the mountains. These minerals drew men to the states over a hundred years ago. Oil and natural gas are other resources found in the Rocky Mountain states.

Water is an important natural resource in the West because many locations lack water. But several major rivers do flow through these states. The Missouri and the Colorado Rivers are the most important water sources. Rivers provide food through fishing. They can also be used to create electricity.

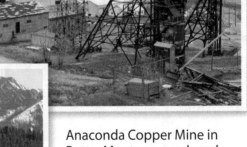

Anaconda Copper Mine in Butte, Montana, produced 94,900 tons of copper between 1881 and 1947 (top).

Cattle ranch in the Rocky Mountain region (left)

Resources and Products of the Rocky Mountain States

Washington

Columbia R.

Oregon

Idaho

Montana

Missouri R.

North Dakota

South Dakota

Wyoming

Snake R.

Nevada

Great Salt Lake

Nebraska

Platte R.

California

Utah

Colorado

Colorado R.

Kansas

Arkansas R.

KEY

Cattle	Gold	Natural gas	Silver
Coal	Grain	Oil	Sugar beets
Copper	Iron ore	Potatoes	Trees
Fish	Lead	Sheep	

What is a tundra?

Making a Living

Natural resources provide an important foundation for jobs in many of these states. Jobs in Idaho are centered on the land. Farming provides most of the jobs. Potatoes, wheat, and sugar beets are the most important crops raised there. The timber industry is also important for Idaho. This industry cuts down trees and makes them into boards, paper, and other products.

Jobs in Montana are also centered on the land. Many people grow wheat, barley, hay, and sugar beets. Many others work as cattle ranchers. Some work in the mines, and still others work as **lumberjacks**. Tourism also provides jobs as more people come to Montana to see its natural beauty.

The Timber Industry

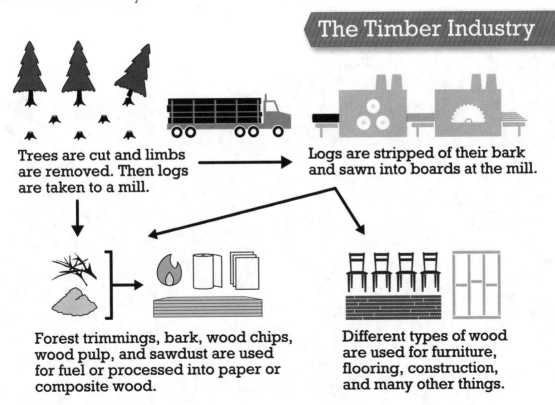

Trees are cut and limbs are removed. Then logs are taken to a mill.

Logs are stripped of their bark and sawn into boards at the mill.

Forest trimmings, bark, wood chips, wood pulp, and sawdust are used for fuel or processed into paper or composite wood.

Different types of wood are used for furniture, flooring, construction, and many other things.

Life in Wyoming is similar to that in Montana. Cattle ranching is the biggest business in Wyoming. Because this is cowboy country, people come to see rodeos. This state has large coal mines and oil and natural-gas drills. Hunting and fishing opportunities as well as Yellowstone National Park attract visitors to the state.

Many people in Colorado work in ranching and mining as well. Tourism is also a major industry in this state. Pikes Peak is a famous mountain that tourists often visit. Many people come to hike, climb, ski, and bike in the Rocky Mountains. White-water rafting and trout fishing in mountain streams are also popular activities. Some people try to climb one of the many fourteeners in Colorado. Mountains that are over fourteen thousand feet tall are called fourteeners.

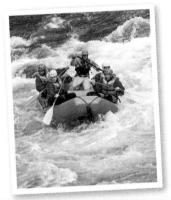

White-water rafting in Colorado

Since many people today are moving to live in Colorado, real estate is an important job. Real estate agents help people buy and sell land and houses. Colorado also manufactures goods such as scientific instruments and processes foods. Jobs in communications and medicine are also important for Colorado's economy.

Utah and Nevada are drier states where there is some farming and ranching. But service industries, such as banking, are more important. In Nevada, printing books and making food are important businesses. Sadly, gambling also provides work for many in Nevada.

Fly-fishing in the Rocky Mountains

Pikes Peak

What is the biggest business in Wyoming?

Cities and Sites

The Rocky Mountain states are not known for their cities. In some states even the capital cities are not large when compared to other US cities. This is true of Helena, Montana; Cheyenne, Wyoming; and Boise, Idaho. Still, cities play an important role in every state. Three cities stand out in the Rocky Mountain states—Denver, Las Vegas, and Salt Lake City.

The United States Mint in Denver, Colorado, manufactures more than fifty million coins a day.

Coins made in Denver are stamped with a small "D" to mark where they came from.

Denver, Colorado

Denver sits northeast of the center of Colorado. It is called the Mile High City. A mile is 5,280 feet long, and Denver is about that many feet above sea level. Important cities, such as Denver, are built next to rivers or by ocean ports.

Denver began as a mining town during gold-mining days. In the early 1900s the United States built a mint in Denver. This mint still makes coins. Coins produced in the Denver Mint have a small *D* stamped on them.

Today Denver is the largest city in the Rocky Mountain states. Denver serves as a transportation hub in the West. It is home to an important airport. Its location provides a tie between the cities of the West and the Midwest. Its place in the **Mountain Standard Time Zone** helps certain businesses. Some companies work in both the Pacific Standard Time Zone and the Central Standard Time Zone. Denver is in the middle, making communication between the time zones easier.

Las Vegas, Nevada

Las Vegas has a sad nickname. It is called Sin City. Las Vegas was originally a normal western town built near a fort and a railroad. Today it is a big city because of the many casinos there. A casino is a place for gambling. In the past, reformers had pressed the states to pass laws that would stop gambling. Nevada was one state that permitted it. The reformers wanted to ban gambling because it hurts people. Often money that should be used to support a family is lost. Casinos often attract criminals. Other sins, like drunkenness, usually go along with gambling.

The Bible tells us to look out for other people's good and not just our own. Because of this command, Christians oppose gambling. The gambler does not act in love toward his neighbor. He tries to take money from his neighbor. But the leaders of Las Vegas refuse to stop the gambling. They like the money that casinos bring to the city.

A landmark sign welcomes visitors

Salt Lake City is the capital of Utah. The Wasatch Mountain Range provides a beautiful backdrop for the city.

Salt Lake City, Utah

Salt Lake City is the largest city in Utah. It was founded by the Mormons in 1847. In the eastern United States, the Mormons had trouble wherever they went. They claimed that all churches were false except their own. They also claimed that God had spoken to their leaders and added more to the Bible. There were reports that Mormons were going to marry more than one wife at the same time. These things made many Americans uneasy and led to violent arguments. After the Mormon leader Joseph Smith was killed, Brigham Young led the Mormons west. They settled down to live in Salt Lake City. At the center of the city, they built a large temple, and the streets of the city spread out from it.

The Mormons wanted to get away from other Americans. But the transcontinental railroad was built near Salt Lake City. The westward movement of American people kept the Mormons from getting away by themselves. Salt Lake City remains the center of Mormonism, but many other kinds of people now live there as well.

Where in the Rocky Mountain states would you like to live?

Of the People, By the People, For the People

Many people have lived in the Rocky Mountain states over the years. Nomadic Indians roamed the Great Basin. Cliff dwellers built impressive cities in the mountain clefts, or tiny openings in the cliffs. Today many American Indians live in these states. Montana especially has a large population of American Indians.

Farmers and ranchers moved west over one hundred years ago. They also remain an important part of Western life to this day. The Mormons have a significant influence on states such as Utah and Idaho. In some parts of those states, the Mormons make up the majority of the population. Some parts of the Rocky Mountain states still have an old-frontier feel to them. Other parts are modern cities with people from all over.

Anasazi Ruins where ancient Pueblo people lived. These cliff dwellings were designed so entry ladders could be lifted during enemy attacks.

The people who settled in the Rocky Mountain states shaped its culture. People who live here tend to like outdoor activities such as hiking and skiing. There is also an independent streak in many people. They are used to relying on themselves. In the recent past these states have tended to vote Republican. Colorado and Nevada, however, have become more likely to vote for the Democratic Party. These shifts may reflect the changes in population. Many people continue to move west from other parts of the country.

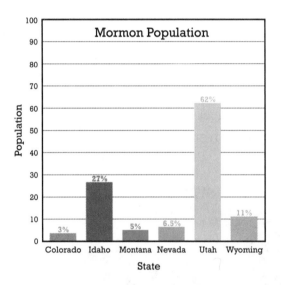

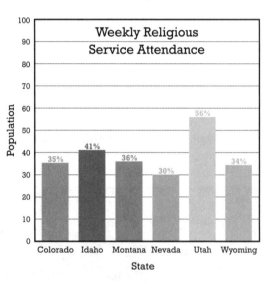

There are many different views of religion in the Rocky Mountain states. Fewer people attend any kind of religious services in Nevada and Wyoming from week to week than in many other states. Utah and Idaho are states with large Mormon populations. They have higher rates of attendance at religious services, while Nevada is in the bottom five. Colorado and Montana fall in the middle.

These facts give the Christian something to think about. These states need a Christian witness. In some of these states, people do not want much to do with religion. But they need to hear about their need for a Savior from sin. In other states the people are very religious. But many are worshipping false gods. They need Christians to tell them the good news about Jesus. Jesus died to save people from their sins and rose again so people can have peace with God.

Salt Lake Temple is the largest Latter Day Saints church and is located in Utah.

Starting churches in the Rocky Mountain states is hard. Mormons are often very committed to remaining Mormons. Also, people in these states sometimes live great distances apart. Like the churches in the Southwest, churches here are often small. But even now there are Christians starting churches in these states. Maybe one day you can go and help them.

Small Christian church in Brighton, Colorado

What shows that there is a great need for a Christian witness in the Rocky Mountain states?

17 The Pacific States

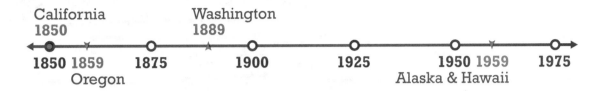

California
1850

Washington
1889

1850 1859   1875   1900   1925   1950 1959   1975
      Oregon   Alaska & Hawaii

America's westernmost states represent much diversity in history, landscape, and people. Three of these states are in the continental United States. Two other states in the Pacific region are farther away. Alaska and Hawaii are separated from the other forty-eight states on the continent. Hawaii is made up of islands. These five states all border or lie in the Pacific Ocean.

Shaped by Its Past

Spanish explorers came to California, Oregon, and Washington in the 1500s. These men met many Native American tribes. Many different tribes lived in California. Two were the Pomo and the Chumash. Many tribes lived in the western areas of the Pacific region. These included the Coast Salish, the Klamath, and the Nuu-chah-nulth, or Nootka.

Immigrants also helped shape California's history. The Spanish settled in parts of California, but they did not move into the northwestern area of the Pacific region. Spanish priests built many missions. As in the Southwest region, the priests wanted to convert the Native Americans to Catholicism. Today many of

Pacific States

California's cities and towns have Spanish names. These names often reflect the Catholic beliefs of the Spanish. During the 1900s people came to California from Asia and Latin America. They have added to the cultural changes brought by other immigrants.

Few Europeans moved to the northwestern Pacific region upon its discovery. Eventually French fur traders came from eastern North America. Then British traders arrived. In the early 1800s, fur companies set up permanent posts in this region. Soon after, missionaries from the United States moved west. They wanted to share the gospel with the native peoples.

During the mid-1800s all three of these states joined the United States. In 1846 the United Kingdom agreed that Oregon and Washington should be part of the United States. Then Mexico lost the Mexican War. In 1848 it had to agree to sell California. California became a state in 1850. Oregon joined in 1859, and Washington joined in 1889.

Europeans learned of Alaska and Hawaii later than they did these three. The first people to live in Hawaii were Polynesians. They traveled by boat across the Pacific. These first Hawaiians arrived between AD 300 and 800. Hawaii's volcanic islands were good spots to settle because of the rich soil. The first European to see the islands was James Cook. In 1778 this British captain sailed to the island of Kauai. After learning of the island, Europeans and Americans moved there. During the Spanish-American War, the United States gained Hawaii. It became the fiftieth state in 1959.

Aerial view of Hawaii from a NASA satellite

Alaska's native people came in several waves. The first group traveled through Alaska and settled in other parts of the Americas. Later, other people came whom Europeans called "Eskimo." But they prefer to be called by their own tribal names. In the late 1700s Russians claimed Alaska. The United States bought Alaska after the Civil War. Like Hawaii, Alaska became a state in 1959.

What geographic feature borders the Pacific states?

All Things Bright and Beautiful
Hawaii

Hawaii is known for its unique birds that live on the islands. Most famous is the nene, or Hawaiian goose. The i'iwi, a small red-and-black bird, drinks nectar with its curved bill. Many sea birds such as albatrosses, petrels, and terns visit the islands. These islands are the only land the birds will find for hundreds of miles.

Hawaii is also famous for its wonderful plants. The yellow hibiscus is the state flower. Silversword plants grow even on the high, dry mountains. The large koa tree can be used to make furniture, surfboards, canoes, and musical instruments.

Not all of Hawaii's plants and animals are native to the islands. The beautiful plumeria was brought to Hawaii in the mid-1800s. Its blooms are made into necklaces called leis, which are sold to tourists. Some other things brought to the islands were not as beneficial. Early settlers brought pigs that often destroyed native plants.

i'iwi

plumeria

silversword

koa

Alaska

Alaska is famous for its birds, bears, and fish. Many bald eagles nest in Alaska. They often eat the salmon and trout in Alaska's rivers. Massive Kodiak bears, a type of brown bear, enjoy the fish as well. In the polar regions, Alaskan animals adapt to the cold. Polar bears, arctic hares, arctic foxes, and caribou thrive in the cold. Alaska has many sea creatures. Fur seals, whales, and walruses can be found on the Alaskan coast.

Just like the animals, Alaska's plants thrive in cold and wet areas. The warmer areas have heavy forests. Sitka spruces and other evergreen trees fill the woods. There are also deciduous trees such as birches. Farther north fewer plants grow. The tiny arctic willow grows close to the ground and provides food for animals of the tundra.

bald eagle

arctic willow

arctic fox

walruses

Pacific Northwest: Washington and Oregon

Washington and Oregon share similar plants and animals. The dry eastern part of both states has grass, scrublands, and some forests. Pines, spruces, and quaking aspen fill the forests. The forests support wildflowers and many animals. Brown bears catch the fish swimming to the ocean. Deer, moose, elk, bears, and coyotes live in this part of the region.

California

California has many plants and animals. Perhaps it is most famous for its gigantic redwood and sequoia trees. The tallest of these is almost 380 feet high. It would tower over the Statue of Liberty! In the redwood forests live many animals. The banana slug is usually a mustard-yellow color. It can grow up to seven inches long. These slugs eat whatever falls to the forest floor. This process is like an organic recycling plant.

California's varied climate supports many different species. Along the coast California has killer whales, seals, and sea otters. The deserts have Joshua trees and cacti. California also has mountain goats in its high eastern mountains.

brown bear

Joshua tree

redwood

banana slug

Why do you think Hawaii has such unique plants and animals?

State Trees, Flowers, and Birds of the Pacific States

	Tree	Flower	Bird
California	coast redwood and sequoia	California poppy	California Valley quail
Washington	western hemlock	coast rhododendron	willow goldfinch
Oregon	Douglas fir	Oregon grape	western meadowlark
Alaska	Sitka spruce	forget-me-not	willow ptarmigan
Hawaii	kukui	yellow hibiscus	nene

The Nature of the Place
Physical Geography

The five Pacific states have some of the most striking geography in the United States. Each state has high mountains, productive valleys, and beautiful coastlines. Although all the states share landforms, each has distinct features.

Hawaii is famous for its volcanoes and beaches. All eight main Hawaiian islands were once live volcanoes. Now most are either **dormant** or nonexistent. Kilauea and Mauna Loa are both active. Fortunately for Hawaiians, their volcanoes are **shield volcanoes**. This type of volcano rarely erupts violently. Instead, it produces runny lava. This lava flows slowly, giving people time to escape danger. Hawaii also has peaceful spots of natural beauty. Its beaches attract many visitors. One beach even has olive-green sand.

Kilauea volcano is one of the most active volcanoes in the world and has been erupting since 1983.

Mendenhall Glacier in Alaska is about twelve miles long but is receding and forming Mendenhall Lake.

Alaska's natural beauty offers much variety. The highest mountain in North America is **Mount McKinley**. It stands nearly four miles high. Many **glaciers** flow in Alaska. Glaciers are rivers of ice. Other rivers cut through the land and provide homes for fish. Alaska has two major chains of islands, or **archipelagos**. These are in its southwest and southeast. This combination of mountains, rivers, and islands makes Alaska stand out compared to other states.

Oregon and Washington share similar landscapes. Their eastern regions are dry. In the west, two ranges of mountains run through the states. Many people live in river valleys between the Coastal Range and the Cascades. Between the two states, the Columbia River flows to the ocean. The Puget Sound sits in northwest Washington. This inlet of the Pacific Ocean gives people a place to fish and sail.

California's geography creates climate extremes. California has many mountains. The Coastal Range and the inland Sierra Nevada are the most important. Between them lies the huge Central Valley where many Californians live. In the state's east, Death Valley has record-setting heat. California also has beautiful beaches such as in Malibu and Monterey.

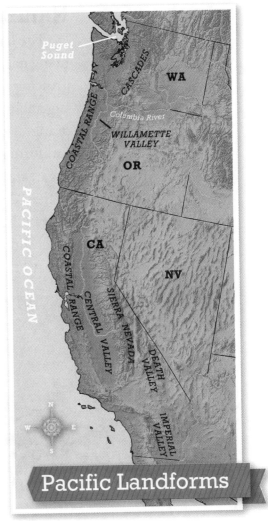

Pacific Landforms

Natural Resources

The lands and waters of the Pacific states provide many natural resources. California enjoys a long growing season and is able to produce fruits and vegetables for the United States. Many of the nation's oranges, grapes, lettuce, tomatoes, and nuts come from California. Some of Hawaii's main crops are pineapples, sugar, and coffee. Washington and Oregon grow grain in their dry eastern parts. They also have apple and pear orchards. Alaska has a limited growing season due to its climate. However, Alaska does produce oil and gas. All these states have good fishing grounds as well.

Gold-processing plant in Bodie, California, where "stamp mills" crushed rock to powder, leaving behind gold and silver (left).

The mild weather and volcanic soil on Big Island, Hawaii, allow coffee trees to grow well (right).

These states also produce other resources. The Pacific region's northwest is known for forests. Gold rushes occurred in both California and Alaska in the 1800s. Now Alaska produces much black gold, or oil.

All five Pacific states enjoy the resource of great natural beauty. Tourists visit each of these states hoping to experience its special sights. Residents can visit the sights on a daily basis.

Resources and Products of the Pacific States

Washington

Montana

Columbia R.

Oregon

Snake R.

KEY

Apples	Grain	Pineapples
Coffee	Harbor	Sugar
Fish	Natural gas	Trees
Fruits	Oil	Vegetables
Gold	Pears	

ARCTIC OCEAN

Nevada

Hawaii

PACIFIC OCEAN

Alaska

California

PACIFIC OCEAN

Arizona

Colorado R.

PACIFIC OCEAN

What limits agriculture in Alaska?

409

Making a Living
Getting Raw Materials

Agriculture, fishing, logging, and mining provide many jobs in the Pacific states. California in particular has many farming jobs. Some workers travel from California to the northwestern area to harvest various crops at different times of the year.

Making Things

Turning raw materials into a more complete product gives many jobs in the Pacific states. Food processing provides industrial jobs in Hawaii and Alaska. Raw foods are prepared there and are then shipped throughout the United States. All three of the other states produce electronic equipment. Some of the world's largest computer companies are found on the West Coast. Washington State is also famous for its aircraft industry. Both Washington and Oregon have thriving **lumber** industries. These jobs turn trees into useful wood products, such as houses, paper, cardboard, and furniture.

Food Processing

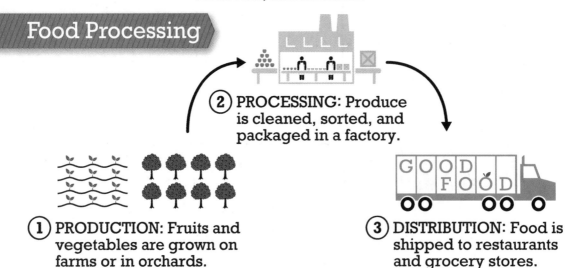

① PRODUCTION: Fruits and vegetables are grown on farms or in orchards.

② PROCESSING: Produce is cleaned, sorted, and packaged in a factory.

③ DISTRIBUTION: Food is shipped to restaurants and grocery stores.

Helping People

Service industries provide the Pacific states with many jobs. Some of these jobs are in education, medicine, and government. Tourism also provides jobs. Hawaii receives millions of visitors each year. Many come from Asia. Alaska also attracts

Many tourists admire Alaska's Hubbard Glacier from a cruise ship.

many tourists. Each summer people take cruises along the state's coastline. Some people visit Alaska to hunt or fish. The Pacific Northwest attracts visitors who enjoy hiking, camping, and boating. Mountains such as Mount Hood and Mount Rainier are popular with tourists. Tourists even hike Mount St. Helens, a volcano in southern Washington. This mountain violently erupted in 1980. California also draws in millions of tourists every year. Many come from foreign countries. The beaches, mountains, valleys, and cities of California are full of things to do.

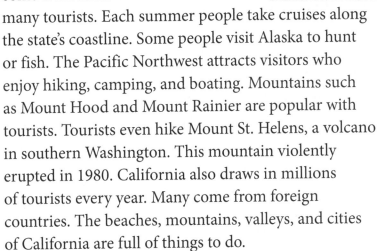

The Golden Gate Bridge is a suspension bridge in California between San Francisco and Marin County.

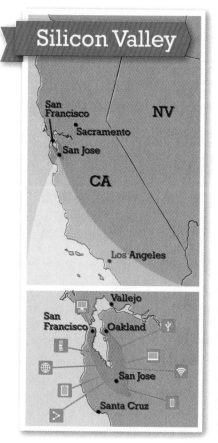

Silicon Valley

Computer design and programming form another important West Coast service industry. These services are sometimes called the **tech industry**. Companies based in California, Oregon, and Washington design computers, tablets, and cell phones used around the world. An area of California called Silicon Valley has companies that write computer programs and apps. Computer engineers and programmers help people around the world.

Many television shows and movies are made in California. The beautiful weather in southern California helped the city of Hollywood to become the center of American moviemaking. Sadly, many television shows and movies present a false picture of life. They show people finding true happiness without knowing Jesus. But not all movies make this mistake. Christians produce movies that show the joy and peace found only in Christ.

The Hollywood sign in Los Angeles, California, on Mount Lee is a landmark that is forty-five feet tall and three hundred and fifty feet long (right).

What major industry do California, Hawaii, and Alaska share?

Cities and Sites

Los Angeles, California

Los Angeles is the country's second-largest city. The city sits in the heart of southern California. It was founded by the Spanish in 1781. Some of its biggest industries are education and the shipping of goods. Tourists like visiting the many museums. The Page Museum displays the bones of saber-toothed cats, dire wolves, and many other animals. They were preserved in the La Brea Tar Pits. For centuries the tar kept these animals from rotting.

Today visitors can explore Hancock Park in Los Angeles, California, where the La Brea Tar Pits are located.

San Francisco, California

San Francisco is midway up the California coast. It is the focus of the cities around the San Francisco Bay. Alcatraz Island, a former prison, sits in the bay. Over 800,000 people live on a hilly peninsula between the bay and the Pacific Ocean. The Golden Gate Bridge connects the city to the rest of the state. San Francisco is known for Chinatown, streetcars, and the Fisherman's Wharf. Despite suffering from several major earthquakes, the city has prospered.

Elevated trams are one of the many modes of transportation in San Francisco, California.

The Hawthorne Bridge in Portland, Oregon, is a lift bridge where a portion of the bridge rises for boats to pass under.

Portland, Oregon

The capital of Oregon has a mild, wet climate. Its nickname is the City of Roses. Portland has a large technology industry. Many sportswear companies also work from Portland. The city sits across the Columbia River from Fort Vancouver. This fort was the center of fur trade on the Pacific coast in the nineteenth century.

Seattle, Washington

Located on a beautiful harbor, Seattle has a mild climate. The Space Needle stands 600 feet high over the city. People enjoy visiting Pikes Place Market and drinking the city's famous coffee. Seattle also has the only major-league baseball and football teams in the American Northwest.

Many tourists enjoy camping in Alaska (left) or visiting the Arizona Memorial at Pearl Harbor in Honolulu, Oahu, Hawaii (below).

Anchorage, Alaska

Alaska's largest city began as a railroad station and port. Many goods still ship through the city's port and its airport. After an earthquake in 1964, the city was rebuilt. Now its inhabitants enjoy many outdoor activities.

Honolulu, Hawaii

Located on the island of Oahu, Hawaii's capital has much for people to see. Waikiki Beach is a popular destination. People can visit the Pearl Harbor Memorial. The beautiful Iolani Palace was the home of Hawaii's last queen. The Bernice Pauahi Bishop Museum exhibits the story of Hawaii's people.

What is the second-largest city in the United States?

Of the People, By the People, For the People

People and Cultures

Americans of many backgrounds live in the Pacific states. Many Hawaiians and Alaskans are descendants of the original occupants. All five states have large populations of people with Asian ancestry. Of course, many Americans of European descent live in these states as well. The Pacific states enjoy a wide variety of people and cultures. This is especially true of California. California's location encourages immigrants from Central America. More than one of every four people there were born outside the United States. This mixture of cultures can remind Americans that their nation is sometimes called a melting pot. Because of its location and resources, more people live in California than in any other American state.

People Groups of the Pacific States

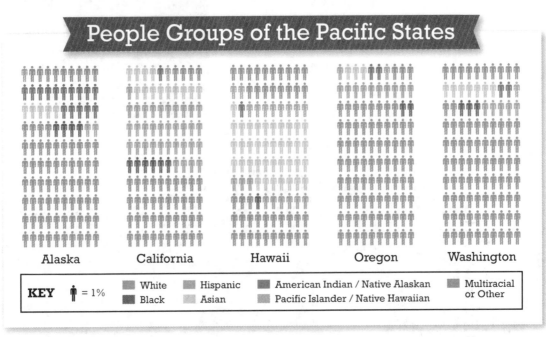

Alaska — California — Hawaii — Oregon — Washington

KEY	♦ = 1%	White	Hispanic	American Indian / Native Alaskan	Multiracial or Other
		Black	Asian	Pacific Islander / Native Hawaiian	

Politics

The Pacific states are more alike in their politics than in their cultures. Most voters normally support the Democratic Party. These voters want the government to make many laws. They hope laws about schools, the environment, and business will improve the world. Alaskans normally vote for Republicans. They often believe that fewer laws are better. Probably the most famous politician from the Pacific states was Ronald Reagan. He was a movie actor in California who liked politics. Eventually he became president of the United States.

Religion

These states have a variety of religious beliefs. Few people regularly attend religious services. Some practice non-Christian religions, such as Hinduism or Buddhism. Many believe that there is no God. However, each state has some churches where God's truth is believed and taught.

Christians in the Pacific states have many opportunities to tell of God's love. Jesus told His disciples to be light in a dark world. People everywhere are looking for truth to believe in. Only the gospel fully satisfies that need. Only by knowing the Creator can anyone truly appreciate the beautiful world of people, land, and sea that is the Pacific states.

What is the greatest need in the Pacific states?

18 Territories

American Samoa
1899

Northern Mariana Islands
1947

1898 1900
Puerto Rico & Guam

1917
US Virgin Islands

1925

1950

Other United States Lands

The United States has other lands in addition to the fifty states. These lands are called **territories**. Territories are like the fifty states in many ways. People who live in territories are United States nationals. In some territories the residents are US citizens at birth. People in all territories enjoy the protection of the US government. Residents of territories can serve in the US military. They can travel back and forth to the states without a passport. They use the US postal system. But territories do not have all the same privileges that a state would have. Their people do not vote in national elections. In Congress, representatives from territories do not have the same voting rights as representatives from states do.

The United States has five main territories. It also has some other islands. Not all these islands have people living on them. This chapter will focus on the territories where people live.

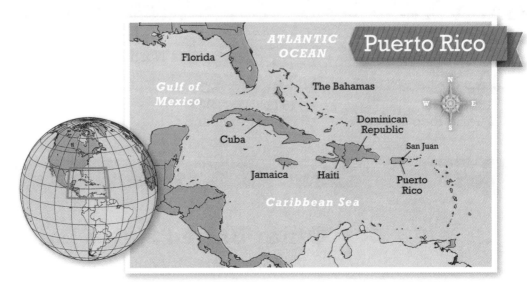

Puerto Rico

Puerto Rico is an island in the Caribbean Sea southeast of Florida. A few smaller islands around the main island are also part of Puerto Rico. The name is Spanish for "rich port." Early Spanish explorers called the island by this name because they found gold there.

History and Culture

The Taíno Indians were some of the earliest people to live in Puerto Rico. They were farmers, fishermen, and sailors. Europeans first arrived in 1493. Christopher Columbus and his crew stopped on Puerto Rico during his second voyage to the Americas. They claimed the island for Spain. The Spanish brought African slaves to the island. The slaves helped produce crops like tobacco, coffee, and sugar cane. Slavery on the island did not end until 1873.

After the Spanish-American War, the United States gained Puerto Rico from Spain. It has been a US territory ever since. In the 1950s Puerto Rico became a **commonwealth**. The people adopted their own constitution, giving them more freedom to govern themselves. However, the island is still part of the United States. Its people are US citizens.

The Puerto Rican people are known for their friendliness. They greet visitors with a welcoming "Hello!" or "Hola!" Both English and Spanish are spoken in Puerto Rico, but the main language is Spanish. The people celebrate Spanish holidays. Spanish influence can be seen in their music, literature, and art. Pastel-colored buildings and tile roofs give the cities a Spanish look. However, Puerto Rico also has traditions all its own. One of these unique traditions is its food. Puerto Rico has its own style of cooking with island fruits, vegetables, seafood, and spices.

Puerto Rican citizens in traditional carnival costumes

People

Most Puerto Ricans are descendants of Taínos, Europeans, or Africans. More than three-and-a-half million people live in Puerto Rico. The population is one of the densest among islands of the world. Many Puerto Ricans come to the United States to find better jobs. New York City has a large number of Puerto Ricans.

Puerto Ricans do not have a vote in US elections. Some of them would like to have more say in the national government. For many years Puerto Rico has considered becoming America's fifty-first state. A growing number of Puerto Ricans support this idea.

The largest religion on the island is Roman Catholicism. About two-thirds of the people are Catholics. Puerto Rico has Baptist churches and schools as well. Puerto Rican students can even attend a Christian college on their island. At this college they can prepare to serve the Lord as pastors, teachers, missionaries, or other kinds of Christian workers.

Climate and Natural Resources

Puerto Rico has a tropical climate. Like many islands, it has warm weather all year. The air is humid, and rainfall is heavy during certain seasons. Sometimes hurricanes strike the island.

Southern Puerto Rico has steep mountains and hills. The mountains block most of the rainfall from reaching the south coast. Not as many plants and trees grow in this dry coastal area. It is considered a rain shadow.

Puerto Rico has some natural resources such as copper, gold, forests, and fish. Its primary resource is its natural beauty. The beautiful scenery brings many tourists to the island.

Photos comparing northern and southern Puerto Rico reveal the climate difference caused by the rain-shadow effect.

Flora and Fauna

Tropical plants grow well in Puerto Rico. Many unusual orchids and flowering trees are found there. The island also has a variety of birds. The rainforest has birds like parrots and cuckoos. Sea birds like pelicans and sandpipers live on the coasts. Insects, lizards, and frogs are common on the island. A tree frog called a coquí is named after the sound it makes. Coquís call to each other with the sound "ko-KEE!"

A smaller island off the east coast of Puerto Rico is home to hundreds of monkeys. Scientists use the island as a research station to study these monkeys.

Industries

In the early 1900s Puerto Rico's biggest industry was agriculture. Manufacturing is now a much larger business on the island than farming. Puerto Rico produces electronics, medicines, and machines.

Tourism is also a large industry. People love to visit the white-sand beaches. Visitors also find much to see and do in the large, busy capital city of San Juan.

Some Puerto Ricans have left the island in search of higher-paying jobs. But many of them love their island home and are happy to stay.

parrot

coquí

Cayo Santiago, off the eastern coast of Puerto Rico, is also known as Monkey Island.

What European country has greatly influenced Puerto Rico's culture?

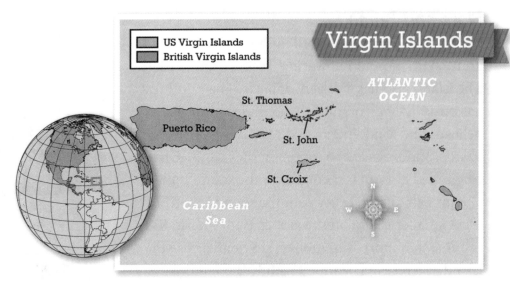

US Virgin Islands
British Virgin Islands

ATLANTIC OCEAN

St. Thomas

Puerto Rico

St. John

St. Croix

Caribbean Sea

US Virgin Islands

Just east of Puerto Rico in the Caribbean Sea is another United States territory. The US Virgin Islands are a group of three main islands surrounded by smaller islands called **cays.** Most of these cays have no one living on them. The main islands are Saint Thomas, Saint John, and Saint Croix. Great Britain owns another group of the Virgin Islands. Their islands are known as the British Virgin Islands.

History and Culture

The Virgin Islands' early settlers were Indians. Caribs and Arawaks lived there. Christopher Columbus visited the islands in 1493. When Spanish settlers began to live on the islands, they brought diseases that the Indians had never had before. The Indians could not fight off these diseases. Many Indians died. Others fled the islands to avoid becoming slaves. There are no more Caribs or Arawaks in the islands today.

A number of European countries tried to set up colonies on the Virgin Islands. By the 1700s Denmark had taken over all three of the main islands. They were called the Danish West Indies. The islands were filled with sugar plantations, and African slaves provided labor. The slaves were finally freed during the 1800s.

The United States bought the islands from Denmark in 1917. The US military stationed troops on them during World War I to protect the Panama Canal. The islands are now an official US territory. They remain under the US government, but the islands' residents elect their own local governor.

Children dressed for a special festival in the US Virgin Islands

The main language of the US Virgin Islands is English. But the culture still keeps its Danish heritage. Many streets have Danish names. The islands are the only territory in the United States where people drive on the left side of the road. African culture has influenced the islands' folk music. The local food is a mixture of European, African, and native Caribbean dishes.

People

About three-fourths of US Virgin Islanders are of African descent. Some were born in the Virgin Islands. Others have moved there from other Caribbean islands. People from American, Latin American, and Asian backgrounds also live there. In addition to English, French and Spanish are spoken in some parts of the islands.

This costume represents the Mocko Jumbie, a mythical spirit-being from Virgin Islands folklore.

In the US Virgin Islands, more than 40 percent of the people claim to be Protestant Christians, particularly Baptists. Another major religious group is Roman Catholics. Sometimes Christian beliefs are mixed with belief in magic and island myths or legends. Christians in the islands must rely on God's Word to keep truth separate from error.

Climate and Natural Resources

Like Puerto Rico, the Virgin Islands have a tropical climate. They have a rainy season during the fall months. Rain does not usually last for an entire day. Short rain showers come at different times throughout the day. Hurricanes are a danger. The months of June through November are considered hurricane season.

Natural resources in the islands include beautiful hills and valleys, beaches, and coral reefs. A large portion of the island of Saint John is a national park. The park preserves resources like fish and sea plants. It also protects shoreline plants like mangroves. Mangroves support unique kinds of wildlife.

Flora and Fauna

The Virgin Islands, especially Saint John, are mostly covered with trees. Coconut palms and tropical fruit trees are common. The trees provide homes for birds like the bananaquit and the hummingbird.

Mangrove trees are found along the shorelines. These trees create a **habitat** for many young animals and plants. Their roots grow close together underwater.

Mangrove trees provide habitats above and below water.

These tight thickets provide shelter from predators. Many kinds of plants and animals live in these mangrove roots. Sponges, corals, anemones, urchins, sea stars, and many kinds of fish make their homes there. Some fish use the mangrove roots as "nurseries." Their young stay there until they are grown and better able to protect themselves.

The islands also have many kinds of colorful flowers. Orchids and hibiscus grow there. The yellow trumpetbush is the official flower of the territory.

trumpetbush

Industries

The main industry of the Virgin Islands is tourism. Many people work in restaurants, hotels, and resorts. The island of Saint Croix also has a large oil-refining industry.

What kind of tree creates a special habitat on shorelines of the US Virgin Islands?

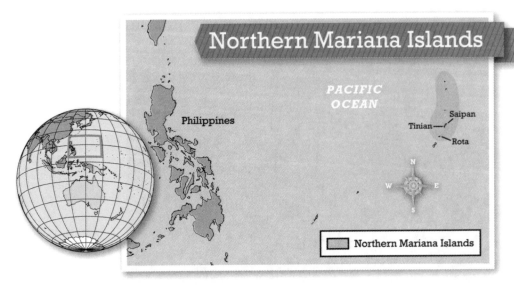

Northern Mariana Islands

The Northern Mariana Islands are a commonwealth like Puerto Rico. The islands lie in the Pacific Ocean, east of the Philippines. Many small islands make up this territory. The three main islands are Saipan, Tinian, and Rota. The Northern Mariana Islands have belonged to the United States since World War II. They began to govern themselves as a commonwealth in 1978.

History and Culture

The Chamorro people were some of the earliest settlers on the islands. Their ancestors landed there while exploring in canoes. Ferdinand Magellan found the islands in 1521. He claimed them for Spain. Spanish missionaries came and taught Roman Catholicism to the Chamorros.

People from the nearby Caroline Islands also came. These Carolinians lived among the Chamorros. People from both groups still live in the Northern Mariana Islands today.

After Spain, Germany and then Japan took control of the islands. The United States captured them from the Japanese during World War II. The islands were used as US military bases near the end of the war. Planes flew from a base on Tinian to drop two atom bombs on Japan. The bombing brought about the end of the war. Afterward, the US Navy took charge of the islands. Later, the island people wrote their own constitution. They now elect their own governor every four years. They also send a representative to the United States Congress.

Today the islands' culture is a blend from many different peoples. The Spanish have left their mark on the religion. Americans have influenced the language and customs. Japanese, Spanish, and Chamorro foods are popular. American food is also becoming more common.

The Northern Mariana Islands contain many reminders of the lives sacrificed in World War II. This war memorial in Saipan is one of them.

People

The Northern Mariana Islands' people are Chamorros, Carolinians, and Asians. Most of them live on the island of Saipan. Many people speak both Chamorro and English. Some speak other languages from nearby islands.

Roman Catholicism is still the main religion. However, there are Protestant Christians on the islands. There are also a number of Buddhists.

orchid

Climate and Natural Resources

The climate of the Northern Mariana Islands is tropical. The islands are warm year-round and often receive heavy rain. Some of the small islands are volcanic. The deepest point in the world's oceans is located east of the islands. The **Mariana Trench** is between six and seven miles deep.

Natural resources on the islands are few. Many kinds of tropical fish live in the coral reefs. The islands also have good land for growing fruit, vegetables, and coconuts.

Flora and Fauna

The forests of the islands are a good place to see many kinds of plants and trees. The red-flowering flame tree is the official tree of the commonwealth. Coconut palms, papaya trees, and mango trees grow there as well. Tropical flowers such as orchids and plumeria thrive in the warm climate.

The Northern Mariana Islands have a variety of birds and fish. Some birds are native to the islands. The Mariana fruit dove and the Tinian monarch are two native

coconut palm

unicornfish

430

birds. Rabbitfish, unicornfish, and rays are found off the islands' coasts. Sea turtles, whales, and dolphins also live in these waters. A special program is in place to keep the Northern Mariana Islands free of snakes. Snakes are the greatest enemy of many other forms of wildlife on the islands.

The Northern Mariana Islands attract people who enjoy fishing and snorkeling.

Industries

Tourism is the largest industry of the Northern Mariana Islands. The capital is located on Saipan. This is the island that draws the most visitors. Some come to enjoy restaurants, golf courses, and beautiful beaches. Others come to visit World War II history sites. Many visitors like to go snorkeling around the coral reefs.

The clothing industry is also important in the islands. Some people come from China and the Philippines to work in clothing factories. These factories have recently come under stricter laws. The US government wants to be sure that factory workers are paid fairly. They want to see that employers treat workers justly.

Fishing and agriculture are smaller industries in the islands. God has given the people fish and farmland as natural resources. The people are using these resources wisely.

What important geographical site is located east of the Northern Mariana Islands?

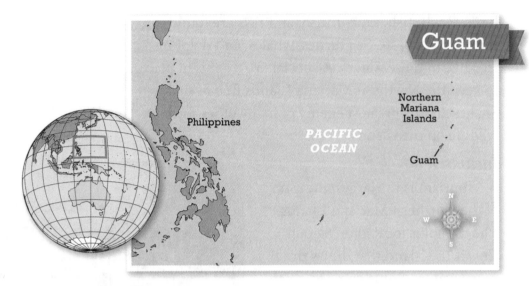

Philippines

Northern
Mariana
Islands

PACIFIC
OCEAN

Guam

Guam

The island of Guam is one of the Mariana Islands. It is south of the Northern Mariana Islands. Guam is the largest of all these islands and is a separate US territory.

History and Culture

For hundreds of years the Chamorros lived on Guam. Spain took over the island in the 1500s. The Spanish controlled Guam for more than three centuries. Then Guam was given to the United States at the end of the Spanish-American War.

The Japanese captured Guam for a short time during World War II. Then the Americans recaptured it. They set up military posts on the island. After the war, Guam wanted more independence. It became a US territory. The people began to elect their own governor. Guam now has the right to make many of its own laws. The US government oversees the local government of Guam.

Guam and the Northern Mariana Islands have similar cultures. Both are a blend of Spanish, American, Asian, and Chamorro cultures. Immigrants from nearby islands have also brought their traditions to Guam. But the Chamorros have had the strongest influence. Chamorro culture teaches respect for elders. Chamorros also value native music, foods, and legends.

Ancient latte stones are a common sight on the island of Guam.

On Guam and other Mariana Islands, stone pillars from ancient buildings are still standing. Early Chamorros built homes on these **latte stones**. These tall stone pillars have cup-shaped tops. Latte stones remind Guam's people of their Chamorro history.

People

Guam has the largest population of all the Mariana Islands. Its people are Chamorros, Asians, Americans, and Pacific Islanders. A common greeting in Guam is "Hafa adai!" This Chamorro phrase means, "How are you, friend?" Chamorro and English are the main languages on the island of Guam.

The largest religious group in Guam is Roman Catholics. A smaller group is Protestant Christians. Some Christians in Guam are able to attend a Bible college on the island. These students learn to take the gospel to Guam and other surrounding islands.

Climate and Natural Resources

Guam has a tropical climate. Sea winds affect the weather on the island. Rainfall varies during different seasons. December through June is often a drier season. The island receives more rain in July through November. A hurricane-like storm in this part of the Pacific Ocean is called a typhoon. Guam sometimes experiences typhoons and tropical storms.

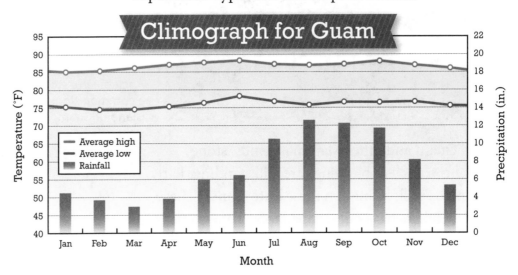

Guam's natural resources are its fish and other ocean wildlife. Many people visit the island to go snorkeling and scuba diving. There are rare sights to see under the water. Coral, algae, sea grass, sea turtles, and colorful fish can be found just off the coast of Guam.

Flora and Fauna

Guam has many of the same plants and animals as the Northern Mariana Islands. The official tree of Guam is the ifit. The ifit tree was once common on the island. For many years its wood was used to build houses and furniture. Now it is illegal to cut down ifit trees because they are rare.

water buffalo

bougainvillea

brown tree snake

fruit bat

Guam's climate is good for tropical flowers and shrubs. A common flowering plant is the bougainvillea. It blooms in several different colors. It also has long, sharp thorns. Some people plant bougainvillea shrubs as "fences" to protect an area from intruders.

Guam has land animals as well as fish. In some parts of Guam there are carabao, or water buffalo. Small lizards, frogs, and sea birds are common. The Mariana fruit bat is protected in a wildlife reserve. Unlike the Northern Mariana Islands, Guam is not free of snakes. The brown tree snake has become a problem for Guam. Scientists are working to control it and to keep it from preying on native birds.

Industries

The US military has several different bases on the island of Guam. The men and women serving on these bases are an important part of Guam's economy. They bring income to Guam's businesses. Tourism is another major industry on the island. Restaurants, hotels, stores, and other businesses depend on tourists. Construction is also a large industry in Guam.

What are the major industries on the island of Guam?

435

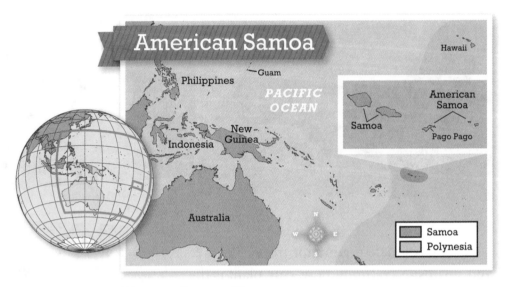

American Samoa

The Samoan Islands are a chain of islands in the South Pacific Ocean. They are east of Australia and south of Hawaii. American Samoa is made up of the easternmost islands in this chain. The territory has five main islands and two atolls. An **atoll** is a ring-shaped island made of coral.

History and Culture

John Williams

The early people in Samoa were Polynesians. Polynesia is a name for all the islands in that area. The native people of these islands had similar cultures.

British missionaries visited the islands of Samoa in the 1830s. John Williams was the leader of the missionaries and preached the gospel. Many of the Samoan people turned to Jesus Christ. Williams was later killed by cannibals on another Pacific island. American Samoans still honor him for bringing the gospel to their islands.

Various countries in Europe tried to set up colonies in Samoa. The United States finally took control of

American Samoa. These islands became a US territory in 1900. Like the other territories, American Samoa now has its own governor. The western Samoan Islands remain independent.

For many years the United States has had military bases on the islands of American Samoa. Samoans served as Marines during World War II. They helped defend their islands against the Japanese.

The family is very important in the American Samoan culture. Family groups have leaders called chiefs. These groups usually keep close ties throughout life. They help each other in times of need. Young people are taught to respect their elders and the cultural traditions. Music, art, dance, and several kinds of sports are important in the culture. On an October holiday called White Sunday, children wear white clothing and perform songs and plays in church services.

Children perform at a White Sunday celebration

People

More than 90 percent of the people in American Samoa are Polynesians. Both English and Samoan are spoken in the islands. Samoans greet each other by saying, "Talofa!" It is a way of expressing friendship as well as saying hello.

Christianity is still the main religion in the islands. Sunday is set aside as a day to go to church, and offices and shops are closed. In some villages, people observe a special time of prayer in the evenings.

Climate and Natural Resources

The islands of American Samoa have about seventy-six square miles of land. All the land put together is a little smaller than the state of Rhode Island. Like on other tropical islands, the climate is warm and humid all year. The amount of rainfall is usually high.

All five of the main islands are volcanoes. None of the volcanoes has erupted since the 1800s. Tropical cyclones and earthquakes sometimes threaten the islands. In 2009 an undersea earthquake caused a **tsunami**, or giant wave, to strike the Samoan Islands.

American Samoa has a variety of natural resources. Its capital city, Pago Pago, has one of the best natural harbors in the Pacific Ocean. Beautiful beaches bring tourists to the islands. A type of volcanic rock called **pumice** is also an important resource. Pumice is used in items like soap and construction materials.

Damage to a Samoan church as a result of the 2009 tsunami

The harbor of Pago Pago

438

Flora and Fauna

Large portions of the islands are covered with tropical rainforests. Many trees and flowers grow in these forests. Breadfruit trees, coconut palms, and pandanus trees are common. Pandanus leaves are used as a flavoring in cooking. They are also used to make baskets, mats, and grass skirts. Tropical flowers like hibiscus, plumeria, and passionflower also grow well.

Part of American Samoa is a national park. Animals such as fruit bats, lizards, and toads live in the park. Dolphins and humpback whales can sometimes be seen from the shore. The park also protects the many kinds of wildlife in the coral reefs.

pandanus

hibiscus

Industries

One of the largest industries in American Samoa is tuna canning. Fishermen catch tuna in the waters around the islands. Many American Samoans work in canneries. Canneries are places where the tuna is packed in cans to be exported.

The tourism industry is also growing in American Samoa. As on other tropical islands, visitors enjoy scuba diving, snorkeling, and swimming at the beach. Many people are also interested in learning more about the Samoan traditions and way of life.

dolphins

How did Christianity come to the islands of American Samoa?

Being a Good Citizen

The regions and territories of the United States all have one thing in common. They all need citizens who will live as God wants people to live. Christians are citizens of the kingdom of heaven. They are waiting for Jesus to return and rule the earth. But even while they are waiting, Christians should be good citizens now wherever they live. How can you be a good citizen of your community, your state, and your country?

First, you can pray for your government leaders. First Timothy 2:1–4 tells us to pray for all who are in positions of leadership. God desires for all people to be saved and to know the truth. Christians can pray that God will save our leaders so that they can truly be wise, just rulers.

Second, you can live as a citizen of God's kingdom here on the earth. You can look for ways to help people in your community. You can be a good neighbor. You can be honest and dependable in your work. You can look out for those who are in need and have no one to help them. You can tell your friends and neighbors about the Lord Jesus Christ. You can faithfully attend your church and invite other people to go with you.

If you are a believer in Jesus Christ, you have a responsibility. You must be the best citizen you can be. But you do not have to do it all by yourself. You have God's Holy Spirit to help you. With His help, you can live as a good citizen for Christ.

How can you be a good citizen?

Resource Treasury

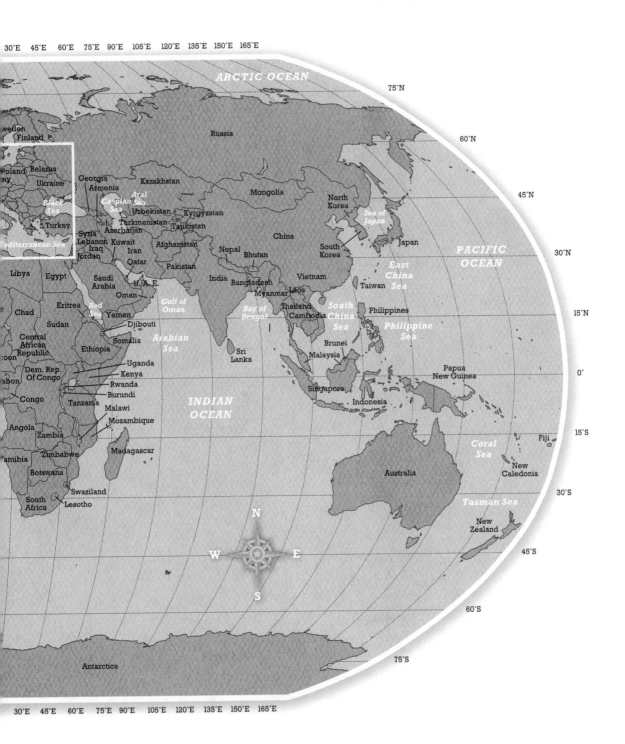

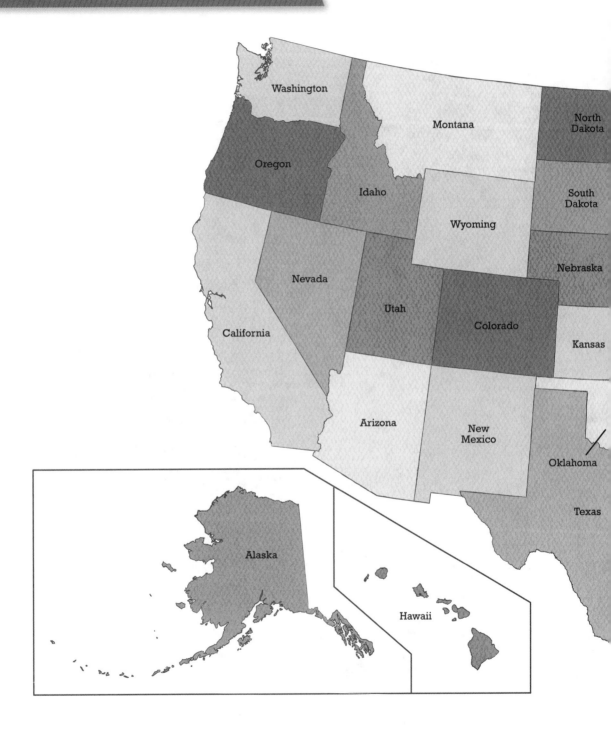

Minnesota

Vermont

Maine

New Hampshire

Massachusetts

Wisconsin

New
York

Michigan

Rhode Island

Iowa

Pennsylvania

Connecticut

New Jersey

Illinois

Ohio

Delaware

Indiana

Maryland

West
Virginia

Virginia

Missouri

Kentucky

North
Carolina

Tennessee

Arkansas

South
Carolina

Georgia

N

Alabama

W

E

Florida

Louisiana

Mississippi

S

Minnesota

Wisconsin

Michigan

Iowa

Illinois

Indiana

Ohio

Missouri

Kentucky

West
Virginia

Pennsylvania

New
York

Vermont

Maine

New Hampshire

Massachusetts

Rhode Island

Connecticut

New Jersey

Delaware

Maryland

Virginia

Tennessee

North
Carolina

Arkansas

South
Carolina

Georgia

Alabama

Florida

Mississippi

Louisiana

N

W   E

S

United States: Regions

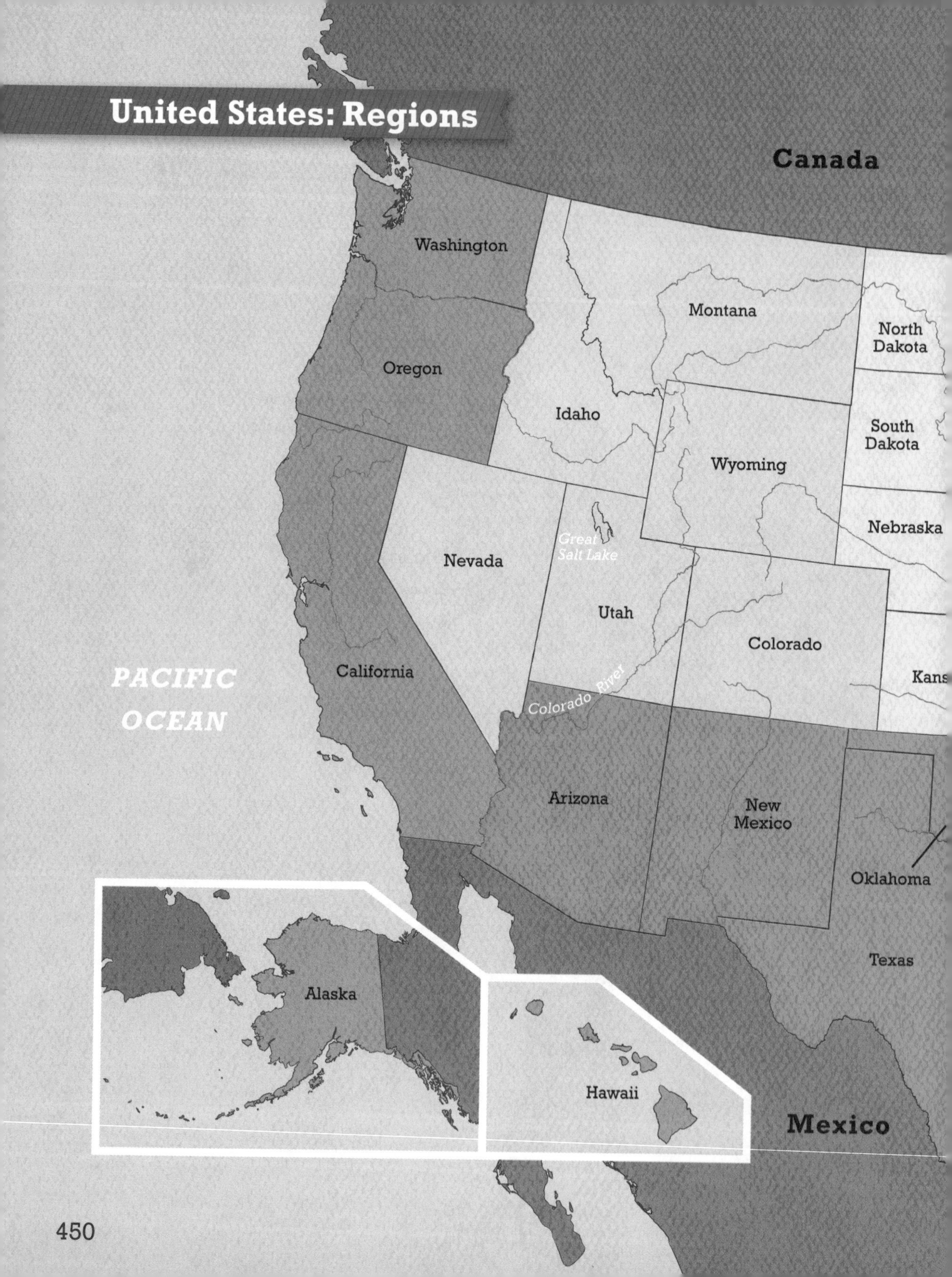
Canada
Washington
Montana
North Dakota
Oregon
Idaho
South Dakota
Wyoming
Nebraska
Great Salt Lake
Nevada
Utah
Colorado
PACIFIC OCEAN
California
Kans
Colorado River
Arizona
New Mexico
Oklahoma
Texas
Alaska
Hawaii
Mexico

Northeast · Southwest · Southeast · Rocky Mountain states · Midwest · Pacific states

Minnesota

Lake Superior

Wisconsin

Lake Michigan

Lake Huron

Michigan

Iowa

Illinois

Indiana

Ohio

Lake Ontario

New York

Hudson River

Vermont

Maine

New Hampshire

Massachusetts

Rhode Island

Connecticut

New Jersey

Delaware

Maryland

Lake Erie

Pennsylvania

Missouri River

Missouri

Ohio River

West Virginia

Kentucky

Virginia

Arkansas

Tennessee

North Carolina

South Carolina

ATLANTIC OCEAN

Mississippi River

Alabama

Georgia

Louisiana

Mississippi

Florida

N

W   E

S

Gulf of Mexico

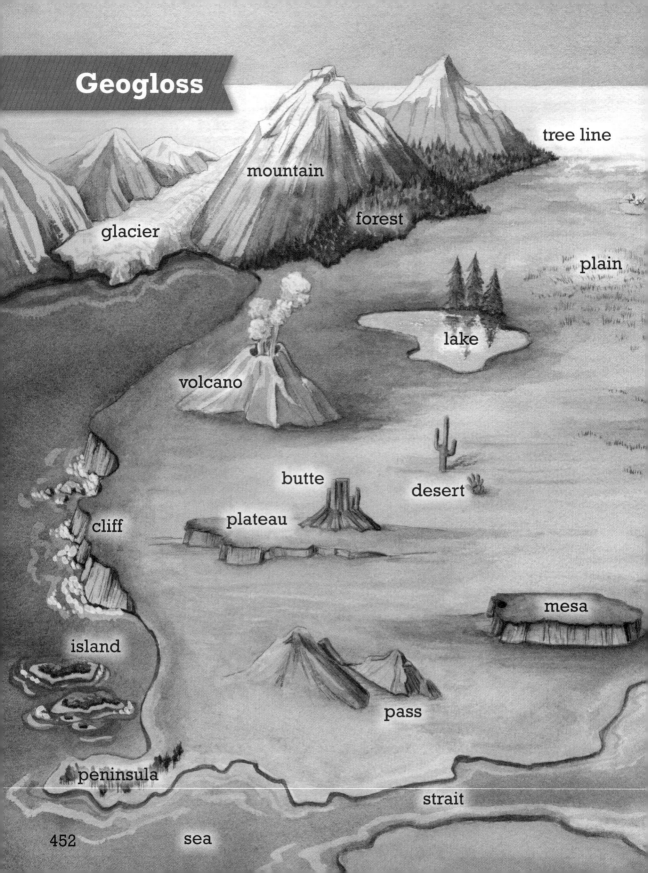

Geogloss

tree line

mountain

glacier

forest

plain

volcano

lake

butte

desert

plateau

cliff

mesa

island

pass

peninsula

strait

452

sea

sea level

ocean

tundra

valley

river

harbor

bay

basin

prairie

hill

piedmont

coastal plain

archipelago

bog

wetland

coast-land

gulf

Gazetteer

A gazetteer is a geographical dictionary or glossary. Entries do not have complete definitions like a normal dictionary. Instead each place is followed by helpful information you learned in this book. Many descriptions end with the page number of a map that shows the place.

A

Abilene, Kansas The town in which Joseph McCoy set up the first cattle-shipping yard. (m. 64)

Africa One of the seven continents of the world. (m. 7, 151)

Alaska A very cold land on the northwestern tip of North America, sold to the United States by Russia. (m. 137, 409)

American Samoa A chain of islands in the South Pacific Ocean that is a territory of the United States. (m. 436)

Anchorage, Alaska Alaska's largest city.

Appalachian Mountains The largest mountain range in the Northeast, stretching from Alabama up into Canada. (m. 319)

Asheville, North Carolina The city where George Vanderbilt built Biltmore House and Gardens in the late 1800s.

Asia The largest of the world's seven continents. (m. 7, 151)

Atlanta, Georgia A city in the South that led in building factories and businesses after Reconstruction ended and has become a center of communication. (m. 18)

Atlantic Ocean The ocean to the east of North America. (m. 444, 451)

B

Australia One of the seven continents of the world; located between the Pacific and Indian Oceans. (m. 7, 151)

Austria-Hungary A member of the Triple Alliance before World War I; the country whose archduke was assassinated by a terrorist group. (m. 110)

Belgium A European country that was neutral during World War I. (m. 110, 187, 199)

Belleau Wood A wooded area in France where a major World War I battle was fought.

Bering Strait A narrow area of water between Alaska and Asia that most historians believe people used to cross from Asia to North America. (m. 7, 137)

Black Hills A mountain range in South Dakota that once belonged to the Sioux Indians; site of the richest lode of gold found in the United States. (m. 67, 76)

Boston, Massachusetts The capital of Massachusetts; a center of resistance during the Revolutionary War; home of the Patriot leaders. (m. 11, 18)

Boulder, Colorado A boomtown that grew during the Pikes Peak Gold Rush and is now a large city.

Britain *See* Great Britain.

C

California An area that originally belonged to Mexico; was important for access to the Pacific Ocean; attracted many people in the gold rush of 1848; entered the United States as a free state in 1850. (m. 20, 409)

Canada A country in North America located north of the United States and extending from the Atlantic Ocean to the Pacific Ocean. (m. 137, 290, 312, 334)

Carribbean, the A group of islands in the Caribbean Sea that President Grant wanted to purchase from Santo Domingo. (m. 137, 143)

Central America The part of North America between Mexico and South America.

Charleston, South Carolina An important and valuable port city; site of the first battle of the Civil War; one of the oldest towns in the South; nicknamed the "holy city"; cultural center that hosts the Spoleto Festival. (m. 7, 18)

Charlotte, North Carolina A city where some gold mines were discovered; operated a mint in the early nineteenth century; is a center for the banking industry.

Château-Thierry A town in France located near the Marne River where Americans battled the Germans during World War I.

Chicago, Illinois The city in which Al Capone based his organized crime; the biggest and most important city in the Midwest; home of the first skyscrapers in the world. (m. 18)

China An Asian country that Europe traded with for spices and other goods; country attacked by Japan during World War II. (m. 266, 271, 282)

Chisholm Trail The trail that was used to drive cattle to the shipping yards in Abilene, Kansas; named after Jesse Chisholm. (m. 64)

Cincinnati, Ohio The original Midwest center of trade; home of the first professional baseball team, the Red Stockings. (m. 18)

Cleveland, Ohio An industrial city of the Midwest founded on Lake Erie. (m. 18)

Colorado A destination for cattle drives farther west than Kansas; site of a gold rush about ten years after the California gold rush; part of the Rocky Mountains; became part of the Union in 1876. (m. 64, 388)

Coney Island America's first amusement park; located on the Atlantic Coast near New York City.

Confederacy, the The Confederate States of America; the states that chose to secede from the United States, sparking the Civil War; the focus of Reconstruction after the war.

Cuba The largest and most important of the Caribbean Islands; claimed by Spain but gained independence; focus of the Spanish-American War. (m. 137, 143, 151)

Czechoslovakia A country in Europe that was conquered by Hitler before World War II. (m. 260, 264, 268, 287)

D

Denmark A country in Europe that extends north from Germany. (m. 110, 260, 264, 268, 281, 287)

Denver, Colorado A boomtown that grew during the Pikes Peak Gold Rush; called the Mile High City; today serves as a transportation hub in the West and is the largest city in the Rocky Mountain states. (m. 64)

Detroit, Michigan The second most important city in the Midwest; known as "Motor City" because of all the cars that are manufactured there. (m. 18)

Dodge City, Kansas A railroad town that became a shipping point for the cattle trade; one of the best-known cow towns in the West. (m. 64)

Dutch East Indies A colony conquered by Japan during World War II; now known as Indonesia. (m. 266, 271, 282)

E

Ellis Island, New York The site of the US immigrant station in New York Harbor.

Ellsworth, Kansas A railroad town that became a shipping point for the cattle trade; one of the best-known cow towns in the West. (m. 64)

England Part of Great Britain; the country from which the Pilgrims and Puritans came to the New World. *See* Great Britain. (m. 110)

Erie Canal A waterway across New York extending from Albany to Buffalo.

Europe The continent from which most of the original inhabitants of America came; one of the continents that founded many colonies in new lands; continent split by the alliances formed before the start of World War I. (m. 7, 110, 151, 260, 268)

Everglades The region in Florida that has the largest combination of swamps and marshes in the United States.

F

Four Corners The point where the borders of New Mexico, Arizona, Utah, and Colorado meet; original home of the Ancestral Pueblo Indians.

France A European country; trade rival with Britain that helped America during the Revolutionary War; member of the Triple Entente before World War I; country invaded by Germany during World War II. (m. 110, 187, 199, 260, 264, 268, 281, 287)

G

Germany A European country; member of the Triple Alliance before World War I; country that was blamed for starting World War I and had to pay war costs according to the Treaty of Versailles; country controlled by Hitler and the Nazi Party before World War II; member of the Axis Powers during World War II. (m. 110, 187, 199, 260, 264, 268, 281, 287)

Goodnight-Loving Trail A trail created by Charles Goodnight and Oliver Loving that was used to drive cattle to Colorado and Wyoming. (m. 64)

Grand Canyon A canyon in Arizona formed as a result of the Flood; more than 250 miles long, 18 miles wide at its widest point, and more than a mile deep in some parts.

Great Britain The nations of England, Scotland, and Wales; trade rival with France that claimed much land in the New World; member of the Triple Entente before World War I; one of the Allies during World War II. (m. 187, 199, 260, 264, 268, 281, 287)

Great Lakes Five lakes that include Lakes Superior, Huron, Erie, Ontario, and Michigan; located between Canada and the United States; later connected to the Atlantic Ocean by the Erie Canal.

Great Plains The area between the Mississippi River and the Rocky Mountains; mostly flat grasslands where many Indians lived and hunted; "America's Breadbasket." (m. 56)

Great Salt Lake The largest saltwater lake in North and South America; located in the Great Basin in Utah.

Green Mountains A smaller range of the Appalachian Mountains located in Canada and Vermont.

Guam An island of the Caribbean formerly owned by Spain; controlled by the United States after the Spanish-American War. (m. 151, 266, 271, 282, 432)

H

Havana, Cuba The capital of Cuba; location of the harbor where the USS *Maine* blew up.

Hawaii A group of islands in the Pacific Ocean between the United States and the Philippines; originally controlled by the United States to help protect shipping to the Philippines during the Spanish-American War. (m. 271, 282, 409)

Hiroshima, Japan The Japanese city where an American plane dropped the first atomic bomb to end World War II. (m. 282)

Honolulu, Hawaii The state capital of Hawaii, located on Oahu; site of the Pearl Harbor Memorial.

Houston, Texas The largest city in the Southwest; the fourth-largest city in the nation; one of the largest ports in the world and the leading center of oil and gas production in the United States; home of the Johnson Space Center.

Hull-House A settlement house in Chicago, Illinois, begun by Jane Addams to help immigrants in poor living conditions.

I

Ireland A large island in the Atlantic Ocean west of Great Britain. (m. 110, 260, 264, 268, 281, 287)

Italy A European country; member of the Triple Alliance before World War I but changed alliances during the war; country controlled by the Fascist Party after World War I; country allied with Germany before World War II; member of the Axis Powers during World War II. (m. 110, 260, 264, 268, 281, 287)

Iwo Jima An island of Japan in the Pacific Ocean; conquered by the Allies during World War II in order to more easily bomb Japan. (m. 266, 271)

J

Jamestown The first successful English colony or settlement in the New World; traded with the Indians.

Japan Attacked and conquered China during World War II; sought to control most of East Asia as an empire; was a member of the Axis Powers during World War II. (m. 266, 271, 282)

L

Little Bighorn River The site of the battle between Custer, his men, and the Sioux Indians; Custer's Last Stand. (m. 76)

Los Angeles, California The second-largest US city; founded by the Spanish in 1781 and located in the heart of southern California.

Louisiana Territory The Midwestern area of the United States sold to the country by France in what was called the Louisiana Purchase.

M

Mariana Trench Crescent-shaped trench located east of the Mariana Islands in the western Pacific Ocean; the deepest point in the world's oceans.

Marne River A river located in France where battles in World Wars I and II were fought. (m. 187, 199)

Mexico The country south and west of the United States that fought to keep control of Texas and refused to sell California but lost both in wars with the United States; country asked by Germany to fight against the United States in World War I. (m. 143, 290, 331, 334, 356, 378, 400)

Midway A small Pacific island where the United States fought a battle that became an important turning point in World War II. (m. 266, 271, 282)

Midwest The US region made up of Illinois, Indiana, Iowa, Kansas, Michigan, Minnesota, Missouri, Nebraska, North Dakota, Ohio, South Dakota, and Wisconsin. (m. 290, 312, 334, 356, 378, 400)

Minneapolis, Minnesota A city that first boomed with many sawmills and flour mills; grew together with St. Paul to become the largest urban area in the United States.

Mississippi River The longest and most important river in the United States. (m. 18, 56, 319)

Mount McKinley The highest mountain in North America, standing nearly four miles high.

Mount Rushmore A monument located in the Black Hills of South Dakota with likenesses of presidents Washington, Jefferson, Lincoln, and Theodore Roosevelt engraved in the rock.

N

Nagasaki, Japan The Japanese city where an American plane dropped the second atomic bomb, leading to Japan's final surrender and ending World War II. (m. 282)

Netherlands A country invaded by Germany during World War II; home of Corrie ten Boom and her family, who hid Jews. (m. 110, 187)

Nevada The site of the Comstock Lode; joined the Union in 1864; was the one state to permit gambling when people tried to outlaw it. (m. 67, 388)

New Orleans, Louisiana A large port city at the end of the Mississippi River that was controlled by Spain and then France before the United States bought it; site of the battle that occurred after the treaty of the War of 1812 was signed; important in trade; one of America's largest urban communities.

New World The name for the land that Columbus first discovered; includes North, South, and Central America. (m. 7)

New York, New York The largest US city; home of Wall Street, location of many immigrants; city made up of five counties, or boroughs: the Bronx, Manhattan, Queens, Brooklyn, and Staten Island. (m. 11, 18)

Niagara Falls A group of waterfalls shared by the United States and Canada that produces energy for nearby power plants.

Normandy A region in France where all the Allies, except the USSR, landed troops to trick Germany on D-Day and free Europe during World War II. (m. 281)

North Africa A region that the Axis Powers tried to conquer but was freed by Allied forces during World War II.

North America A continent first settled by Indian tribes and then discovered and colonized by Europeans. (m. 7, 151)

Northeast The US region made up of Connecticut, Delaware, Maine, Maryland, Massachusetts, New Hampshire, New Jersey, New York, Pennsylvania, Rhode Island, and Vermont. (m. 290, 331, 334, 356, 378, 400)

Northern Mariana Islands A US commonwealth consisting of a group of islands east of the Philippines that was captured by American forces during World War II. (m. 428)

O

Okefenokee Swamp The largest swamp in North America; found in parts of Georgia and Florida.

Oklahoma A state in the Midwest; site of the Land Rush of 1889; provides important natural resources such as fertile soil and grassland for farming and grazing. (m. 356, 365)

Oklahoma City, Oklahoma The state capital and the largest city in Oklahoma; city formed during the Land Rush of 1889; important in oil production, food processing, and manufacturing; Horse Show Capital of the World.

Omaha, Nebraska The city from which the Union Pacific Railroad Company began laying track westward for the transcontinental railroad. (m. 56)

Ozark Mountains A mountain range found in Arkansas and neighboring Southeastern states. (m. 319)

P

Pacific Ocean The ocean to the west of North America. (m. 444)

Pacific States The US region made up of Alaska, California, Hawaii, Oregon, and Washington. (m. 290, 312, 334, 356, 378, 400)

Pearl Harbor, Hawaii The location of a surprise attack by Japanese naval and air forces during World War II; reason for the United States joining World War II. (m. 266, 271, 282)

Philadelphia, Pennsylvania The city where the Declaration of Independence and the United States Constitution were signed; the fifth-largest US city in population; the "city of brotherly love." (m. 11, 18)

Philippines A country of Asia that wanted independence after the Spanish-American War; country conquered by Japan during World War II. (m. 151, 266, 271, 282)

Phoenix, Arizona The capital of Arizona; the sixth-largest city in the United States; pioneer settlement in the late 1800s; manufacturing center and tourist spot.

Pikes Peak A famous peak located in the Rocky Mountains; site of gold discovery in 1858. (m. 67)

Poland A country in Europe that was fought over during World War II; country invaded by Germany, beginning World War II. (m. 260, 264, 268, 281, 287)

Portland, Oregon The capital of Oregon; a center of technology; nicknamed the City of Roses.

Promontory Summit, Utah The place at which the two tracks of the first transcontinental railroad met. (m. 56)

Puerto Rico A smaller island near Cuba originally owned by Spain but controlled by the United States after the Spanish-American War. (m. 137, 143, 151, 420)

R

Richmond, Virginia The city chosen for the capital of the Confederate States of America; site of many Civil War battles. (m. 18)

Rocky Mountains A major mountain range that spreads through six of the Western states. (m. 56, 67, 76, 290, 334, 356, 378, 400)

Rocky Mountain States The US region made up of Colorado, Idaho, Montana, Nevada, Utah, and Wyoming. (m. 290, 312, 378)

Russia The European country that sold Alaska to the United States; a member of the Triple Entente before World War I; named the USSR, or the Soviet Union, while controlled by the Communist Party after World War I. (m. 110, 137, 260, 264, 266, 268, 271, 281, 282, 287)

S

Sacramento, California The city from which the Central Pacific Railroad Company began laying track eastward for the first transcontinental railroad. (m. 56)

Saint Louis, Missouri The city where Lewis and Clark began their expedition through the Louisiana Territory; known as the Gateway City. (m. 18)

Saint Paul, Minnesota A city near the Mississippi River that grew together with Minneapolis to become the largest urban area in the United States.

Salt Lake City, Utah A city founded by the Mormons in 1847; largest city in Utah today; remains the center of Mormonism.

San Francisco, California A large city midway up the California coast; site of the Golden Gate Bridge and Alcatraz Island. (m. 56)

Santiago de Cuba A city on the southern coast of Cuba; the most important city captured in the Spanish-American War.

Santo Domingo A country in the Caribbean Islands; now called the Dominican Republic.

Savannah, Georgia An important port city in Georgia. (m. 11, 18)

Sicily An island halfway between North Africa and Italy that was used as a jumping-off place for the Allies in World War II. (m. 268)

Singapore An island conquered by Japan during World War II. (m. 266, 271, 282)

South America One of the seven continents of the world; located between the Pacific and Atlantic Oceans. (m. 7, 151)

South Carolina A state in the Southeast; the first state to secede from the United States during the Civil War. (m. 20, 322)

South Dakota A state in the Midwest; site of several battles between the Indians and the US Army; location of the Black Hills; home of Mount Rushmore and the Crazy Horse Memorial. (m. 76, 344)

Southeast, the The US region made up of Alabama, Arkansas, Florida, Georgia, Kentucky, Louisiana, Mississippi, North Carolina, South Carolina, Tennessee, Virginia, and West Virginia. (m. 290, 312, 334, 356, 378, 400)

Southwest, the The US region made up of Arizona, New Mexico, Oklahoma, and Texas. (m. 290, 312, 334, 356, 378, 400)

Soviet Union Russia's name under the control of the Communist Party in the pre-World War II era. (m. 260, 264, 266, 268, 281, 287)

Spain A country in southwestern Europe that fought with the United States over Cuba's independence during the Spanish-American War. (m. 110, 151, 260, 264, 268, 281, 287)

T

Texas A state in the Southwest that first belonged to Mexico and then fought to gain its independence; leading producer of oil and natural gas in the United States. (m. 136, 365)

Tokyo, Japan The capital of Japan that was firebombed during World War II. (m. 282)

U

Union The states that chose to remain a part of the United States when Southern states seceded; states that had more men, factories, and railroads than the Confederacy but had to travel south in order to fight during the Civil War.

United Kingdom *See* Great Britain.

USSR Stands for the Union of Soviet Socialist Republics; *See* Russia and Soviet Union.

US Virgin Islands United States territory located east of Puerto Rico in the Caribbean Sea. (m. 424)

W

Wall Street A place in New York City that handles money interests of the United States; where the New York Stock Exchange is located.

Washington, DC The capital city of the United States, *DC* standing for "District of Columbia"; the city where Congress meets and the president resides. (m. 18)

Western Front The site of a great stalemate between armies in France during World War I. (m. 187)

Western Trail A trail used to drive cattle to the shipping yards in Ogalalla, Nebraska. (m. 64)

West Quoddy Head The point farthest east in the continental United States; located in Maine.

Wichita, Kansas A railroad town that became a shipping point for the cattle trade; one of the best-known cow towns in the West. (m. 64)

Wounded Knee Creek, South Dakota The site of the last major battle between the Indians and white men. (m. 76)

Biographical Dictionary

A

Adams, John Quincy The sixth president of the United States; son of John and Abigail Adams.

Addams, Jane Started Hull-House in Chicago, Illinois, to help immigrants in poor living conditions.

Alcott, Louisa May An American writer during the Gilded Age; famous for her two well-known novels, *Little Women* and *Little Men*.

Anna, Santa A general in the Mexican army who became the president of Mexico in the 1830s.

Anthony, Susan B. An advocate who spoke out openly for women's rights during the Gilded Age.

B

Bell, Alexander Graham Immigrated to the United States from Scotland; became a teacher for the deaf; is credited with inventing the first telephone.

Birdseye, Clarence Improved methods for freezing food.

Bly, Nellie The name used by a reporter pretending to be insane so she could report on the conditions of an insane asylum.

Booth, John Wilkes The actor who shot and killed President Abraham Lincoln.

Bryan, William Jennings A famous Democratic politician who supported the government's case against John Scopes in the Scopes Trial.

Bunyan, Paul A legendary hero from Minnesota famous for logging in the state's woods.

C

Capone, Al Led organized crime in Chicago during the 1920s; was caught in the early 1930s.

Carnegie, Andrew Became the most important steel manufacturer in the United States during the Gilded Age; gave much of his wealth away to benefit other people; spoke out against the United States taking control of other lands.

Cassatt, Mary An artist during the Gilded Age known for her paintings of mothers and children.

Cather, Willa A progressive author who wrote about life in the Nebraska prairies.

Chiang Kai-shek The head of the Chinese Nationalistic government from 1928 to 1949; supported Western ideas and led the non-Communist Chinese fighters to defend their country during World War II.

Chisholm, Jesse A trader who used a popular cattle trail to carry goods to Abilene, Kansas; Chisholm Trail was named after him.

Churchill, Winston A famous politician from Great Britain who led the nation in fighting Hitler during World War II.

Clark, William The explorer who went with Meriwether Lewis on an expedition through the Louisiana Territory to the Pacific Ocean.

Cleveland, Grover Served as the twenty-second and twenty-fourth president of the United States; spoke out against the United States taking control of other lands.

Cody, William "Buffalo Bill" Put together a traveling show during the Gilded Age about life in the Wild West.

Cohan, George Wrote a popular song called "Over There" about American soldiers entering World War I.

Columbus, Christopher An explorer for Spain who discovered what is now called the Americas.

Cook, James The first European to see the Hawaiian islands.

Coolidge, Calvin Served as vice president of the United States under President Harding; became the thirtieth president after Harding's death; focused on business during his presidency.

Coronado, Francisco Vásquez de A Spanish explorer who explored much of New Mexico and parts of Arizona while looking for gold and silver.

Crazy Horse A Sioux chief who helped lead his people against the United States government when treaties made with the American Indians were broken.

Custer, Colonel George The leader of one of the US forces that fought against American Indians in the West; was killed at the Battle of the Little Bighorn.

D

Darrow, Clarence The lawyer who defended John Scopes and used the Scopes Trial to try to prove that the Bible was full of errors.

Darwin, Charles The naturalist whose theories of evolution became widely accepted during the Gilded Age.

de Lôme, Enrique Dupuy The Spanish ambassador to the United States whose offensive letter caused tension and helped lead to the Spanish-American War.

Dempsey, Jack A famous boxer during the 1920s.

Dewey, George The commander of a small US fleet that defeated the Spanish Pacific fleet at Manila Bay during the Spanish-American War.

Dickinson, Emily A poet during the Gilded Age who was not well known during her life but is now famous for her poems.

Dixon, A. C. The pastor of a New York City church who preached against some of the shows and activities at Coney Island.

Doolittle, Jimmy A US colonel who led US airmen in successfully dropping bombs on Tokyo, Japan, during World War II.

Du Bois, W. E. B. The first black American to earn a PhD; supporter of ending segregation right away; founder of the National Association for the Advancement of Colored People.

Dvořák, Antonín A Hungarian composer who taught music in America during the Gilded Age and is famous for his New World Symphony.

E

Ederle, Gertrude A well-known American swimmer during the 1920s; first woman to swim the English Channel.

Edison, Thomas An inventor who set up his own lab during the Gilded Age; inventor of the light bulb and the phonograph.

Einstein, Albert A famous scientist of the 1920s who won the Nobel Prize in Physics and helped scientists understand how light works.

Eisenhower, Dwight A US general during World War II who became the supreme allied commander in Europe; leader of the Allies in pushing the Germans back to Germany to end World War II.

F

Ferdinand, Archduke Francis The heir to the throne of Austria-Hungary whose assassination by a terrorist group from Serbia sparked World War II.

Fisher, Ezra Traveled west to be a missionary in Oregon and California during the 1840s.

Fitzgerald, Francis Scott A popular author during the 1920s who is known for his novel *The Great Gatsby.*

Foch, Ferdinand Commanded the Allies during World War I; met with German leaders to sign the armistice at the end of the war; did not believe World War I would be the war to end all wars.

Ford, Henry Made the automobile that most people bought during the Progressive Era; made his cars affordable by using interchangeable parts and assembly lines.

Franklin, Benjamin An inventor and a founding father of the United States who lived in Philadelphia.

G

Gershwin, George An American composer who combined traditional classical music with modern jazz during the 1920s.

Glidden, Joseph A farmer who invented barbed wire for fences in the West in the 1800s.

Goodnight, Charles Created the Goodnight-Loving Trail with Oliver Loving to drive cattle to Colorado and Wyoming.

Grant, Ulysses S. A Union Civil War general who became the eighteenth president of the United States in 1868.

H

Harding, Warren G. The twenty-ninth US president; worked out an independent treaty with Germany after World War I.

Hayes, Rutherford The nineteenth president of the United States; spoke with Chief Joseph about the Nez Perce people in the 1870s.

Hearst, William Randolph Worked as the journalist and publisher of the *New York Journal* during the Gilded Age; stretched the truth in his stories to sell more newspapers.

Henry, Patrick An American Revolutionary leader who is known for saying, "Give me liberty, or give me death."

Hickok, "Wild Bill" The marshal of Abilene, Kansas, after Tom Smith, and probably the most famous lawman of the West.

Hirohito The emperor of Japan during World War II; believed by most Japanese people to be a living god.

Hitler, Adolf The dictator of Germany in the 1930s during World War II; the Führer, or the leader, of the Nazis; believed the Germans were a superior race and wanted to destroy Jewish people.

Homer, Winslow A famous artist during the Gilded Age who is best known for painting scenes from everyday life.

Hoover, Herbert Was in charge of the US Food Administration during World War I; served as Secretary of Commerce during the 1920s; became the thirty-first president of the United States in 1929.

J

Jackson, Andrew The seventh president of the United States; broke treaties with the American Indians and removed them from their lands.

Johnson, Andrew Served as Abraham Lincoln's vice president; became the seventeenth president after Lincoln's death; faced many decisions about Reconstruction.

Johnson, James Weldon Promoted the Harlem Renaissance through writing and speaking; worked to help improve the lives of black Americans.

Joplin, Scott An African American composer during the Gilded Age who wrote ragtime music.

Joseph, Chief A Nez Perce chief who tried to lead his people to freedom in Canada.

K

Key, Francis Scott Wrote the poem "The Star-Spangled Banner," which later became America's national anthem.

King, Martin Luther, Jr. Led the civil rights movement in the South.

L

Lewis, Meriwether An explorer who led an expedition through the Louisiana Territory to the Pacific Ocean along with William Clark.

Lincoln, Abraham The sixteenth president of the United States; president during the Civil War who brought about the emancipation of the slaves and was killed by John Wilkes Booth.

Lindbergh, Charles An American aviator during the 1920s; first person to fly solo across the Atlantic.

Loving, Oliver Created the Goodnight-Loving Trail with Charles Goodnight to drive cattle to Colorado and Wyoming.

M

MacArthur, Douglas A US general during World War II who led US troops in defending the Philippines.

MacDowell, Edward A classical American composer during the Gilded Age who is best known for his piano piece "To a Wild Rose."

Machen, J. Gresham The most respected Fundamentalist teacher of the 1920s; teacher at Princeton Seminary who wrote many books defending the Christian faith.

Mao Zedong Served as leader of the Communist Party in China in 1935 and as chairman of the People's Republic of China from 1949 to 1976.

Matzeliger, Jan Immigrated to the United States from South America; built a shoe-lasting machine during the Gilded Age that made shoes more affordable.

McCoy, Joseph Set up a cattle-shipping yard in Abilene, Kansas, to help cowboys avoid driving cattle through settlers' lands.

McKinley, William Served as the twenty-fifth president of the United States during the Spanish-American War; did not want to help Cuba in its war against Spain, but wanted to help the two countries make peace.

Montgomery, Bernard A US general during World War II who successfully fought the Germans in western Egypt and pushed them west.

Moody, Dwight L. Left the shoe business to preach the gospel; was used by God to win thousands of people to Christ during the Gilded Age.

Moore, Annie The first immigrant to be received at the immigrant station on Ellis Island, New York, on New Year's Day in 1892.

Morse, Samuel Developed the telegraph in the 1840s.

Mussolini, Benito The prime minister and leader of the Fascist Party in Italy during World War II; leader who wanted to make Italy the center of a new Roman Empire.

N

Nast, Thomas A political cartoonist during the 1800s whose work made fun of corrupt people and influenced the thinking of many Americans.

Nimitz, Chester The admiral who led the US Navy in recapturing the small Pacific islands that had been occupied by the Japanese during World War II.

O

Oakley, Annie A performer in Buffalo Bill's Wild West Show known for her shooting skills.

P

Pasteur, Louis The French chemist who discovered how to kill bacteria in milk in the 1860s; process of pasteurization named after him.

Patton, George A US general during World War II who led US troops in pushing the Axis forces east out of North Africa.

Payne, Daniel A free black American educator of the Civil War era; the first African American to become president of an American college.

Penn, William A Quaker who planned and named the city of Philadelphia, Pennsylvania.

Pershing, John J. The commander of the first American soldiers who arrived in France in the fall of 1917 to help fight World War I.

Polk, James K. The eleventh president of the United States; was elected in 1844; purposely stirred up conflict with Mexico to gain more land for the United States.

Proctor, Redfield An American senator who visited Cuba and reported on the conditions to the Senate; encouraged Congress to favor helping Cuba gain independence from Spain.

Pulitzer, Joseph Worked as the journalist and publisher of the *New York World* during the Gilded Age; stretched the truth in his stories to sell more newspapers.

R

Reagan, Ronald A movie actor in California who liked politics and eventually became the fortieth president of the United States.

Reed, Walter A US Army pathologist and bacteriologist during the 1800s who proved that mosquitoes spread yellow fever.

Rickenbacker, Eddie The top American flying ace during World War I who shot down twenty-six enemy planes.

Rockefeller, John D. Became the most important man in the oil industry during the Gilded Age; gave much of his wealth to medical research and schools.

Roosevelt, Eleanor A diplomat, First Lady, and delegate to the United Nations; married to Franklin D. Roosevelt.

Roosevelt, Franklin D. A Progressive Democrat and great speaker on the radio; president who promised the

American people a New Deal; thirty-second president of the United States.

Roosevelt, Theodore Served as the Assistant Secretary of the Navy; volunteered to fight for Cuba in the Spanish-American War; led a cavalry unit called the Rough Riders; later became the twenty-sixth president of the United States and encouraged Progressive ideas.

Rosie the Riveter Represented the American woman who filled in the workforce in factories during World War II.

Ross, Betsy An American flag maker whose house is a popular place to visit in Philadelphia, Pennsylvania.

Ruth, Babe The most famous baseball player of the 1920s; helped the New York Yankees reach the World Series six times in ten years.

S

Sacco, Nicola An Italian immigrant tried and convicted with Bartolomeo Vanzetti for murder in the 1920s; believed to be innocent by many people.

Sankey, Ira A singer and composer of gospel songs; traveled with D. L. Moody and led music for Moody's evangelistic meetings during the Gilded Age.

Sargent, John Singer One of the most successful portrait painters during the Gilded Age.

Schurtz, Carl Reported on the progress and effects of Reconstruction in the South after the Civil War.

Scopes, John A teacher who broke the law and taught evolution in a public school during the 1920s. His trial was called the Scopes Trial.

Seward, William Appointed Secretary of State by President Abraham Lincoln; bought Alaska, keeping Russia from controlling land in North America.

Sholes, Christopher A newspaper publisher who invented the first modern typewriter during the Gilded Age.

Sitting Bull A Sioux chief who helped lead his people against the United States government during the Battle of the Little Bighorn; was killed at the Battle of Wounded Knee.

Smith, Al A Democratic candidate from New York; lost to Herbert Hoover in the thirty-first presidential election.

Smith, Tom One of the first marshals of Abilene, Kansas; was killed while on duty.

Sousa, John Philip Composed popular marches during the Gilded Age, including "The Stars and Stripes Forever."

Spencer, Herbert Believed in Social Darwinism; invented the phrase "survival of the fittest."

Squanto A Native American who helped the Pilgrims survive in America.

Stalin, Joseph Led the Communist Party in Russia during the 1930s; killed anyone who did not obey him or make him happy; tried to end all religion in Russia.

Stanton, Elizabeth Cady An advocate who spoke out openly for women's rights during the Gilded Age.

Stratemeyer, Edward Hired groups of authors to write series of children's books during the Progressive Era.

Sunday, Billy The most famous of the Fundamentalist preachers during the 1920s; former baseball star who became an evangelist.

T

Taft, William Howard The twenty-seventh president of the United States; caught between Progressives and conservatives in the 1912 election and did not please either group.

ten Boom, Corrie Hid Jews in her family's home in the Netherlands during World War II.

Tiffany, Louis Famous for making stained-glass objects during the Gilded Age.

Tilghman, Bill A marshal of Dodge City known for his honesty and courage; later a lawman in Oklahoma.

Tojo Hideki A general and prime minister of Japan in the 1930s; led the country in building a large military and in attacking and conquering parts of China.

Truman, Harry Became the thirty-third president of the United States after President Roosevelt died of a stroke; used the atomic bomb on the Japanese when they refused to surrender during World War II.

Twain, Mark An American writer during the Gilded Age; famous for his novels about Tom Sawyer and Huckleberry Finn; speaker against the United States taking control of other lands.

V

Vanderbilt, Cornelius Became rich through the railroad and through shipping during the Gilded Age.

Vanzetti, Bartolomeo An Italian immigrant tried and convicted with Nicola Sacco for murder in the 1920s; believed to be innocent by many people.

W

Warfield, Benjamin Breckinridge An important Bible teacher at Princeton Seminary; defended the Bible against the teachings of the liberals from the late 1800s to the early 1900s.

Washington, Booker T. A freed slave who worked hard to gain an education during the Progressive Era; thought that ending segregation gradually would be better for black Americans than ending it right away.

Washington, George The first president of the United States; influenced the country more than any other American of his time.

Whitefield, George A preacher who traveled throughout the American colonies and helped spread the Great Awakening.

Wilder, Laura Ingalls Traveled west and lived as a homesteader with her family; wrote several books during the Progressive Era about her life growing up in the Midwest.

Williams, John The leader of the British missionaries that visited the Samoan Islands in the 1830s.

Williams, Roger An English preacher who bought land from the Narragansetts and started his own colony which became Rhode Island.

Wilson, Woodrow The twenty-eighth president of the United States; supported both groups within the Democratic Party, thus winning the election of 1912 because the Republicans were divided; believed the United States should stay neutral during World War I; wanted a League of Nations to help keep other wars from starting.

Wright, Orville Built and flew the first successful airplane with his brother, Wilbur, in 1903.

Wright, Wilbur Built and flew the first successful airplane with his brother, Orville, in 1903.

Y

York, Sergeant Alvin Drafted to fight in World War I; opposed fighting in the war at first but decided it was his duty; was awarded the Congressional Medal of Honor for his bravery in battle.

Young, Brigham The Mormon leader who led his followers to Utah in the 1840s.

Glossary

A

adobe Building material made of clay and straw that dries and hardens in the sun.

alliance An agreement between two or more parties to join together for a common purpose.

Allies Alliance between Great Britain, France, the United States, Russia, and other countries during World War II.

ambassador A person who goes to another country to represent his own.

American Expeditionary Force The first American soldiers to arrive in France during World War I.

anarchist A person who believes that there should not be any form of law or government.

ancestor Any person from whom one is descended.

apartment A set of rooms within a building that a person or family can rent to live in.

aquifer A reserve of water deep under rich soil; layers of sand, gravel, or bedrock that hold or move the ground water, making the soil fertile.

arable Land where farmers can grow crops.

archipelago An island group or chain of islands.

arid A dry climate.

armistice An agreement between two or more parties to stop fighting.

assassinate To murder someone who is of political importance.

assembly line A process where a product passes from one worker to the next, with each worker adding one piece to the product.

atoll A ring-shaped coral island or a string of coral islands.

atom bomb A bomb made by splitting atoms, causing great destruction.

auditor A person who checks business records.

Axis Powers Alliance between Japan, Germany, and Italy during World War II.

B

bank run When a large number of people take their money out of the bank in fear of it failing.

bankrupt Condition when a person is not able to pay money that is owed.

Black Tuesday The name for October 29, 1929, when prices on the stock market collapsed.

blitzkrieg A fast-moving military attack, usually involving both land and air forces working together; also called a lightning war.

boomtown A town in the West that grew quickly because of sudden wealth.

borough One of five counties that make up New York City.

brand A symbol burned into a cow's hide to identify its owner.

bribe A gift of money or favor to cause someone to make a decision.

bull market The term for rising stock prices.

butte A small hill with steep sides.

C

capitalism An economic system in which the people own the country's goods and businesses.

carpetbagger A Northerner who went south to get government jobs after the Civil War.

catechism A book of questions and answers that teaches about God and the Bible.

cattle drive Moving a herd of cattle.

cay A small island composed of sand or coral.

Central Powers Alliance between Germany and Austria-Hungary during World War I.

chemical weapon An instrument that uses chemicals to cause death or harm to people.

chickee A thatched-roof home without walls that was built by the Seminoles.

child labor The use of underage children to work full-time.

Chinese Exclusion Act An act passed by Congress in 1882 forbidding Chinese people from the working class to enter the United States.

Civil War The long war in the United States between the Union Army and the Confederates; lasted from 1861 to 1865.

civilian A person who is not serving in the armed forces.

coastal plain Flat land stretching up from the coast.

commonwealth A nation or state governed by the people; a self-governing state voluntarily associated with the United States.

continental Located on a continent.

Continental Divide Mountains extending from Alaska to Mexico, mostly in the Rocky Mountains, from which the river water flows out in two different directions.

corruption Dishonesty.

cow town A town where cattle were driven to be shipped by train.

creole A form of cooking that mixes foods from European, African, Caribbean, and American cultures.

culture Customs, beliefs, arts, and institutions of a group of people.

D

Dawes Act An act passed in 1887 that allowed individual American Indians to own land and live as farmers in the West.

decade A period of ten years.

deciduous Having leaves that fall once each year.

delta The mouth of a river where it flows into a larger body of water.

demographics The study of people who live in a certain area.

dense Being close together; crowded.

deposit To put money in a bank for safekeeping.

dictator A leader who controls everything in a nation.

diphtheria A throat infection that can lead to death.

direct primary A meeting of registered voters in which the direct vote of the people nominates candidates for political office.

district An area of land marked out for a special purpose.

dormant Being inactive for a period of time.

doughboy The name given to a soldier who was in the American Expeditionary Force.

draft The process of selecting people for duty in the armed forces.

E

employer A person or an organization that pays people to work.

evangelist A preacher who travels from city to city preaching the gospel.

expert A person who knows much about a specific part of life.

extraction The act of obtaining with some effort or difficulty, as in obtaining oil from the ground.

F

fauna Animals and birds that live in a region.

firebomb A bomb used to start a fire.

flora Plants, flowers, and trees in a region.

fourteeners Mountains that are over fourteen thousand feet above sea level.

freedman A person freed from slavery during the Reconstruction Era.

Freedmen's Bureau An organization created to help anyone who had lost his home during the Civil War.

frontier Land that has not been settled.

fundamental Something of basic importance.

G

ghost town A town in the West that was abandoned when people could no longer make a living from mining.

Gilded Age A period during the late 1800s when the population and economy grew quickly in America.

glacier A river of ice that is formed by tightly packed snow.

Great Awakening A time period in the eighteenth century when there was a powerful social, political, and religious force that changed the course of American history; a special time when many people turned to Christ for salvation.

Great Depression The economic crisis beginning with the stock market crash in 1929 and continuing through the 1930s, resulting in millions of people losing their jobs.

H

habitat A place where an animal or plant lives and grows.

hogan A Navajo home that was dome shaped and made of wooden poles, tree bark, and mud.

Holocaust The killing of many Jews and others by the Nazis during World War II.

Homestead Act An act signed by President Lincoln that promised citizens ownership of 160 acres if they lived on and made improvements to the land over five years.

homesteader A person who settled and farmed land under the Homestead Act of 1862.

I

imperialism A policy of controlling foreign lands.

income tax A tax begun during World War I that is based on what a person earns each year.

industry The producing of goods or services by businesses and factories for the purpose of making money.

insulin A treatment for diabetes.

interchangeable part Identical part of a product that can be replaced with a new part if broken.

interest Money that banks pay their depositors for using the depositors' money.

internment camp An area where the United States government imprisoned the Nisei during World War II.

iron curtain An imaginary line that separated Eastern Europe and the Soviet Union from Western Europe after World War II.

irrigate To supply land or crops with water by a system of channels.

island hopping The American strategy during World War II to reach and conquer the Japanese islands.

J

journalism The gathering and presentation of news by newspapers and magazines.

just To be honest and fair; always doing what is right toward people.

K

kerosene A thin, light-colored oil made from petroleum.

L

labor union A group of workers that unite to go on strike.

latitude Lines that run east to west around the globe and are used to measure distance in degrees.

latte stones Tall stone pillars with cup-shaped tops that the early Chamorros built homes on.

liberalism (also called modernism) A religious view that the teachings of Christianity must be updated for the present age and that human reason and experience holds authority over the Bible; belief that salvation is gained by helping to improve people and society and is not about saving people from God's judgment.

lode A rich source of precious metals.

longhorns Wild cattle brought to America by Spanish settlers.

longitude Lines that run north to south around the globe and are used to measure distance in degrees.

lubricate To apply oil to make an object move more easily; often used with machinery parts.

Luftwaffe German air force during World War II.

lumber Timber sawed into boards to make useful wood products, such as houses, paper, cardboard, and furniture.

lumberjack A person who chops or saws down trees and takes the logs to a sawmill.

M

machine The name given to a group of people who control the way a city runs.

malaria A disease spread by mosquitoes.

marsh An area covered by shallow water in which small plants grow.

Marshall Plan A program to provide economic aid to European countries damaged by World War II.

mesa A hill with a flat top.

mint A place that makes the coins that people use as money.

mosque A Muslim place of worship.

Mountain Time Zone Standard time zone for the Rocky Mountain states.

muckraker A person who went out of his way to find and write news stories that exposed misconduct.

N

Nisei Americans born of Japanese parents who had relocated to the United States.

nomad A person with no permanent home who moves from place to place in search of food and water.

O

Oklahoma Land Rush An event that occurred on April 22, 1889, when people raced to claim land in Oklahoma.

organized crime Many criminals who work together to break the law.

P

pass A gap between two mountains that makes them easier to get through.

pasteurization A process in which milk is heated to get rid of harmful bacteria.

penicillin An antibiotic made from a mold that stops bacteria from growing.

petroglyph A rock carving made by ancient people long ago.

petroleum Oil drilled from the ground.

phonograph An invention by Thomas Edison that could record and play back the human voice.

piedmont The foothills between the Atlantic coastal plain and the mountains to the west.

pollute To corrupt or make dirty.

portrait A form of art made popular by John Singer Sargent during the Gilded Age; a picture of a person.

prairie Flat grasslands in the Midwest that receive little rain and have few trees.

Prohibition The act of forbidding the making, transporting, and selling of alcohol.

propaganda Information designed to make people think or feel a certain way.

prospector Someone who explores an area for gold or other valuable minerals.

providence The truth that nothing happens apart from God's plan or permission.

pueblo An American Indian village of the Southwest made of stone and adobe buildings built very close together.

pumice A volcanic rock used in items like soap and construction materials.

R

racial discrimination Treating people unjustly because of the color of their skin or their ancestry.

ragtime A popular form of music at the end of the 1800s that mixed classical with African American music styles.

rain shadow An area where there is very little rain due to a mountain barrier that causes the wind to lose moisture.

ration To limit the amount of food or other items available to people.

raw material A resource used to make a product.

Reconstruction The period from 1865 to 1877 when America was being rebuilt by reuniting the nation physically, socially, and politically.

refine To purify.

reservation An area of land set aside by the US government for Native Americans.

row house A house in a row of houses built without any space between them.

rural Outside a city, often having fewer people but more farms and land; characteristic of the countryside.

S

saboteur A person who would do damage to hurt war production.

scalawag A white Southerner who worked with Northerners during Reconstruction.

Second Great Awakening Religious revival after the Revolutionary War; a powerful social, political, and religious force that altered the course of American history.

segregation The act of separating people from the rest of society because of their differences such as skin color or religion.

settlement house Housing to help immigrants in poor living conditions.

shanty A house that is pieced together with scraps of metal, wood, and cardboard.

sharecropping To work or grow crops to share with the landowner, often as a way of paying rent.

shield volcano A type of volcano that produces slow-flowing, runny lava and rarely erupts violently.

Social Darwinism The view that because the fittest are those best suited to survive, governments should not ensure justice for the weak.

Social Gospel The teaching that God's kingdom will be brought about on the earth through personal and social improvement.

social scientist A person who studies societies.

society A group of people who live and work together and have similar cultures and beliefs.

sodbuster A prairie farmer.

speculate To buy stocks and then sell them as soon as the price goes up in an effort to gain wealth quickly.

stalemate A situation when two sides in a fight cannot gain any ground.

stampede A sudden rush of scared animals, such as a herd of horses, cattle, or buffalo.

stockholder A person who owns stock in a company.

strike To stop work in order to get better benefits.

subway An underground railroad.

suffrage Voting rights.

swamp An area covered by water in which large plants and trees grow.

swing state State whose voting swings back and forth between Republican and Democrat.

T

tank A heavily-armored moving vehicle that fires shells and was introduced during World War I.

tech industry A service industry that includes computer design and programming.

tenement Cheap housing that is found in the poorer sections of a city; an old house or building that was divided up into many small rooms.

territory An area of land and waters or region that is under the authority of a government.

terrorist A person who commits violence to introduce fear for military or political purposes.

textile Cloth to be manufactured into clothing.

trail boss A person in charge of a cattle drive.

transcontinental Crossing a continent.

transmit To send a message from one place to another.

Treaty of Versailles The peace treaty between Germany and the Allies that ended World War I.

tributary A river that flows into a larger body of water.

Triple Alliance Alliance between Germany, Austria-Hungary, and Italy at the beginning of World War I.

Triple Entente Alliance between Great Britain, France, and Russia during World War I.

truce An agreement between two or more parties to stop fighting for a period of time.

truck farm A small farm that grows fruits and vegetables to sell.

tsunami A giant ocean wave caused by an underwater earthquake or an eruption from a volcano.

tundra An area in the Arctic region where only small shrubs, mosses, and grasses can grow.

U

unemployment The condition of wanting and needing a job but being unable to find one.

unrestricted submarine warfare A policy that submarines would attack any ship that came into a war zone; the policy the Germans adopted during World War I.

V

vaudeville A popular type of theater in the 1800s made up of short acts of acrobats, clowns, dancers, jugglers, and trained animals.

Veterans Day A holiday celebrating the end of World War I; a day set aside to honor all Americans who have served in America's armed forces; November 11.

W

Western Front A line of trenches between Belgium and France where fighting occurred during World War I.

wetland A bog or swamp area that is soaked with water.

wildlife reserve An area of land set aside by the government for wild animals and plants to live in protection.

World War I (1914–1918) War in which Great Britain, France, the Soviet Union, the United States, and other countries defeated Germany, Austria-Hungary, Japan, and others.

World War II (1939–1945) War in which Great Britain, France, the Soviet Union, the United States, China, and other Allies defeated Germany, Italy, Japan, Hungary, Romania, Bulgaria, and other Axis Powers.

Y

yellow fever A disease spread by mosquitoes.

yeomanette A woman enlisted in the navy who did mostly office work.

Z

zeppelin A large aircraft similar to a blimp used to drop bombs during World War I.

Index

Photo Credits

Chapter 1

4 omgimages/iStock/Thinkstock; **6** © Hugoht | Dreamstime.com; **10** ClassicStock.com/SuperStock; **11** "Gilbert Stuart Williamstown Portrait of George Washington" by Gilbert Stuart/Wikipedia/Public Domain; **12** (all) "Constitution of the United States"/U.S. National Archives and Records Administration/Wikipedia/Public Domain; **13** Public Domain; **14** "Northpt" by Don Troiani/US Army/Wikimedia Commons/Public Domain; **15t** Library of Congress, LC-DIG-pga-01838; **15b** Photo Researchers/Getty Images; **17** SuperStock/ SuperStock; **19tl** ©iStockphoto.com/fotosmania; **19tr** "PSM V03 D423 Morse telegraph"/Wikimedia Commons/Public Domain; **19b** Quint & Lox Limited/ SuperStock; **21** Library of Congress, LC-USZC4-4575; **22** "Abraham Lincoln circa 1860"/Wikimedia Commons/Public Domain; **23** National Archives

Chapter 2

29 Library of Congress, LC-DIG-ppmsca-33070; **30** Otto Herschan/Hulton Archive/Getty Images; **32t** Hulton Archive/Getty Images; **32b** Library of Congress, LC-DIG-ppmsca-05704; **35, 40, 47** North Wind Picture Archives via AP Images; **37** "Tolson's Chapel MD1" by Acroterion/Wikimedia Commons/CC By-SA 3.0; **38t** "Robert Smalls - Brady-Handy"/Library of Congress/Wikipedia/Public Domain; **38c** "Joseph Rainey - Brady-Handy"/Library of Congress/Wikipedia/Public Domain; **38b** "Blanche Bruce - Brady-Handy"/Library of Congress/Wikipedia/Public Domain; **41t** "Hampton Institute - geography" by Frances Benjamin Johnston/Wikimedia Commons/Public Domain; **41b** "Daniel A Payne"/Wikimedia Commons/Public Domain; **42** "Carpetbag" by Sobebunny/Wikipedia/CC By-SA 3.0; **43** Library of Congress, LC-HABS RI,5-WICK,1--13; **45** ©iStockphoto.com/HultonArchive; **46** Kean Collection/Archive Photos/Getty Images; **51** "Ulysses Grant 1870-1880"/Library of Congress/Wikimedia Commons/Public Domain; **53** Public Domain

Chapter 3

57 Pajaro Valley Historical Association; **59l** "East and West Shaking hands at the laying of last rail Union Pacific Railroad" by Andrew J. Russel/Wikimedia Commons/Public Domain; **59r** "The-Golden-Spike-7Oct2012" by Wjenning/Wikimedia Commons/CC By-SA 3.0; **63t** © Beodra | Dreamstime.com; **63c** Greggory Frieden/iStock/Thinkstock; **63b** Michael Rutherford/SuperStock; **65t** Public Domain; **65b** Everett Collection/SuperStock; **66t** © Everett Collection Historical/Alamy;

66b "Colt Flat Top Target" by Hmaag/Wikipedia/CC By-SA 3.0; **67** Courtesy, History Colorado (William Henry Jackson collection, Scan #20100653); **68** ©iStockphoto.com/lcepparo; **69** Baptist Annals of Oregon: 1844-1900/Public Domain; **70** Library of Congress, **71t** Richard and Ellen Thane/Science Source; **71b** © Vintage Images/Alamy; **72** Herbert Hoover Presidential Library-Museum; **73** © Wenling01 | Dreamstime.com; **75t** "Sitting Bull" by David F. Barry/Library of Congress/Wikimedia Commons/Public Domain; **75b** "Custer Bvt MG Geo A 1865 LC-BH831-365-crop"/Library of Congress/Wikipedia/Public Domain; **77** SuperStock/SuperStock; **78** "Woundedkneeencampment" by Miller, James A./Library of Congress/Wikimedia Commons/Public Domain; **79t** JenDen2005/iStock/Thinkstock; **79c** BJU Photo Services; **79b** Justin Williford/Shutterstock.com

Chapter 4

84 Universal Images Group/SuperStock; **86t** Library of Congress, LC-USZ62-118801; **86b** Courtesy of the Lucretia Little History Room, Mill Valley Public Library; **87t** Library of Congress, LC-USZ62-120152; **87b** Courtesy of Minnesota Historical Society-James J. Hill Papers; **88** SuperStock/SuperStock; **89** © Fotoluminate | Dreamstime.com; **91** PhotoQuest/Archive Photos/Getty Images; **95** Library of Congress, LC-DIG-det-4a21395; **96** ©iStockphoto.com/wynnter; **97** Everett Collection/SuperStock; **98** Colin Young/iStock/Thinkstock; **99** © Collection of the New-York Historical Society, USA/Bridgeman Images; **101** "Young Men's Christian Association Building - Cor. 23rd St. and 4th Ave, from Robert N. Dennis collection of stereoscopic views - cropped, jpg version"/ Wikimedia Commons/Public Domain; **102** Historical Center of the Presbyterian Church in America, Photo collection- http://www.pcahistory.org; **103** © James Nesterwitz/Alamy; **104l, r** Public Domain; **106** "Chautauqua Hall Of Philosophy" by Beth Scupham/Flickr/CC By-SA 2.0

Chapter 5

111 sparhawk4242/iStock/Thinkstock; **112** Apic/Hulton Archive /Getty Images; **113t** "Sholes1"/Wikimedia Commons/Public Domain; **113b** Science & Society Picture Library/SSPL/Getty Images; **114t, b** Science and Society/ SuperStock; **114c** Photos.com/Thinkstock; **115t** Library of Congress, LC-DIG-cwpbh-04044; **115b** "Fonograf 2" by Holger.Ellgaard/Wikimedia Commons/CC By-SA 2.0; **116l** "Jan ernst matzeliger"/Wikimedia Commons/Public Domain; **116r** Print Collector/

Hulton Archive/Getty Images; **117** "Cornelius Vander-bilt Daguerrotype2" by Mathew Brady/Wikipedia/Public Domain; **118** "Houston Carnegie Library 1904"/Courtesy of Special Collections, University of Houston Libraries/Wikipedia/Public Domain; **120t** "Child in a Straw Hat by Mary Cassatt c1886"/National Gallery of Art/Wikipedia/Public Domain; **120b** "Edinburgh NGS Singer Sargent Lady Agnew" by John Singer Sargent/Wikimedia Commons/CC By-SA 3.0; **121t** "Snap the Whip 1872 Winslow Homer"/Metropolitan Museum of Art/Wikimedia Commons/Public Domain; **121b** Peter Harholdt / SuperStock; **122t** "Antonín Dvořák 31.7.1870"/Wikimedia Commons/Public Domain; **122c** Michael Ochs Archives/Stringer/Getty Images; **122b** "Mark Twain by AF Bradley"/Wikimedia Commons/Public Domain; **123tl** Public Domain; **123tr** "William Randolph Hearst cph 3a49373" by J.E. Purdy/Library of Congress/Wikipedia/Public Domain; **123bl** Library of Congress, LC-USZ62-116257; **123br** Culver Pictures, Inc. / SuperStock; **124t** David Spindel / SuperStock; **124b** "Annie Oakley with shotgun"/Wikimedia Commons/Public Domain; **125** Universal Images Group / SuperStock; **126t** Hodag Media/Shutterstock.com; **126b** © Mary Evans Picture Library/ Alamy; **127t** SCIENCE SOURCE/Photo Researchers/Getty Images; **127b** "Hull House 2" by Zagalejo/Wikimedia Commons/Public Domain; **128** "Mill Children in Macon 2" by Lewis Hine/Library of Congress/Wikipedia/Public Domain; **129l** "ElizabethCadyStanton-Veeder"/Library of Congress/Wikipedia/Public Domain; **129r** Library of Congress, LC-USZ62-111423; **130** Art Archive, The/SuperStock; **131** Library of Congress, LC-USZC2-2666; **132** The Granger Collection, NYC

Chapter 6

138 Library of Congress, LC-DIG-ggbain-12929; **141** Library of Congress, LC-DIG-highsm-06111; **142** Library of Congress, LC-USZ62-75979; **144** Library of Congress, LC-USZ62-117982; **145** "USS Maine entering Havana harbor HD-SN-99-01929"/Wikipedia/Public Domain; **146** Library of Congress; **147** Library of Congress, LC-USZ62-61877; **148** Library of Congress, LC-DIG-ppmsca-35735; **149** Christie's Images Ltd./SuperStock; **150** © Archive Image/ Alamy; **152** "Katipuneros"/Wikipedia/Public Domain; **154** Library of Congress, LC-DIG-hec-03147; **155** The National Library of Medicine/Public Domain

Chapter 7

158 Everett Collection / SuperStock; **164** Library of Congress, LC-B2- 2236-6; **166** Library of Congress, LC-DIG-nclc-01543; **170t** Culture Club/Hulton Archive/Getty Images; **170b, 171b** Stock Montage/Archive Photos/Getty Images; **171t** Library of Congress, LC-DIG-ppmsca-27845; **172** Library of Congress, LC-DIG-nclc-04529; **173** Library of Congress, LC-DIG-fsa-8a03228; **174l** Buyenlarge/SuperStock; **174r** MPI/Stringer/Archive Photos/Getty Images; **175t**

Library of Congress, LC-USZ62-111278; **175b** Culver Pictures, Inc./SuperStock; **176t** Library of Congress, LC-DIG-ppmsc-06102; **176c** Library of Congress, LC-DIG-ppprs-00683; **176b** Library of Congress, LC-DIG-ppprs-00626; **178t** "Bobbsey Twins in a Great City"/Wikimedia Commons/Public Domain; **178c** "The Rover Boys on the Farm"/Wikipedia/Public Domain; **178b** "Tom Swift and His Aerial Warship"/Wikimedia Commons/Public Domain

Chapter 8

185 Rue des Archives / The Granger Collection, NYC; **186** Archives Larousse, Paris, France/Bridgeman Images; **187** Library of Congress, LC-B2- 3574-11; **189t** Three Lions/Stringer/Hulton Archive/Getty Images; **189c** Library of Congress, LC-USZ62-115014; **189b** Classic Vision/age fotostock/SuperStock; **192** Hulton Archive/Stringer/Getty Images; **194t** Library of Congress, LC-USZ62-42532; **194b** Library of Congress; **195** Library of Congress, LC-USZC4-2950; **196t** Library of Congress, LC-USZ62-51348; **196b, 201c** MPI/Stringer/Archive Photos/Getty Images; **197t** Library of Congress, LC-USZC4-10321; **197b** "School children holding one of the large heads of cabbage"/National Archives/Flickr/Public Domain; **198** Library of Congress, LC-USZC4-9884; **199** Library of Congress, LC-USZC4-3048; **200t** "369th 15th New York"/National Archives/Wikimedia Commons/Public Domain; **200b** Britannicus84/iStock/Thinkstock; **201bg** David De Lossy/Photodisc/Thinkstock; **201t** Hulton Archive/Stringer/Archive Photos/Getty Images; **201b** John Parrot/Media Bakery LLC; **202t** Pictorial Parade/Archive Photos/Getty Images; **202b** Library of Congress, sn85042243; **203** The Granger Collection, NYC; **204** Library of Congress, LC-B2- 4956-10; **205** Private Collection/Photo © Christie's Images/Bridgeman Images

Chapter 9

210l © Jeff Morgan 16/Alamy; **210r** Transcendental Graphics/Archive Photos/Getty Images; **211t, b, 217, 225b** The Granger Collection, NYC; **213** FPG/Retrofile/Getty Images; **214t, 215r** SuperStock/SuperStock; **214b** Keystone-France/Gamma-Keystone/Getty Images; **215l** Popperfoto/Getty Images; **215c** Library of Congress, LC-B2- 5897-15; **218** FPG/Archive Photos/Getty Images; **219** Library of Congress, LC-B2- 636-14; **220** Keystone/Stringer/Hulton Archive/Getty Images; **221l** New York Daily News Archive/New York Daily News/Getty Images; **221r** Underwood Photo Archives/SuperStock; **222** Library of Congress, LC-USZ62-96024; **223** Everett Collection / SuperStock; **224t** Library of Congress, LC-USZ62-60242; **224b** Science and Society/SuperStock; **225t** Hulton Archive/Getty Images; **226t** Library of Congress, LC-DIG-ggbain-38216; **226b** Library of Congress, LC-USZ62-11819; **228t** Library of Congress, LC-B2- 1222-16; **228b** Library of Congress, LC-DIG-bbc-0155f; **229** Used with the permission of the Archives of Montgomery Library at Westminster

Theological Seminary, Philadelphia PA.; **230** (both) MPI/Stringer/Archive Photos/Getty Images

Chapter 10
237 Library of Congress, LC-USZ62-94124; **239, 253** The Granger Collection, NYC; **240** "Herbert Hoover - NARA - 532049"/Wikimedia Commons/Public Domain; **242, 255** AP Photo; **243** "Franklin D. Roosevelt and Hoover in Washington, Washington, D.C - NARA - 196763"/Wikimedia Commons/Public Domain; **248l** Library of Congress, LC-DIG-fsa-8a04960; **248r** National Archives; **249** "National Recovery Administration" by whitewall buick/Flickr/CC By 2.0; **250** "Lancaster, Pennsylvania - Housing. William Heights - squatter colony on edge of town - mostly casual workers - NARA - 518456" by Lewis Hine/Wikimedia Commons/Public Domain; **251** "48-22 3708(11)"/FDR Presidential Library & Museum/Flickr/CC By 2.0; **257** "Eleanor Roosevelt - NARA - 195319"/U.S. National Archives and Records Administration/Public Domain

Chapter 11
260 (both), **261**b, **263**l, **270** Library of Congress; **261**t, **262**l, **275, 279, 280**b, **283, 284**r National Archives; **262**r Harrison Forman/Three Lions/Getty Images; **263**r "Hideki Tojo posing"/Japanese Library of Parliament Digital Archive/Wikimedia Commons/Public Domain; **267, 276**t BACM Research, Paperless Archives, The Library Collection, Paperlessarchives.com; **269**t "Montgomery E010786478-v8"/Library and Archives Canada/Wikimedia Commons/Public Domain; **269**b National Archives/Historylink101.com; **272** "B-25 prior to start on USS Hornet for Doolittle raid" by USAF/Wikimedia Commons/Public Domain; **276**b "To learn how to shop with point stamps, these youngsters in a Fairfax County, Virginia, grade school have set up a play - NARA - 535821"/National Archives/Wikimedia Commons/Public Domain; **277**t "Women aluminum shells WWII"/Library of Congress/Wikimedia Commons/Public Domain; **277**b Provided by BAC software; **278** "The charge of the scrap brigade in Roanoke, Virginia, includes such methods of collecting as this pony cart. NARA - 196336"/National Archives/Wikimedia Commons/Public Domain; **280**t "Dwight D. Eisenhower as a major"/US Army/Wikimedia Commons/Public Domain; **284**l "Judenstern Fürth Schwabacherstr" by Ferdinand Vitzethum/Wikimedia Commons; **285** © RIA Novosti / Alamy; **286**t "General George C. Marshall, official military photo, 1946"/US Army/Wikimedia Commons/Public Domain; **286**b "Reconstruction work of Tokyo station Marunouchi building"/Wikimedia Commons/Public Domain; **287** SuperStock/SuperStock

Chapter 12
291 North Wind Picture Archives via AP Images; **292** ©iStockphoto.com/David Sucsy; **293**t Andrew McLachlan/ All Canada Photos/SuperStock; **293**bl ©iStockphoto.com/Brian McEntire; **293**br ©iStockphoto.com/ferrantraite; **294**t ©iStockphoto.com/keiichihiki; **294**c

PaulReevesPhotography/iStock/Thinkstock; **294**bl RONSAN4D/iStock/Thinkstock; **294**br © Shawn Milne | Dreamstime.com; **295**t RCKeller/iStock/Thinkstock; **295**c © Brian Kushner | Dreamstime.com; **295**bl Cheryl Davis/iStock/Thinkstock; **295**br ©iStockphoto.com/LoriProphoto; **296**lt ©iStockphoto.com/RiverNorthPhotography; **296**lb "Light through White Oak" by Dendroica cerulea/Flickr/CC By 2.0; **296**ct © epantha - Fotolia.com; **296**cb ©iStockphoto.com/Joesboy; **296**r ©iStockphoto.com/Jeff Goulden; **298** "Cranberrys beim Ernten" by Keith Weller/USDA-ARS/Wikipedia/Public Domain; **300** ©iStockphoto.com/Ron and Patty Thomas Photography; **302**l spwidoff/Shutterstock.com; **302**r © Ken Cole | Dreamstime.com; **303** ©iStockphoto.com/tonda; **304** "Independence National Historical Park Franklin Court Ghost Structure"/National Park Service Digital Image Archives/Wikimedia Commons/Public Domain; **305** Stock Connection/SuperStock; **306** S.R. Maglione/Shutterstock.com; **308**t ©iStockphoto.com/ferrantraite; **308**b Universal Images Group/SuperStock

Chapter 13
313 "Gentleman - NARA - 527584" by Mathew Brady/Wikimedia Commons/Public Domain; **314** The Granger Collection, NYC; **315** © Everett Collection Inc./Alamy; **318**lt BarryB/Bigstock.com; **318**lc ©iStockphoto.com/lawcain; **318**lb Gary Corbett/age fotostock/SuperStock; **318**ct ©iStockphoto.com/1MoreCreative; **318**cb ©iStockphoto.com/ earleliason; **318**rt ©iStockphoto.com/Robert Hambley; **318**rc, **318**rb ©iStockphoto.com/megasquib; **320** ©iStockphoto.com/EdStock; **321** ©iStockphoto.com/Ed Metz; **323** ©iStockphoto.com/Toni Scott; **325**t ©iStockphoto.com/Rainer Plendl; **325**b © Georgy Timakov - Fotolia; **326** © Sergey Borisov - Fotolia; **327** ©iStockphoto.com/Paul Giamou; **328** Visual & Written/SuperStock; **329** Inge Johnsson/age fotostock/SuperStock

Chapter 14
335 Mike_Kolesnikov/iStock/Thinkstock; **336** abadonian/iStock/Thinkstock; **337** GordanD/iStock/Thinkstock; **340**l pdb1/Bigstock.com; **340**c © magann - Fotolia.com; **340**rt Thomas Biegalski/iStock/Thinkstock; **340**rc Sarah Jessup/Shutterstock.com; **340**rb DougLemke/iStock/Thinkstock; **341** ©iStockphoto.com/Maxfocus; **342** Jim Reed/SuperStock; **343** ©iStockphoto.com/earleliason; **345**t ©iStockphoto.com/JTSorrell; **345**b Maksymowicz/iStock/Thinkstock; **347** ©iStockphoto.com/Kubrak78; **348** photo .ua/Bigstock.com; **349** ClassicStock./SuperStock; **350** ©iStockphoto.com/DenisTangneyJr; **351** ©iStockphoto.com/Paul Velgos; **352** "Islamic Center of America" by Dane Hillard/Flickr/CC By 2.0

Chapter 15
357 ©iStockphoto.com/Dean_Fikar; **358** Chris Johns/National Geographic/Getty Images; **359**l ©iStockphoto.com/clickstock; **359**c Kenneth Keifer/iStock/Thinkstock; **359**r ©iStockphoto.com/twildlife; **360**t Fuse/